Mudluscious

MUDLUSCIOUS

**Stories and Activities Featuring Food
for Preschool Children**

JAN IRVING

and

ROBIN CURRIE

Illustrated by Robert B. Phillips

1986

Libraries Unlimited   **Littleton, Colorado**

LIBRARIES UNLIMITED, INC.
P.O. Box 263
Littleton, Colorado 80160-0263

Library of Congress Cataloging-in-Publication Data

Irving, Jan, 1942-
    Mudluscious : stories and activities featuring food
for preschool children.

    Includes index.
    1. Food--Study and teaching (Elementary) 2. Nutri-
tion--Study and teaching (Elementary) I. Currie, Robin,
1948-   . II. Title.
TX364.I78   1986   372.3'7   85-23954
ISBN 0-87287-517-2

Libraries Unlimited books are bound with Type II nonwoven material that meets and exceeds National Association of State Textbook Administrators' Type II nonwoven material specifications Class A through E.

To Kathleen
whose lack of enthusiasm for the subject
has inspired us to create an irresistible feast!

And to our families
for living on TV dinners,
carry out, and bare cupboards!

CONTENTS

Introduction xiii

Setting Up the Program xvii

1—Breakfast Starts the Day 1
    Introduction 1
    Initiating Activities 1
    Literature-Sharing Experiences 3
        Books about Eggs 3
        Related Activities about Eggs 4
        Books about Pancakes 5
        Related Activities about Pancakes 6
        Books about Cereal 7
        Related Activities about Cereal 7
        Other Books about Breakfast 8
    Games and Frolics for Breakfast 8
    Craft Experiences for Breakfast 9
    Cooking and Tasting Experiences for Breakfast 11

2—Lunch to Munch 14
    Introduction 14
    Initiating Activities 15
    Literature-Sharing Experiences 16
        Books about Sandwiches 16
        Related Activities about Sandwiches 16

Literature-Sharing Experiences — *continued*
    Books about Picnics..18
    Related Activities about Picnics........................19
    Books about Lunch at Home and On the Go................21
    Related Activities about Lunch on the Go...............22
  Games and Frolics for Lunch...............................25
  Craft Experiences for Lunch...............................26
  Cooking and Tasting Experiences for Lunch.................29

3 — Food to Grow On..34
  Introduction..34
  Initiating Activity.......................................35
  Literature-Sharing Experiences............................35
    Books about Good-for-You Foods..........................35
    Related Activities on Good-for-You Foods................36
    Books about Nutrition...................................39
    Related Activities about Nutrition......................40
  Games and Frolics for Foods to Grow On....................49
  Craft Experiences to Grow On..............................50
  Cooking and Tasting Experiences that are "Good for You"...52

4 — For the Sweet Tooth....................................55
  Introduction..55
  Initiating Activity.......................................55
  Literature-Sharing Experiences............................56
    Books about Ice Cream...................................56
    Related Activities about Ice Cream......................56
    Books about Pie and Cookies.............................59
    Related Activities about Pie and Cookies................60
    Books about Donuts, Candy, and Other Sweet Treats.......62
    Related Activities about Donuts, Candy, and Other Sweet Treats...62
  Games and Frolics for the Sweet Tooth.....................65
  Craft Experiences for the Sweet Tooth.....................66
  Cooking and Tasting Experiences for the Sweet Tooth.......69

5 — Fun and Fantasy Foods..................................71
  Introduction..71
  Initiating Activity.......................................71
  Literature-Sharing Experiences............................72
    Books about Fun Foods...................................72
    Related Activities about Fun Foods......................74
    Books about Fantasy Foods...............................78
    Related Activities about Fantasy Foods..................79
  Games and Frolics for Fun and Fantasy Foods...............86
  Craft Experiences for Fun and Fantasy Foods...............88
  Cooking and Tasting Experiences for Fun and Fantasy Foods...90

6 — Stir and Bake...92
   Introduction..92
   Initiating Activity..93
   Literature-Sharing Experiences...93
      Books about Bread...93
      Related Activities about Bread...94
      Books about Cake..98
      Related Activities about Cake..99
   Games and Frolics for Bread and Cake.............................106
   Craft Experiences for Bread and Cake..............................107
   Cooking and Tasting Experiences for Bread and Cake........109

7 — Soup's On!..111
   Introduction..111
   Initiating Activity..111
   Literature-Sharing Experiences...112
      Books about Soup...112
      Related Activities about Soup.......................................113
      Books about Leftovers..122
      Related Activities about Leftovers...............................123
   Games and Frolics for Soup's On!.....................................128
   Craft Experiences for Souper Dooper Kids.....................129
   Cooking and Tasting Experiences for Soup's On!..........130

8 — I'll Eat You Up!..132
   Introduction..132
   Initiating Activities...133
   Literature-Sharing Experiences...133
      Books about Food that Runs Away..............................133
      Related Activities about Food that Runs Away...........134
      Books about I'll Eat You Up...138
      Related Activities about I'll Eat You Up.......................139
   Games and Frolics for I'll Eat You Up...............................143
   Craft Experiences for I'll Eat You Up................................143
   Cooking and Tasting Experiences for I'll Eat You Up.....145

9 — Magic Pots Cooking 'Round the World.........................147
   Introduction..147
   Initiating Activity..148
   Literature-Sharing Experiences...148
      Books about Cooking Pots...148
      Related Activities about Cooking Pots.........................149
      Books about Many Lands...154
      Related Activities about Many Lands...........................155
   Games and Frolics about Many Lands..............................161
   Craft Experiences about Many Lands...............................162
   Cooking and Tasting Experiences about Many Lands......164

10—Holidays to Celebrate..166
    Introduction 166
    Initiating Activity...167
    Literature-Sharing Experiences...........................167
        Books about Halloween..............................167
        Related Activities about Halloween.................168
        Books about Thanksgiving..........................170
        Related Activities about Thanksgiving..............170
        Books about Christmas.............................173
        Related Activities about Christmas.................173
        Books about Hanukkah.............................176
        Related Activity for Hanukkah.....................176
    Games and Frolics for Holidays............................176
    Craft Experiences for Holidays............................178
    Cooking and Tasting Experiences for Holidays.............183

11—Fussy and Not-So-Fussy Eaters..............................187
    Introduction 187
    Initiating Activities..187
    Literature-Sharing Experiences...........................188
        Books about Fussy Eaters..........................188
        Related Activities about Fussy Eaters..............189
        Books about Not-So-Fussy Eaters..................192
        Related Activities about Not-So-Fussy Eaters.......194
    Games and Frolics for Fussy and Not-So-Fussy Eaters......200
    Craft Experiences for Fussy and Not-So-Fussy Eaters......202
    Cooking and Tasting Experiences for Fussy Eaters.........205

12—Stuffing Mother Hubbard's Cupboard.......................207
    Introduction 207
    Initiating Activities..207
    Literature-Sharing Experiences...........................212
        Books about Shopping and Selling Food.............212
        Related Activities about Shopping..................213
        Books about Finding and Growing Food.............215
        Related Activities about Finding and Growing Food...216
        Books about Kitchen Help..........................218
        Related Activities about the Kitchen and Helping....218
    Games and Frolics for Mother Hubbard's Cupboard........219
    Craft Experiences and Some Things to Grow for
        Mother Hubbard's Cupboard.......................220
    Cooking and Tasting Experiences for Mother Hubbard's Cupboard..................222

Resource Bibliography..223

Skills List...229

Breakdown of Activities by Skills Area...........................230

Alphabetical Index of Activities Showing Associated Skills..........241

Literature Index...256

INTRODUCTION

Mudluscious is a sourcebook for librarians, preschool teachers, and adults working with preschool children. Its purpose is to introduce quality literature that preschoolers will enjoy and to extend the literature through a variety of activities appropriate to preschoolers' interests and attention spans. We have chosen food as the "vehicle" to appreciation of language and literature. Since the English language is especially rich with food expressions, young children will delight in the word play of "eat like a pig," "in a pickle," and "easy as pie." And, food has always been a universal theme in folk literature. Food continues to be such a compelling theme for writers of contemporary stories that we readily identified over 150 picture books on the topic. These books are the springboard for the extending activities.

We believe young children will learn about language and reading from the activities in this book. Reading readiness has become a national concern. Eager parents are reading to children at an earlier age, and "surrogate parents" in daycare centers, preschools, and libraries share increasingly in this responsibility. Recent research confirms what we have known instinctively for years—nothing is as crucial in developing a child's reading interest and later success in school as the early storytime experience. The "live" experience of storyhours is far more effective in a child's language development than video or film presentations. Hearing someone read aloud sensitizes children to "book language," preparing them for reading on their own. And it's likely that children will want to read (and continue reading) if they are read to and invited to participate in story-related activities.

In addition to the language experiences, children will learn cognitive skills and social interaction skills through the activities we have created. The activities have been "child tested" in public libraries and in workshops with librarians and teachers. The skills index located in the appendix will guide you in teaching such skills as counting, following directions, and group cooperation. For example, a specific fingerplay might be used to teach counting, identifying body parts, and following directions. The skills index identifies sixteen skill areas and enumerates the activities in this book you may select if you wish to focus on a specific skill.

Finally, children will learn about food and establishing good eating habits from *Mudluscious.* Our overall approach to the "food issue" has been to take a light-hearted tone. The chapter "Fussy and Not-So-Fussy Eaters," for example, introduces books that generally treat children's eating problems with a sense of humor so that we might laugh at ourselves. This approach will, in the long run, provide young children with more open-minded attitudes about food and learning. Or, considering another issue: we live in a world with catchy television jingles promoting sugared cereals and candy bars. To ignore this or to deny the fact that children enjoy sweets is simply unrealistic. We've included the chapter "For the Sweet Tooth" not because we endorse whole-hog consumption of sugar; rather, we take a more balanced approach. Consider Cookie Monster's example as a "teachable moment" to appeal to what children like, but help them discover other delicious fare.

Mudluscious is the kind of resource book you should plunge right into. Though you may want to browse through the book to get a sense of its organization, you'll probably linger over a poem, sample a story, discover a game, and then go on to another place to find inspiration for your own activities. The chapters are identically structured. After an introduction and an initiating activity come literature-sharing experiences. Games, crafts, and cooking/tasting experiences extend the literature experiences. Each chapter introduces a different food theme. The books and activities for each chapter develop that theme. There is overlap—in "Lunch to Munch" and "Soup's On," for example—so you might find ideas in different chapters that work quite effectively together. There is no prescribed way to proceed in using this resource book!

Each chapter introduction briefly presents the scope of the chapter and its relevance to young children. The initiating activity both summarizes the overall theme and may be used as a warm up. These activities are flexible, often an "add on" game or participatory song that can be used as children arrive for the day's events.

Literature-sharing experiences are presented first since books and language experiences are the springboard for the learning activities that follow. Annotated bibliographies for subthemes of each chapter introduce the librarian or teacher to a variety of picture books that may be read to young children. Books have been selected that are well written and notable for the quality of illustration. Since young children may not be as attentive in a group, longer picture books have generally been excluded even though they might be excellent choices for older children. The titles are in print or readily available in most good children's libraries. And books can be requested through interlibrary loan if they are not in a nearby library. More books have been listed than will probably be used on a single theme. The intent is for the teacher or librarian to select a few titles, then choose among the related activities that follow each book list. Activities, including songs, poems, chants, media-enhanced stories from flannelboards to puppet skits, extend the literature experiences. In this respect, *Mudluscious* is unique. Most program guides introduce books and outline activities for teachers but do not include related fingerplays or "storytime stretches" for children.

Since very young children love rhythm and rhyme, there are dozens of poems and songs. The songs are set to the tunes of traditional folksongs children may already know so everyone can participate with little difficulty. Some stories suggest flannelboard or puppet presentation since younger preschoolers respond better when story is enhanced with visual techniques. Other activities directly involve children as characters in stories—often with the aid of masks or simple props. In our experience, participatory storytelling most effectively helps children remember the story, and, rather than threatening the shy, is begged for again and again. We've included "leader prompting" along with the story so you can recreate this kind of story experience with children even if you've never tried creative dramatics before.

Games and frolics follow the literature section and build on the overall themes. They may be a way to "get the wiggles out" after children have been sitting during storytime. Active games provide opportunities for large-motor-skill development as well as practice in following directions. Many games are adaptations of such traditional favorites as "Simon Says" and "Duck Duck Goose," but with a food twist. An effort has been made to emphasize cooperation over competition in a "new games" spirit so that children will learn that play is fun when everyone can share in the winning.*

Crafts will give children creative opportunities to turn everyday materials into simple projects they take home to remember the program long after it's over. Most of the projects use such inexpensive items as paper plates, sandwich bags, and construction paper. If your budget is too tight to purchase these items, children might be asked to bring some supplies from home. Local merchants are generally willing to contribute small items too. Fast-food establishments, for example, will give away paper cups and sandwich boxes that become treasured puppets with a child's creative touch.

Since this book explores the subject of food, it would not be complete without cooking and tasting experiences. Some institutions have better facilities than others for actual food preparation. With a little ingenuity, however, the adult can improvise quite well with appliances such as an electric skillet or blender. Obvious safety precautions need to be taken when using electricity or sharp knives. But, more and more, teachers are showing young children how to work with utensils and learn good judgment. Most of the food preparation in *Mudluscious* is simple. If you wish to try more elaborate recipes, consult the resource bibliography for cookbooks to use with children. Ambitious teachers and librarians may prepare food ahead or ask a parent to demonstrate the cooking of a special dish. The chapter on food from many lands is a perfect opportunity to invite a father who "cooks Chinese" or a mother who makes homemade pasta to share their expertise. Young children feel especially proud when their own parents make a "guest appearance." Local grocers will often contribute food, especially if they are mentioned in newspaper articles informing the public about your programs. Explore your community for possible field trips: a trip to the bakery or dairy, for example, or a visit to a turkey farm. You might initially think these requests are impositions, but enthusiastic requests planned well in advance bring surprisingly eager responses. People not only love to explain their work but look forward to return visits when they see the excitement it brings to a group of bright-eyed children.

We would like to thank the many people who encouraged and helped us during this project. Those who provided special assistance are Paula Brandt, Director of the Curriculum Laboratory, College of Education, The University of Iowa; Jim Rice, Associate Professor, School of Library and Information Science, The University of Iowa; Carole Elbert, Youth Services Coordinator, Ames Public Library, Ames, Iowa; Lorna Caulkins, Director, Ginny Cameron, Leslie Czechowski, Jean Jones, and the entire staff of Stewart Public Library, Grinnell, Iowa; Debbie Lease, home economics teacher, Grinnell Junior High School; Terry Burkhead, Director of the Grinnell Day Care Center; and Linda Hill, typist.

---

*For more information on the approach to games that emphasizes cooperation over competition see Terry Orlick's *The Cooperative Sports and Games Book* (Pantheon 1978).

SETTING UP THE PROGRAM

We suggest books and activities so that you might create your own program. Your final selection of the type and length of activities and stories should be based on your own situation. But here are a few sample programs the way we might set them up. The programs are derived from chapters 1 and 11.

BREAKFAST STARTS THE DAY

Sample Program*

Initiating Activities:	Begin with "Glass of Sunshine Fingerplay" (p. 3) as children arrive. Repeat this several times until children can participate easily. Then, when all children have come, sing "The Breakfast Song" (p. 1).
First Story:	Read the longest story of the day, *What Shall We Have for Breakfast?* by Zimelman (p. 3). Children listen most attentively when they are fresh, so save shorter stories for later.
Related Activities:	Follow up this egg story with three egg activities—"Eggs and More Eggs—Surprise!" (p. 4), "Humpty Dumpty Triple Treat" (p. 4), and "Unhatched Egg" (p. 5). The first will give children a chance to stretch and use their bodies; the second tells a favorite Mother Goose rhyme with an unexpected ending; and the third will help them settle down for the next story.
Second Story:	Read the *Three Bears* by Galdone (p. 7).

---

*Based on chapter 1.

xviii / Setting Up the Program

Related Activities:	Follow up this familiar tale with three cereal activities—"Peas Porridge Hot" (p. 8), "The Soggy Cornflake Song" (p. 7), and "Snap, Crackle, Pop Around" (p. 7). The first activity will remind children of the bears' porridge. The second song will relate to their everyday experience of eating cereal. And the third activity will help them follow directions in playing a game.
Third Story:	"Read" *Pancakes for Breakfast* by de Paola (p. 5). Since this is a wordless book, ask children to help tell it in their own words.
Related Activities:	Follow up this final story of the day with a dramatic play activity "Pancake Stack" (p. 6). It will give children a chance to move after they've been sitting, and it also uses counting skills!
Final Activities:	You may not have time to do all three of these activities, but they follow up the three stories about eggs, cereal, and pancakes and also introduce a game, a craft, and a tasting experience. Game: "Cereal Surprises" (p. 9). Craft: "Humpty Dumpty Together Again" (p. 10). (Don't leave this out if you do the "Humpty Dumpty Triple Treat" activity!) Tasting: "Pleasing Pancakes" (p. 12).
Final Song:	Sending children off with a song always ends the day on a happy note so we suggest you come full circle and sing "The Breakfast Song" again.

FUSSY EATERS

Sample Program*

Initiating Activity:	Begin with "Food for Thought" game as children arrive (p. 187). This is a good add-on activity that children can quickly follow. It is also a good introduction to the first story.
First Story:	Read *Gregory the Terrible Eater* by Sharmat (p. 189).
Related Activities:	Follow up this story about a picky eater with a flannelboard story about another one, "Picky Paul" (p. 189). This story can be used to teach a number of skills including sequencing, size and shape, and counting. Then, sing "The Fussy Eaters' Song" (p. 191).
Second Story:	Read *Mrs. Pig's Bulk Buy* by Rayner (p. 189). The pigs in this story eat too much of one thing with disastrous results. The craft that is suggested next will graphically demonstrate this result.
Craft:	"Why Pigs Are Pink" (p. 203).

*Based on chapter 11.

Game:

By this time, children will need some exercise, so allow them a fun way to follow directions and work together by playing "Crumb Catcher" (p. 200). Then, when you have "cleaned up all the crumbs" in the game, give children a chance to all be piggies and enjoy a "Pig Party" tasting experience (p. 205).

Tasting:

Pig Party Guaranteed to Turn Picky Eaters into Pigs.

Since you've read a story about pigs and done a flannelboard story about Picky Paul and his pizza, be sure to make the pig tails (p. 206) and Picky Paul Pizza (p. 206).

Final Activity:

Now that you've turned your picky eaters into piggies, sing the "Glutton Feast Song" (p. 198).

1.
BREAKFAST STARTS THE DAY

INTRODUCTION

Young children are usually enthusiastic about breakfast and will try most of the traditional fare—cereal, eggs, and pancakes. Capitalize on this enthusiasm with a breakfast program.

Young children love to serve breakfast on trays to their parents, so you might arrange the materials for this program on a breakfast tray. Set the table to get children into the habit of placing utensils properly on the right and on the left. (Refer to p. 220-21 of chapter 12, "Stuffing Mother Hubbard's Cupboard," for a placemat that will show children how.) The Egg Carton Art (p. 10) suggested in this section will make appealing table decorations, and you can stack the children's name tags on the tray, ready to pin on the children as they arrive.

Because children come to the preschool and library at different times, you might like to begin with some of the songs and frolics to get them involved in the hum of activity. (It's far more constructive than asking lively children to "Please settle down!") Practice "The Breakfast Song" below so everyone will be all ready to sing with gusto when the formal program begins. After the song, use fingerplay and poem to introduce the program. When everyone is settled, read some of the picture books on eggs, pancakes, or cereal. Then extend the book experience through the songs and action rhymes in this chapter, and try a craft and a tasting experience. Remember: the games will allow young children to "get the wiggles out."

INITIATING ACTIVITIES

The Breakfast Song
(To the tune of "My Bonnie Lies over the Ocean")

My breakfast is calling this morning,	(Motion with right hand.)
My bacon is crisp in the pan,	
My pancakes are doing a flip-flop,	(Hop.)
I'm running as fast as I can.	(Run in place.)

Get up! Get up!   (Raise each arm high.)
Oh, roll yourself out of the bed,   (Roll hand over hand.)
    the bed.
Get up! Get up!   (Raise each arm high.)
Oh, don't be an old sleepy head!   (Stretch!)

(End this with a cheery "Good Morning!")

What Do You Like to Start the Day?
(A Breakfast Bill of Fare)

What do you like
When you roll out of bed?
A nice warm slice
Of homemade bread?
    Dip it in egg,
    Slop it in cream,
    Fry it in butter,
    Or whipped mar-jar-een.
    Pour on a syrup
    You like the most
    Love that breakfast
    With warm French toast!

(Leader: Have children clap
hands or snap fingers to
get into the rhythm!)

What do you like
When you first get up?
A tall glass of milk?
Cocoa in a cup?
Maybe some juice,
Like a glass of sun,
That'll start your day
All ready for fun!

What do you like
For a breakfast crunch?
Snap, crackle,
Pop! Pop!
Chew and munch!
Pour on the milk,
And eat it quick
Unless you like
Rice puffs that are ick!

What do you like
Cooked in a pan
Sausage or bacon
Or country ham?
What about eggs
Sunny-side up?
Or once over easy
Just lick 'em up!

Love that breakfast
Most any way,
Super start
To a happy day!

Glass of Sunshine Fingerplay

Pick an orange	(Reach high and grab.)
Round like the sun,	(Bring fingertips of right and left hands together.)
Slice it open	(Hit side of one hand on other palm.)
To make two from one,	(Hold out both hands cupped.)
Get a glass,	(Hold imaginary glass in hand.)
Then twist and squeeze,	(Rub fingers of other hand over glass.)
Orange juice sunshine	(Hold up "glass.")
From a tree!	(Drink juice.)

LITERATURE-SHARING EXPERIENCES

Books about Eggs

Hoban, Russell. **Egg Thoughts and Other Frances Songs.** Illustrated by Lillian Hoban. Harper & Row, 1972.

Frances's mournful verses about eggs soft boiled, sunny-side up, sunny-side down, poached and hard boiled are fun and familiar reactions of many children.

Seuss, Dr. **Scrambled Eggs Super!** Random House, 1953.

Peter T. Hooper brags about his concoction of scrambled eggs made from the eggs of the Ruffle-Necked Sala-ma-goox! But the fun doesn't stop there. Peter adds the eggs of a strange assortment of creatures to his "Scrambled Eggs Super-dee-Dooper-dee-Booper/ Special de luxe ala-Peter T. Hooper."

Seuss, Dr. **Green Eggs and Ham.** Random House, 1960.

Sam-I-Am tries every possible way to convince his friend to try something new. Finally, in desperation, the friend tastes the strange food and is surprised at the result. Everyone who has been conned into "just one bite" and liked the new flavor will appreciate the message. Seuss's endless repetition and rhymes make this story unforgettable.

Zimelman, Nathan. **What Shall We Have for Breakfast?** Illustrated by John Paul Richards. Steck-Vaughn, 1969.

John Jaspar Jones, tired of candied rose petals, wants something different for breakfast. He asks for soft boiled dinosaur eggs, but his mother has only duck, chicken, goose, and turtle eggs. The small grocery and supermarket are also out of them. So is the Natural History Museum—at least it doesn't have fresh eggs. Finally, at Mr. McGooliap's farm they find ostrich (dinosaur) eggs for John Jaspar Jones's breakfast!

Related Activities about Eggs

Eggs and More Eggs—Surprise!
(A Fingerplay)

Turkeys make big ones,   (Stretch arms out wide.)
Robins make small   (Place hands close together.)
Bright blue eggs   (Touch fingers to form circle.)
The prettiest of all.

Duck eggs are dandy,   (Place arms under arm pits to form
    wings.)
Owl eggs are round,   (Circle eyes with fingers.)
The ostrich lays an egg   (Hold arms straight out, interlock fingers,
That weighs three pounds.   and bend knees to show weight of
    egg.)

Teeny is a hummingbird   (Form circle with finger and thumb.)
Great is a goose   (Touch fingers to form circle.)
They lay eggs   (Nod.)
How about a moose?   (Touch thumbs to head, spread fingers for
    antlers, shake head "no.")

But a chicken-sized egg   (Cup hands for nest.)
Seems just about right   (Nod.)
Crack it open   (Clap.)
Surprise! Delight!   (Put arms in air, wave fingers.)

Humpty Dumpty Triple Treat

For this activity prepare two egg faces on the two halves of a panty hose egg-like container. Fill the egg with lots of yellow confetti for the surprise ending.

Humpty Dumpty sat on the wall
(Leader: Show this egg face:)

Top half

Humpty Dumpty had a great fall.
(Leader: Then show this egg face:)

Bottom half

All the King's horses and all the King's men,
Couldn't put Humpty together again!
(Leader: Open the egg and sprinkle confetti on the children's heads!)

Egg Frolic

Pretend you're an egg, sunny-side up.	(Frame face with hands, smile.)
Now be an egg, sunny-side down.	(Bend head down.)
Now you're scrambled.	(Turn around.)
Now you're hard boiled, in a shell,	(Crouch down, curl up.)
On an Easter Egg roll!	(Roll over.)

Unhatched Egg

This is a good action rhyme to use just before you want children to settle down and listen for the next story.

Make a noise like a rooster.	(Crow.)
Make a noise like a hen.	(Cluck.)
Make a noise like a chick.	(Peep.)
Make a noise like an unhatched egg.	(Silence.)
Good! And now you're ready to listen.	

Books about Pancakes

Carle, Eric. **Pancakes, Pancakes.** Knopf, 1970.
> Hungry Jack asks his mother for a large pancake breakfast. She agrees to make it if he will help. Jack cuts down the wheat, takes it to the miller to be ground, gathers an egg, milks the cow, mixes the batter, and helps his mother fry the pancake. But he needs no help to eat it. Bright collage illustrations tell the sequence of events.

De Paola, Tomie. **Pancakes for Breakfast.** Harcourt Brace Jovanovich, 1978.
> An old woman wakes on a cold morning with dreams of a stack of pancakes. She is thwarted in her efforts by missing ingredients and the intrusion of her pets. Finally she follows aromas from a neighbor's house and invites herself in for pancakes for breakfast. This wordless story can be "read" by the children in their own words.

Please note other pancake stories in chapter 8, "I'll Eat You Up."

Related Activities about Pancakes

Pancakes, What a Treat!
(A Fingerplay)

Flapjacks	(Clap.)
Flapjacks	(Clap.)
Hot-on-the-griddle cake!	(Throw arms in air.)
Pancakes	(Clap.)
Pancakes	(Clap.)
Flip-over-easy cakes!	(Turn hands: palms up, then down.)
Blueberry	
Buckwheat	
Buttermilk	(Squat lower on each word.)
What a treat!	(Jump high with arms raised.)

Pancake Stack

Children form a semicircle around the leader who does actions of pouring the batter and flipping the pancakes with an imaginary spatula.

Is everybody ready to make pancakes?	
Here is our pan.	(Motions to the "inside circle," the space in the middle of the circle of children.)
First, I'll pour in the batter.	(Makes pouring motion.)
Everybody put in two round spoonfuls.	(Prompts children to put out two rounded fists.)
Good. Just right.	
Look at that! You're starting to spread.	(Children spread out fists to show two flat palms.)
You're GOOD LOOKING PANCAKES!	
I can see lots of bubbles coming.	(Children wiggle fingers.)
You're ready to turn over.	
Pancakes, flip!	(Children flip palms over.)
Pancake one—stack.	
Two—stack.	
Three—stack.	

(Count as each child puts hands on top of each other's, each child stacking a hand on top of another's hands until everyone has made one big pancake stack.)

Just what I wanted for a morning
    snack!
I LOVE PANCAKES!   (Leader hugs the pancake hand
                                                        stack.)

Books about Cereal

Galdone, Paul. **Three Bears.** Houghton Mifflin, 1972.
    While their breakfast porridge cools and the bears are out, Goldilocks (who is missing a front tooth in this version) tries out their food, chairs, and beds. The bears return, notice the changes, and find Goldilocks who escapes out the window.

McPhail, David. **The Cereal Box.** Little, Brown, 1974.
    The purchase of green cereal begins a breakfast of strange creatures punctuated by inattentive adult comments.

Related Activities about Cereal

The Soggy Cornflake Song
(To the tune of "Eentsy Weentsy Spider")

Mommy put some cornflakes   (Wiggle fingers as if cornflakes are
In my favorite bowl.   being sprinkled.)
Then she poured the milk in   (Make large pouring action.)
Good and fresh and cold.
But I didn't eat it   (Shake head sadly.)
Fast enough I guess.
So I'm looking at my cornflakes   (Shake hands, palms up.)
What a soggy mess!

Snap, Crackle, Pop Around

Divide children into three groups. One group says the word "snap" and snaps fingers. The next group says "crackle" and slaps legs. The last group says "pop" and claps hands. Practice with each group. Then, to the beat of a spoon on a pan, create a breakfast cereal symphony of "Snap, snap, snap, snap, crackle, crackle, crackle, crackle, pop, pop, pop, pop." This can be tried as a round or with all sounds at the same time. Repeat several times.

Peas Porridge Hot

The traditional way of doing this with slapping alternate hands often doesn't work with very young children, so try it with simpler actions like this:

Peas Porridge hot!	(Slap legs, raising hands high on "hot.")
Peas Porridge cold.	(Clap hands, rubbing hands together on "cold.")
Peas Porridge in the pot,	(Clap hands, rubbing tummy on "pot.")
Nine days old.	(Hold up nine fingers, thrusting hands forward for emphasis.)

Other Books about Breakfast

Kwitz, Mary De Ball. **Little Chick's Breakfast.** Harper & Row, 1983.
Little chick awakens early and visits many friends before the sun comes up and her breakfast of dried corn is served. An easy-to-read format that reads well aloud.

Weissman, Cynthia. **Breakfast for Sammy.** Four Winds, 1978.
Herbert tries to make Sammy's breakfast when Mama is sick. Although he is not able to do it "the way Mommy does," the brothers share a good meal and start the day happily.

GAMES AND FROLICS FOR BREAKFAST

Piggy Piggy

Children love a game of tag. This action rhyme is a variation. The leader acts as "pig caller." Instruct children they cannot move until the words are over. Then all children run away. When one child is caught by the pig caller, everyone freezes again. The child who is tagged becomes the pig caller; everyone freezes; the pig caller says the rhyme; and play continues.

Piggy piggy
Oink, oink
Piggy piggy
Squeal!
Who will be
My breakfast meal?
Sausage
Pork Chop
Bacon
Ham —
I will catch you
If I can!

Cereal Surprises

Use eight or so varied cereal boxes. Each box should contain a small amount of cereal and one word from a surprise message. Some suggested messages: "What a way to start the day," "Good morning," "Start the day with a good breakfast."

Let one child at a time choose a cereal to try. The child pulls out the surprise word (and tries some cereal if desired). Another child takes a turn. When all surprise words are found, the message is assembled.

CRAFT EXPERIENCES FOR BREAKFAST

Eggs and egg cartons can offer endless possibilities for crafts. Blown egg shells are too fragile for young children to work with successfully, but hard boiled eggs can be decorated even if it isn't Easter. Remember the Easter rabbit in the picture book who delivered eggs on the Fourth of July? What about an Easter egg turkey on Thanksgiving? Here are some other ideas for egg decorating.

Pysanky Adapted: Daisy, Daisy, I Love You

This method of decorating eggs comes from Poland and the Ukraine, but it does not involve painting eggs with hot wax in intricate designs. Instead, masking tape is put on the egg in a pattern before the egg is dipped in the dye. The tape is then removed and the undyed portion makes the pattern.

1. Hard boil eggs ahead of time and let cool. Place small strips of masking tape on the egg in a daisy design like this:

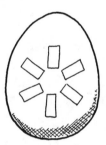

2. Make two dyes—one yellow and one blue—with vinegar and food coloring.

3. Have children dip the eggs in the yellow dye.

4. Let egg dry a few minutes. Now add a piece of tape in the center of the flower to retain the yellow color.

5. Dip egg in blue coloring. The background of the egg should become green. This is a good way to show that yellow and blue make green. Children may wish to make their own designs instead of using the daisy pattern.

Natural Food Dye Decorating

Before the days of commercial dyes, foodstuffs were used for dyes. And, what a perfect way to dye eggs for a program on food!

Assemble beets, spinach, onion skins. For each dye, boil the vegetable about ten minutes. Strain the dye into a bowl. Add about one tablespoon of vinegar to "set" the dye. Let cool. Dip hard boiled eggs into the dyes. Beets make a soft pink, spinach, a soft green, and the onion skins, a soft golden color.

Egg Carton Art

Egg cartons can be cut into sections and painted to make a variety of animals. The cartons are soft enough for children to stick in pipecleaner legs, antennae, paper wings, or beaks. Try your hand at creating egg carton critters à la Dr. Seuss, especially if you read one of the Seuss stories for your program. Or, you might make a simple egg carton baby chick. Here's one approach:

Humpty Dumpty Together Again

And don't forget the egg shells for crafts! If you color eggs first, break up the various colored shells and assemble them into an egg-shell mosaic. Use this activity if you plan to read "Humpty Dumpty."

Draw an egg shape on a piece of paper. Cover the inside of the shape with white glue. Stick on pieces of egg shell to make a brightly colored mosaic.

Label the picture "I Put Humpty Dumpty Together Again!"

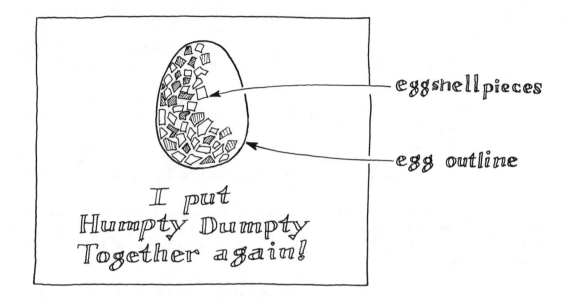

I'm a Good Egg

Name tags give children a nice secure feeling about their place in the library or classroom. And they serve as a useful control device, especially in public libraries where the librarian may not know each child by name. Cut out "whites" of eggs from white construction paper and glue on yellow (or green!) yolks. Then write on the child's name and the slogan "I'm a good egg."

COOKING AND TASTING EXPERIENCES FOR BREAKFAST

Scrambled eggs, often a favorite with young children, are fun to serve, especially if you read *Scrambled Eggs Super!* If you don't have a stove to use in the room, whip up the scrambled eggs in an electric skillet. You might ask an appliance store or electric company to lend you a microwave oven to use for the program. Then you can microwave scrambled eggs and let children watch them magically puff up. Sample both kinds of eggs. Which are creamier? Fluffier?

If you want to try some off-beat egg concoctions try these:

Sam-I-Am Deviled Green Eggs

Deviled eggs might seem strange for breakfast, and so do green eggs. Children will be delighted with the results. Be sure to read *Green Eggs and Ham* (p. 3).

Hard boil eggs. Cut eggs in half and scoop out the yolks. Mash yolks with a fork, adding a bit of mayonnaise, some salt, and a few drops of green food coloring. Fill white egg halves with the green yolk mixture and pass around the results with a straight face (if you can)!

Frances in a Frame

In her egg thoughts, Frances says she doesn't like eggs looking at her (see p. 3). How about framing Frances the egg for an egg in a frame with a new name, "Frances."

Cut the center out of a piece of bread. Spread margarine on both sides of the bread. Put the bread in an electric skillet and brown on one side. Turn the bread over. Carefully break an egg into the picture frame of bread. Don't let the egg yolk break or Frances will look grumpy. Wait just a few minutes until Frances is nicely set. Serve on a plate with a bacon bow tie if you wish!

Almost anyone will come running for pancakes for breakfast. There are pancake stories in this chapter and some runaway pancake stories in chapter 8, "I'll Eat You Up!" so you can do lots of pancake stories and eating. Just so you'll have plenty of pancake batter, here's a recipe for a mix to keep on hand.

Big Batch Pancake Mix

10 cups all-purpose flour
2½ cups instant non-fat dry milk
½ cup sugar
¼ cup baking powder
2 tablespoons salt

Mix the above ingredients and store in large airtight container. Put in a cool, dry place for up to eight months. This recipe will make about 13 cups of pancake mix.

Pleasing Pancakes
Please yourself with your favorite fruit cooked inside these pancakes.

1½ cups pancake mix (above)
1 egg, beaten slightly
1 cup water
3 tablespoons oil

Place pancake mix in medium-sized bowl. Combine remaining ingredients in small bowl. Add liquid mixture to the dry mix and stir just until blended. Let stand 5 minutes. (Children can do all these steps.) Now, pour the mixture on a prepared griddle or electric skillet. Cook 3-4 minutes, turning once. Add your favorite fruit as the pancake is turned—blueberries, sliced peaches, sliced strawberries. This recipe makes between 10 and 12 4-inch pancakes. Serve with warmed applesauce, a sprinkle of brown sugar, or some thawed berries and juice.

Chocolate Pancakes

1 egg
1½ cups milk
1½ cups pancake mix (above)
½ cup Nestle's Quik

Mix ingredients just until blended. Pour onto prepared griddle or electric skillet and cook about 3-4 minutes, turning once. This recipe makes about 10 medium-sized pancakes.

For extra fun, write on the pancakes. Make an extra-thick chocolate batter by adding one tablespoon of pancake mix and 2 tablespoons of Quik to the ½ cup prepared pancake mix. Drizzle onto the uncooked side of pancake just before it's ready to be flipped.

Basic Mix for Granola

If you sing the "Soggy Cornflake Song," you may want to try a different kind of cereal that won't get soggy. Granola is the perfect answer, and it's a really nutritious way to start the day.

10 cups old-fashioned rolled oats
1 cup wheat germ
½ pound shredded coconut
2 cups raw sunflower seeds
1 cup sesame seeds
3 cups chopped almonds, pecans, walnuts, or a combination
1½ cups brown sugar, packed
1½ cups water
1½ cups vegetable oil
½ cup honey
½ cup molasses
1½ teaspoons salt
2 teaspoons cinnamon
3 teaspoons vanilla
Raisins or other dried fruits

Preheat oven to 300 degrees. Combine first six ingredients in a large bowl or pan. Place the brown sugar, water, oil, honey, molasses, salt, cinnamon, and vanilla in large saucepan. Heat just to a boil, stirring to dissolve the sugar. Pour the syrup over the dry mixture and stir until all ingredients are coated. Place in five 9 x 13 inch baking pans. Bake 20-30 minutes, stirring at intervals. If a crunchier texture is desired, bake an additional 15 minutes. Cool, then stir in raisins or dried fruit.

This recipe makes about 20 cups of granola and can be stored up to six months in an airtight container in a cool, dry place.

If you don't have access to an oven in your library or classroom, make up a batch ahead of time, but let children mix in the dried fruit.

2.
LUNCH TO MUNCH

INTRODUCTION

Lunch can be one of the most fun meals for young children. Often it's a mobile meal—eaten on a TV tray, packed in a lunch box or bag (who doesn't love "brown-bagging it"?), or taken along as a picnic. In our fast-paced society, stopping at a fast-food restaurant has become another popular choice. The related activities, games, crafts, and recipes in this chapter focus on these familiar lunch activities.

Since many lunch foods are portable and require little cooking you can easily serve lunch as part of the program. Or, you might invite children to bring their own sack lunch.

Some libraries schedule picnic storytimes in the park during summer months. Stories are enjoyed first, then everyone has lunch together. Since these programs tend to draw large crowds, reading picture books does not work well. Instead, use a participatory story such as "Going on a Picnic," (p. 20), a chant like "Lunchtime Rhyme" (p. 16), and songs like "Fast-Food Quick Trip" (p. 22) and "The Hot Dog Song" (p. 18). Save time to play a few games of the "Teddy Bear Picnic" (p. 25) and "Deviled Eggs—Chicken Legs" (p. 25). If you plan an entire picnic/story series, repeat some of these songs and chants during each program so your group will become old hands by the end of the series. For variety, choose some related participatory stories and songs from the other chapters such as "The Old Woman Who Swallowed a Fly Told Two Ways" (p. 195-98), "The Country Market" (p. 214-15), and "Spider and Fly" (p. 143).

Another twist to the storytime picnic might be a "Teddy Bear Picnic" held in a shopping mall during the winter. Children are invited to bring along their sack lunch and favorite stuffed animal. For this program, be sure to include some of Winnie the Pooh's hums and sing "The Blueberry-Picking Song" from chapter 12, "Stuffing Mother Hubbard's Cupboard" (p. 216) since bears love honey and blueberries!

Even if you don't leave the classroom or library for this lunch program, pack up all the paraphernalia in a picnic basket. It will fit the theme and keep children guessing about what's in store. A mascot puppet for the day might be "Aunt Annie, the Picnic Ant" who goes around asking children what they brought for her to munch on for lunch because she loves everything and everybody who comes on a picnic!

And, since no picnic is complete without a full army of ants, begin and end the program with children marching and singing, "The Ants Go Marching One by One" from Tom Glazer's *Do Your Ears Hang Low?* (Doubleday, 1980). You could also substitute the following parody of this song as an initiating activity as children arrive.

INITIATING ACTIVITIES

The Ants Go Softly Round and Round
(To the tune of "When Johnny Comes Marching Home")

The ants go softly round and round.
Sh! Sh!
The ants go softly round and round.
Sh! Sh!
The ants go softly round and round,
They creep and crawl upon the ground,
And they all move closer,
Eyeing the picnic feast.

Sing this song many times and add children to the marching line as they arrive. You can begin to circle around a picnic basket placed in the middle of the room. When everyone arrives, reach in the basket and take out Aunt Annie, the Picnic Ant puppet (see p. 28), who greets the children.

Lunch is Fun
(An Action Rhyme)

Lunch is fun   (Circle eyes with fingers.)
On a TV tray
Watching cartoons
Any day.

Lunch is fun   ("Drive" car.)
When you go out,
Drive right up,
And take it out.

Lunch is fun   (March in place.)
To take along
In a bag,
Sing a song!

Lunch is fun   ("Pick up" basket.)
If I could pick,
Pack a basket
To go picnic.

But the best lunch time
I like to spend
Is a lunch I share
With all my friends!   (Spread hands in welcome.)

LITERATURE-SHARING EXPERIENCES

Books about Sandwiches

Agnew, Seth M. **The Giant Sandwich.** Illustrated by Barbara Ninde Byfield. Doubleday, 1970.

Mr. Magoffin, struck by a hunger strike, decides to concoct a giant sandwich. To satisfy his hunger, he goes to the butcher, raids the refrigerator, and goes to the garden. After all his work, he decides, in the end, he is no longer hungry.

Gelman, Rita Golden. **The Biggest Sandwich Ever.** Scholastic Book Services, 1980.

Two children on a picnic delight in building a fantastic sandwich. The ingredients are delivered by trucks and planes.

Lord, John Vernon. **The Giant Jam Sandwich.** Jonathan Cape, 1972.

When a giant swarm of wasps invades Itching Down, the citizens create a huge bread and strawberry jam sandwich to trap the pests.

Seymour, Dorothy. **The Sandwich.** Wonder, 1965.

Limited text, but clear pictures show the assembly of huge sandwiches.

Wolcott, Patty. **Tuna Fish Sandwiches.** Illustrated by Hans Zander. Addison, 1975.

Little fish to big fish to fisherman, this simple food chain ends with a tuna fish sandwich.

Related Activities about Sandwiches

Lunchtime Rhyme

Syncopate this chant by clapping out the rhythm. Claps are indicated by slash marks. You can begin and end by ringing a lunch bell.

```
        /                              /         /
Lunchtime,                      Who'll be the ham?
      /                                      /
Munchtime,                          the mustard?
     /         /                            /
What'll we make?                    the lamb?
      /            /                      /        /
Something that starts               the peanut butter?
         /         /                        /        /
With bread we bake.                 and the strawberry jam?
     /        /
You be the first,
    /          /
Ready to spread
        /          /
A nice fat slice
      /              /
Of whole-wheat bread.
```

/   /
Now we need lettuce,
        /   /
    pickles and cheese,
        /   /
    ketchup and onions,
        /   /
    if you please.

/   /
Don't forget the bacon,
            /   /
    the salami and spread,
        /   /
    gobs of mayonnaise
        /   /
    next on the bread.

/   /
Tuck in tomato
        /   /
And a tuna fish,
    /   /
What a handy dandy kind
            /   /
    of lunchtime dish!

/   /
Don't forget to pop
        /   /   /
On the top, top, top,
    /   /
One piece of pumpernickel,
    /   /
Now, let's stop.

(Ring bell.)

And—Diiiggg in! (Leader waves both arms over head as everyone sits down.)

More-Than-Enough Sandwich

(A Fingerplay)

Let's make a sandwich,
Here's the bread,   (Hold palm flat.)
Nice and soft
Like a feather bed.
Next there's bologna
And lettuce on that,   (Lay hand on top, progressively
Swiss cheese   spreading farther apart as lunch
And tomato, round and fat.   gets bigger.)
Ham slice and mayo,
Limburger, salami,
Turkey and mustard,
Cucumber, pastrami,
Now bread on top—

Fit for a pig!
I can't eat my sandwich,
It's gotten too big!
SQUEEZE!   (Press hands together.)
CHOMP!   (Take big bite.)
YUM!   (Rub stomach.)

The Hot Dog Song
(To the tune of "I'm a Little Tea Pot")

I'm a little hot dog   (Hands out, palms up.)
On a bun.
Squirt on the mustard,   (Right hand squeezing.)
Oooo! That's fun!   (Shiver all over.)
Pour on the ketchup,   (Pour with left hand.)
Pickles too,   (Wave fingers of both hands.)
Now you know
Just what to do—   (Bow.)
BITE IN!

Books about Picnics

Berger, Terry. **The Turtles' Picnic and Other Nonsense Stories.** Illustrated by Erikki Alanen. Crown, 1977.

It takes Father, Mother, and Baby Turtle three months to pack a picnic and three years to get to the forest. Just as they are about to eat, Mother says they forgot the can opener. Baby Turtle goes back for it but makes them promise not to touch anything. Mother and Father wait three years. They begin to get ravenous, and finally, after six years they start to eat. Baby Turtle jumps out of the bushes saying he knew they'd cheat!

Brandenberg, Franz. **A Picnic, Hurrah!** Illustrated by Aliki. Greenwillow, 1978.

Elizabeth and Edward plan a picnic, Father shops, Mother prepares the food, but just as they step outside, it starts raining. They make the necessary adjustments to have the picnic indoors, and everyone declares it was the best picnic ever!

Gordon, Margaret. **Wilberforce Goes on a Picnic.** Morrow, 1982.

In succinct text, Wilberforce and his family pile into the car to enjoy a leisurely picnic until the weather takes a turn for the worse.

Kennedy, Jimmy. **The Teddy Bears' Picnic.** Illustrated by Alexandra Day. Green Tiger Press, 1983.

The romping lyrics of a familiar song (the record is included with the book) are perfectly suited to the softly humorous illustrations depicting teddy bears going on a picnic in the woods.

McCully, Emily Arnold. **Picnic.** Harper & Row, 1984.

This wordless picture book tells the moving tale of a little mouse lost on the way to a picnic with her family. No one can eat until she is found, but the reunited family have a happy feast in the end.

Vincent, Gabrielle. **Ernest and Celestine's Picnic.** Greenwillow, 1982.

Ernest the bear makes honey sandwiches for himself and cheese sandwiches for his friend Celestine the mouse, but rain threatens their picnic. Rather than giving up, the two set up a tent and enjoy an almost perfect picnic.

Welber, Robert. **The Winter Picnic.** Illustrated by Deborah Ray. Pantheon, 1970.

Adam's mother is too busy to have a winter picnic until she sees all the preparations he has made. They enjoy sandwiches, chips, and lemonade together in the snow.

Related Activities about Picnics

Let's Go and Pack a Picnic
(To the tune of "Go In and Out the Window")

This song can be performed two ways. First, it works well as a flannelboard activity. A large outline of a picnic basket is first placed on the flannel board. During the song, the children add felt cutouts of the foods mentioned in the song. A second way is to place a picnic basket in the middle of a circle of children. Children can put pictures of the foods mentioned in the song into the basket. Everyone then runs to the center of the circle for the last line and claps.

Let's go and pack a picnic,
Let's go and pack a picnic,
Let's go and pack a picnic,
So we'll have food to eat!

Who will bring the chicken?
Who will bring the chicken?
Who will bring the chicken?
So we'll have food to eat!

Who will bring the lemonade?
Who will bring the lemonade?
Who will bring the lemonade?
So we'll have food to eat!

Who will bring the cupcakes?
Who will bring the cupcakes?
Who will bring the cupcakes?
So we'll have food to eat!

Who will bring the watermelon?
Who will bring the watermelon?
Who will bring the watermelon?
So we'll have food to eat!

Now who will come and get it?
Now who will come and get it?
Now who will come and get it?
(Big pause)
(Say this in a loud chorus:)
WE WILL!
Have good food to eat!

Going on a Picnic

This is a new rendition of the popular lion-hunt participatory story. The leader tells the story and everyone does the appropriate actions.

Do you want to go on a picnic?
Well, let's get out the basket.

What'll we put inside?
Chicken—nice and brown,
Bread and cheese,
Deviled eggs. And salt—I like salt on eggs, don't you?
Potato salad,
Beans and ketchup—I like ketchup on beans, don't you?
Celery,
Carrots,
Don't forget the lemonade and the cupcakes.
(Put down the lid.)
Uh-oh—we forgot the cups.
(Open basket, put in imaginary cups, close lid again.)
Uh-oh—we forgot the plates.
(Open basket, put in plates, close lid again.)
Do we need anything else?
(Children may suggest things to add.)
O.K. Everything's ready.
Let's go!

Oh, it's such a lovely day, let's walk!
Down the road. (Walk in place.)
Up the hill. (Take high steps.)
Higher steps—it's a steep hill. (Take higher steps.)
Now—down the hill. (Walk with hands out to balance.)
Around the river?
No, over the bridge! Tramp, tramp, tramp!
And across the field.

Look—over there by the trees.
Let's just sit down here and open up our picnic.
Here's the cupcakes
And the lemonade,
The plates and the cups.
Carrots, celery,
Ketchup, beans,
Potato salad, deviled eggs,
Salt,
Bread and chesse,
And the chicken!

Doesn't everything look good?
My, I'm hungry, how about you?
Let's get started.   (Pretend to munch.)

Oh NO! Did you feel something?   (Touch head, put hands up.)
It's starting to rain!

QUICK! Got to put everything back in the basket—
Chicken
Bread and cheese
Deviled eggs
Salt
Potato salad
Beans
Ketchup
Celery
Carrots
Cups
Plates
Lemonade
Cupcakes
Slam down the lid! Let's go!

Across the field,
Over the bridge—tramp, tramp, tramp!
Down the hill
Up the hill—
No, that's wrong—
Up the hill and
Down the hill.
Down the road—
Hurry, we're getting soaked!

Run home!
Here we are—inside!
Say—I'm hungry!
I know—let's have a picnic inside!

Books about Lunch at Home and On the Go

Carle, Eric. **What's for Lunch.** Philomel, 1982.
   A play-and-read book introduces ten fruits as a possible lunch for a monkey who is swinging on a vine.

Daly, Kathleen. **My Lunch Box.** Illustrated by Jane Palecek. Golden Press, 1977.
   On his way to school, David wishes he had something different in his lunch box. He meets a variety of animals who offer him their lunches—catnip salad, dog biscuits, cold carrot pie, prickly briar, cheese rinds, corn kernels, potato peeling stew, and hickory nut

biscuits. When David meets a friend with the same kind of lunch as his, they all agree they have the lunch that's right for them.

Lemerise, Bruce. **Sheldon's Lunch.** Parents, 1980.

Sheldon's mother makes his favorite lunch—blueberry pancakes. When his friends come and eat them up, Sheldon proceeds to make more. His friends add "a little bit of everything" until the batter covers everyone. Finally, they follow a recipe and it all comes out fine. Sheldon's recipe is included.

Watanabe, Shiego. **What a Good Lunch!** Illustrated by Yasuo Ohtomo. Collins, 1978.

Bear sets out to eat lunch all by himself but manages to spill soup, get jam on the table, and tangle the spaghetti. His messy but happy solution will please young children who are not yet neat eaters.

Related Activities about Lunch on the Go

Fast-Food Quick Trip
(To the tune of "Jingle Bells")

Pickles, pies
Fish and fries
Shakes and soda pop
Burgers, cheese
No onions, please
Ice cream with fudge on top.

Plastic box
Paper bag
Straw stuck in a cup
Drive right up
And pick it up
Now eat it up
Real fast—gulp!

I Like What's in My Lunch Box

I have a shiny lunch box,
I like to fill with treats,
Like a peanut butter sandwich,
An apple and some sweets.
It has a little thermos
For milk or lemonade.
I like what's in my lunch box,
But I also like to trade!

Lunchtime Surprise
(A Cut-and-Tell Story)

Use an 8½ x 11 piece of paper and fold according to the following directions while you tell the story.

My mother gave me lunch the other day in a box, a plain box that looked like this. (Step 1: fold the paper in half and hold up.)

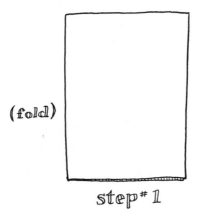

(fold)

step #1

I couldn't tell what was inside. "Open it," my mother told me. "It's a surprise." So I opened one corner (Step 2: fold one corner of the closed side of paper toward you) and I began to imagine what could be in that box.

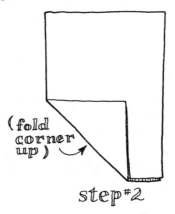

(fold corner up)

step #2

(Pick up scissors.) Was it some long skinny spaghetti? I love spaghetti! (Step 3: from angled edge cut a long cut to the corner. Make this round, and come half way up, cutting a narrow strip.)

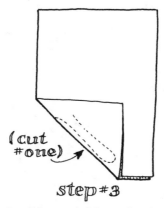

(cut #one)

step #3

It might be spaghetti like this (show children the first cut) or a hot dog. Hot dogs are great! (Step 4: cut back toward open edge, round end and come back to top of folded section.)

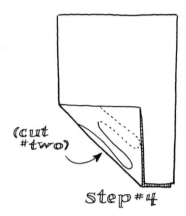

(cut #two)

step #4

That would look like this (show second cut). Or maybe it was a big scoop of ice cream (Step 5: above the fold, through only two thicknesses of paper cut a large half circle ending at the top of the paper). That would look like this. (Show last cut.)

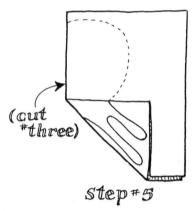

(cut #three)

step #5

Well, I finally opened the box, and lunch was a surprise all right. I only have one question now. (Step six: slowly open shape.)

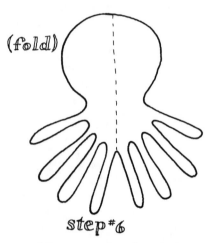

(fold)

step #6

Opened shape reveals octopus

How do you eat an octopus?

GAMES AND FROLICS FOR LUNCH

Giant Musical Sandwich Game

This is a variation of musical chairs, but rather than eliminating children from the fun, you add them to the game.

Begin play with two children standing next to each other. They are the "slices of bread." Leave a little space so the other children can pass through the bread slices. Begin music and have children go through the bread in a line. When the music stops, the child who is between the bread stays and tells what kind of filling he or she is adding to the sandwich. Music continues and children move through the sandwich and filling, and when the music stops again, another filling is added. Music and play continue until you have one giant sandwich with everyone in it!

Deviled Eggs—Chicken Legs Game

This is a variation of the popular "Duck Duck Goose" tag game.

The leader asks children to sit on the floor in a circle making a round picnic basket. In the basket will be lots of deviled eggs, but the chicken leg wants to run away. The leader walks around the outside of the circle and taps each child on the head. With each tap the leader says, "deviled egg," "deviled egg." Then the leader taps a child and says, "chicken leg!" The chicken leg child jumps up and runs around the circle and tries to get back to the empty space before the leader catches her or him. The last one back to the empty space becomes the leader and gets to name the "deviled egg—chicken leg" on the next round.

Teddy Bear Picnic Game

This is a variation of "Simon Says," the kind of game that helps young children listen for directions.

Teddy bears don't take a picnic with them. They find their picnic all around them. Let's all be Teddy bears going on a picnic. When I say, "Teddy bears, jump," you all jump. But if I don't say "Teddy bears," you just stand still.

O.K. Let's try it. "Teddy bears, jump."
 "Teddy bears, touch toes."
 "Sit down."
Oops! Now, "Teddy bears, sit down!"

O.K., now we're ready to get our picnic food.
Teddy bears, get up—we're going to get honey.
Teddy bears, climb a tree.
Teddy bears, shoo those bees.

Now, get the honey!
Oops, too fast.
Teddy bears, get that honey.

Jump down the tree.
Not so fast!
Teddy bears, jump down.
Now let's go get berries.
Teddy bears, squat down low.
Teddy bears, crawl under a bush.
Teddy bears, eat some berries.

Crawl back out of the bush.
No, not yet.
Teddy bears, crawl back out of the bush.

Let's get a drink.
Teddy bears, all look to the right.
No (shake head), no stream there.
Teddy bears, all look to the left.
No (shake head), no stream there.
Teddy bears, look in front of you.
There's our stream!
Teddy bears, all take a drink.
Slurp, slurp, slurp.

Now, Teddy bears are all tired and full.
Teddy bears, stand up and stretch.
And Teddy bears, all sit down.

CRAFT EXPERIENCES FOR LUNCH

Muncher

Any lunch will be more fun if you take it along in a bag. Children are happy with an ordinary brown lunch bag, but they will be delighted with a decorated one like this.

Fold down the top of a lunch bag and write "MUNCHER," in big letters with a crayon or magic marker. Draw a face like the one shown below. Draw big googlie eyes for your critter. And make a big mouth with even bigger teeth so your muncher can munch lunch.

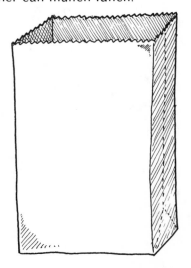

My Lunch Box

If you read the picture book, *My Lunch Box,* this craft activity will be especially fun. Use a center-cut file folder and color or draw around the tab so it will look like the handle on a lunch box. Provide children with beige triangles for sandwiches, yellow circles for apples, brown circles for cookies, and a red rectangle for a thermos. Have children glue the food to the inside of the file-folder lunch box. When they open the folder, they will find a good lunch inside!

Sandwich Sign

Children may not be familiar with sandwich signs that people wear to advertise events, but this is the perfect opportunity to introduce them. Make up your sandwich as a model so they can see a sandwich sign before they make their own.

Use light tan or beige posterboard and color the "crusts" with brown crayon or magic marker. If you want to be fancy, draw some filling sticking out. And what is the filling for the sandwich? You! What kind will you be? Tuna fish? Cheese? Peanut butter? Liverwurst? Add a slogan to the sign such as "Munch me for lunch" or "I'm a Hero." (The "hero" may need some explanation.) Be sure to have a front and a back slice of "bread." Punch holes in the tops of the bread and insert elastic or fat, soft yarn so children can wear the sandwich signs over their shoulders.

Aunt Annie, the Picnic Ant
(A Stick Puppet)

Make a simple cutout of an ant (using the sample pattern below) from black posterboard or tagboard and mount on a narrow craft stick. Now, give Annie a proper "home" by placing her in a plastic food container (the kind that strawberries are sold in). Insert the stick through one of the holes in the bottom and move Annie up and down to show her eating. If you wish to conceal the stick, just line the basket with some checked material or a bandanna.

Aunt Annie

Aunt Annie pops out of her own basket!

Gobble Up: Fast-Food Lunch Muncher
(A Rod Puppet)

Use the sandwich box from any fast-food restaurant. Copy large eyes on a square of paper for children to color and glue to the top of the box. You may wish to leave a folded part so the eyes stand up. Add big teeth cut from a jagged strip of paper and glue around the open edges of the box. Punch a hole in the bottom of the box and insert a soda straw. Bend the end of the straw and attach to the inside top of the box.

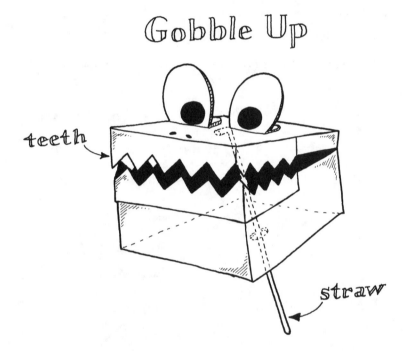

To make Gobble Up eat, hold the bottom of the box in one hand and use the other hand to move the straw up and down. This simple rod puppet is easy enough for young children to manipulate and is very inexpensive to make.

COOKING AND TASTING EXPERIENCES FOR LUNCH

Trail Mix

Here's a tasty treat for picnics or lunch boxes. It's perfect for a hike.

Mix together some of the following ingredients and store in small plastic bags:

dried apples or apricots
sunflower seeds
pumpkin seeds
almonds
walnuts
raisins
coconut
dates or figs

Peanut Butter Wallop

This recipe gets its name because it packs a wallop of nutrition into the favorite lunchtime spread—peanut butter. Spread on whole grain bread for an extra boost.

Mix the following ingredients:

1 cup peanut butter
½ cup wheat germ
¼ cup non-fat dry milk
¼ cup honey

Place in an airtight container and store in refrigerator. About 3 tablespoons of this mixture is about right for one serving. This recipe makes 1½ cups.

SandWitches You Can Make

Peanut Butter and Jelly SandWitch

First, take a slice of bread and spread it with peanut butter for the witch's face.

Next, cut another piece of bread into a

Now, spread your witch hat with grape jelly or blackberry jam.

Put your witch hat on top of the witch head like this:

Add raisin eyes and mouth like this

Don't you want a lot of stringy hair?
Then add some celery sticks.

That's some Sticky Stringy SandWitch!

Scram Ham SandWitch

First take a slice of bread and cover it with a slice of ham for your witch's face.

Next, cut another slice of bread into a

and cover it with a piece of cheese cut into a

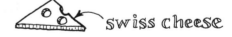

to fit on top of the hat.

Now put the face and hat together like this:

Add big black olives for eyes and a pickle slice for a mouth like this:

You can make hair for your Scram Ham SandWitch out of lettuce or cabbage leaves like this:

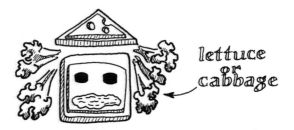

If anybody tries to eat your witch, say "Scram!"

I-Scream Cream Cheese SandWitch

First, take a slice of bread and spread it with cream cheese for your witch's face.

Next, cut another slice of bread in a

and spread it with cream cheese, too.

Add olives (green ones cut in half) for the eyes and mouth like this:

Give your witch lots of carrot curls for hair.

She will look like this:

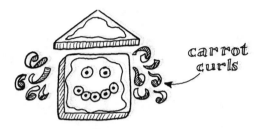

carrot
curls

If you think your witch looks a little pale, just remember she's a "scream cheese" witch, and she just saw a ghost. Booooooo!

3.
FOOD TO GROW ON

INTRODUCTION

Once upon a time Mother Goose rhymes were our common cultural heritage. But thanks to the jazzy rhymes of mass media, children today will grow up rattling off the latest sugared cereal song or soft drink jingle instead. And some of these messages promote products with little or no nutritional value. Early exposure to poor nutrition may be too entrenched to turn around completely, but early-childhood educators, librarians, and parents need to begin their own counter-attack nutrition program long before children begin kindergarten.

The focus of this chapter is on eating a balanced diet, choosing foods from the basic food groups, and selecting healthful foods over a junk diet. Other chapters in this book, especially the ones on fussy eaters and Mother Hubbard's cupboard, also teach good eating and food sources.

Unfortunately, few good picture books have been written on the subject of good nutrition. Here's a challenge to the many talented authors of children's books. Teach—don't preach, but please give us more books about "good" food! In order to supplement the few books on healthy eating for young children, we have included a play, "The H Team vs. the Junk Food Junkies" (p. 40). for use with puppets. The short-lived *P.I.E. News* (Puppets in Education) devoted a lively issue to the use of puppets in nutrition education some years ago. Their philosophy is worth repeating. Preaching, rather than teaching, is almost second nature to adults, especially in this area. (We all succumb to the "Eat it, it's good for you" school sometime.) But puppets can carry such "messages" without children turning them off.

Nutrition programs appropriately include lots of tasting experiences. One of the tasting activities in this chapter, "The Eating of the Green" (p. 52), is used regularly by an elementary teacher we know, and it can inspire you to try many more "try-it-you'll-like-it" times. And let children prepare and bring in their own healthy snacks. Even confirmed junk-food junkies can't resist their own creations!

INITIATING ACTIVITY

If You Want to Grow Up Healthy

Here's a rousing song to begin your program on nutrition. Just about everyone knows "If You're Happy" and one of the best ways to stay happy is to eat right. Try this new version of the song with young children and act it out with your whole body to show strong and healthy versus weak and puny. Let children draw two pictures, "Strong and Healthy Me" and "Weak and Puny Me," after singing the song.

If you want to grow up healthy, eat like this.
Eat a carrot and an apple and a fish.
Don't leave your mashed potatoes,
Or that slice of red tomato.
If you want to grow up healthy, eat like this.   (Make fist to show muscle.)

If you want to grow up puny, eat like this.
Snack on pop and cake and bags of tater chips.
Make room for gooey candy.
Oh, it's oh so very dandy.
If you want to grow up puny, eat like this.   (Droop shoulders, arms
                                                                              limp.)

But if you want to grow up healthy, eat like this.
Try the things your mom puts upon your dish.
Try fruits and vegetables,
Bread and whole grain cereal.
You can grow up strong and healthy if you wish!   (Make fist to show muscle.)

LITERATURE-SHARING EXPERIENCES

Books about Good-for-You Foods

De Paola, Tomie. **The Popcorn Book.** Holiday House, 1978.
  Two kids set out to make popcorn, and while they're cooking, read about its fascinating history and lore. They end up in a blizzard of popped corn but dig in happily. Two recipes for popcorn are included at the end. Humorous illustrations make the factual text come alive.

Krauss, Ruth. **The Carrot Seed.** Harper & Row, 1945.
  A simple story about a little boy who defies all the pessimistic predictions of those larger than he is, and from a tiny seed, grows a great carrot.

Orbach, Ruth. **Apple Pigs.** Collins World, 1976.
  Rhymed verse explains how a family got rid of too many apples by inviting animals to eat, and finally, making apple pigs. Instructions for apple pig assembly are included.

Preston, Edna Mitchell. **Pop Corn and Ma Goodness.** Viking, 1969.

> Preston's story of how Pa and Ma met, married, and shared a lifetime of joys and sorrows romps along in folk ballad verse. The rhythm and alliteration invite lots of hand clapping and foot tapping.

Westcott, Nadine. **Giant Vegetable Garden.** Little, Brown, 1981.

> The mayor enters his poor town in a vegetable-growing contest. When the harvest is brought in, the huge vegetables win. But dividing the prize money is disappointing for the individuals. In the end, they combine their bounty in a huge salad and pie for a community feast — at which the mayor suggests growing contest flowers! The cartoon-like drawings of gigantic vegetables are perfect complements to the text.

Related Activities on Good-for-You Foods

Let Us Make a Salad Bowl
(An Action Rhyme Acted Out by Kids)

Let us make
A salad bowl,
Veggies line up
All in a row.   (Make circle with arms to form bowl.)

One bunch of lettuce,   (Hold up one finger.)
Spray your head.
Two ripe tomatoes,   (Hold up two fingers.)
Sliced and red.
Three cucumbers,   (Hold up three fingers.)
Bumpy and green.
Four long carrots,   (Hold up four fingers.)
Five string beans.   (Hols up five fingers.)
Six stalks of celery,   (Hold up six fingers.)
Chopped so fine.
Sweet little onions,
Seven, eight, nine.   (Hold up seven, eight, nine fingers.)
Ten is the radish,   (Hold up ten fingers.)
We put on top,
Now let's all get ready
To toss —

Up, up, up   (Hold arms up.)
Round and round   (Go around in circle with arms up.)
Ooops, we forgot   (Stop in place.)
The final touch —
Dressing for the salad,   (Wiggle fingers down.)
Here it comes!
Everybody hungry?
Salad's done!

So dig in!   (All sit down.)

Carrots for Every Bunny

(A Cut-and-Tell Story)

Before you tell this story, fold a piece of paper (6 inches long and 8¼ inches wide) back and forth accordian fashion. At the end of the story, you will have a carrot chain.

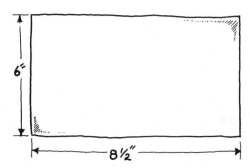
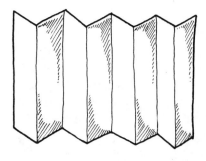

Buzzy Bunny was always into mischief! One day he hopped up the road to find something to eat. (Begin the first long cut like this:)

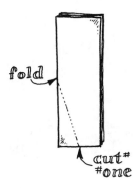

At the end of the road he stopped. (Leave a little space on the fold to hold the carrots together and make a short cut to the center like this:)

There was Mr. MacIntosh's apple orchard. Buzzy Bunny sneaked under the fence, but then he saw Mr. MacIntosh. And Mr. MacIntosh saw him! (Now begin cutting the jagged carrot top as you tell the next part.)

. . . .

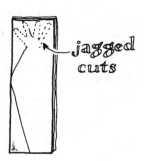

In and out, back and forth Buzzy ran, ziggedy zaggedy through the trees until he reached the fence on the other side. He wiggled right under! Quick as a bunny he ran straight for home. (Now cut the other side of the carrot like this:)

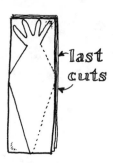

(Put carrot down in lap.)

He was so tired and so hungry and so sad because he didn't have any of those good apples to eat. Just then, Magic Wish Bunny appeared.

"Make a wish," she whispered.

"I wish I had something good to eat," said Buzzy.

(Hold up carrot, folded up to show one.)

"This is something good for you," said Magic Wish Bunny.

But Buzzy shook his head. "It's not enough to share with all my brothers and sisters."

Magic Wish Bunny wiggled her nose and there were two carrots.

(Unfold to make two carrots.)

Buzzy shook his head. "But I have a LOT of brothers and sisters," he said.

So Magic Wish Bunny wiggled her nose again, and there were three carrots.

(Unfold another carrot.)

Again Buzzy shook his head. By this time, the Magic Wish Bunny's nose was all wiggled out. Maybe you boys and girls can help her. When I count to three, wiggle your noses and we'll see what happens. 1—2—3—wiggle!

(Open up all folds to show all eight carrots.)

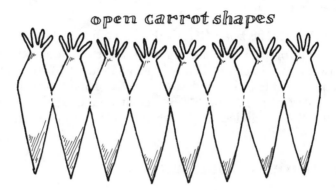

Buzzy clapped for joy.

"Now there are enough carrots for every bunny!"

Fruit Fun
(Face- and Hand-Action Verse)

Follow this verse with children naming as many fruits as they can.

Bananas peel   (Peel imaginary banana.)
Apples crunch   (Bite into imaginary apple.)
Prunes wrinkle   (Wrinkle up face.)
Grapes bunch   (Make two fists with hands on top of
                                                     each other.)

Lemons pucker   (Pucker up face.)
Oranges squeeze   (Squeeze hands together.)
Can you name
More than these?   (Put hands up, questioning.)

Pop Goes the Popcorn
(To the tune of "Pop Goes the Weasel")

Sizzle goes the popcorn oil,   (Wiggle fingers over head.)
Click-clack go the kernels,   (Snap fingers.)
Now we're waiting,   (Squat lower and lower.)
When will it start?
Pop! goes the popcorn!   (Jump up, arms outstretched.)

Books about Nutrition

Barrett, Judy. **An Apple a Day.** Atheneum, 1973.
    Jeremy hates apples so much he hides them in his room to avoid eating them. When the room fills to capacity, he is forced to gluttonous measures with predictable results. The next night at dinner he gets—a pear!

Burningham, John. **Avocado Baby.** Crowell, 1982.

Mr. and Mrs. Hargraves are not very strong so they hope their new baby will be. The baby doesn't like to eat, so the other children suggest giving it an avocado. The baby eats it and grows so strong that he breaks out of his high chair and cot (crib), chases away a burglar, and grows stronger every day eating avocados. A wonderful new version of the Popeye-type character.

Cauley, Lorinda Bryan. **The Bake Off.** G. P. Putnam's, 1978.

All the animals prepare for the autumn Bake-Off contest. Mrs. Beaver is convinced her secret recipe for chocolate cake will win again. Mr. Hare tries his hand even though he specializes in vegetable dishes and knows sweets usually win. His bright idea, a carrot cake, combines the best of both, and Mr. Hare wins the Bake Off. The nutritious recipe for Mr. Hare's carrot cake includes whole wheat flour, wheat germ and a honey-cream cheese frosting.

Related Activities about Nutrition

The H Team vs. the Junk Food Junkies
in
The Race for Health and Happiness

Suggestions for puppets to perform this skit are given at the end of the script.

(The scene opens with the H Team doing exercises to the camp cheer.)

H Team:	We are the H Team. We are tops! We don't snack On soda pop, Candy bars, Or chocolate cake. We don't want A tummy ache! We keep fit On healthy treats. We are the team That's hard to beat! Yeah, Health Team! Yeah, Health Team! Yeah, Yeah, Health Team!
Captain:	Hi Kids! I'm Mickey, Captain Mickey Milk, your best bone-building buddy.
Victoria:	Hello, I'm Victoria Veggie. Dress me up for your favorite salad. I'll make a splash.
Farrah:	Hi ya! I'm the famous and fabulous Farrah Fruit. Just look at my rosy-red apple cheeks and my blue, blue, blueberry eyes, and my curly grapevine locks and—

Victoria:	Hey, Farrah, you're not the only star.
Hollywood:	Star? Did somebody call me? I need no introduction. I'm sure you all know Super Star Hollywood Bread.
Michael:	But don't let it go to your head, Hollywood. I'm the main dish of the Health Team. Everybody knows Michael Meatball. I rock and I roll. What would a plate of spaghetti be without me?
Captain:	Team, team! We'll never beat the Junk Food Junkies in the big race this way. Remember, we all need each other.
Team:	Sorry, Captain.
Captain:	What we need here is more hard work and cooperation.
Hollywood:	But we've worked out all morning. I'd just like to loaf this afternoon.
Captain:	No time for that, Hollywood. The race is tomorrow. Everybody ready for the sound off?

(The Captain lines up the team and begins the next chant.)

Captain:	Sound Off, 1, 2. Sound Off, 3, 4. Sound Off, Health Team Players, Sound Off!
Michael:	We're the team You want to eat, Chicken legs And good roast beef.
All:	Sound Off, 1, 2. Sound Off, 3, 4. Sound Off, Health Team Players, Sound Off!
Farrah:	Apricots And peaches ripe, Don't you want To have a bite?
All:	Sound Off, 1, 2. Sound Off, 3, 4. Sound Off, Health Team Players, Sound Off!

Victoria:
Carrot sticks
Are crunchy fun,
That's what makes
A rabbit run!

All:
Sound Off, 1, 2.
Sound Off, 3, 4.
Sound Off, Health Team Players,
Sound Off!

Hollywood:
Oatmeal, cornflakes,
Whole-wheat bread,
Healthy grains
Will push ahead!

All:
Sound Off, 1, 2.
Sound Off, 3, 4.
Sound Off, Health Team Players,
Sound Off!

Captain:
Milk and yogurt,
Cottage cheese.
Try some Roquefort
If you please!

All:
Sound Off, 1, 2.
Sound Off, 3, 4.
Sound Off, Health Team Players,
Sound Off!

Don't pig out
On any one,
Try each group,
We all are fun!

Sound Off, 1, 2.
Sound Off, 3, 4.
Sound Off, Health Team Players,
Sound Off!

Captain:
There, that's more like it! Now,
1—2—3—4, go—go—go—go!

(The H Team jogs off. Then, in swagger the Junk Food Junkies singing:)

Junkies:
(To the tune of
   "Pop Goes the
      Weasel")
All around the race track
The Junk Food chased the H Team.
The H Team bragged that they would win—
Heh! Junk Food will lick 'em!

Candy bars and chocolate cake—
No one can resist us,
We will kidnap Captain Milk.
Junk Food will lick 'em!

Pop Can: Now, WE'RE the real fun part of this race!
I'm Pop Can. You'll flip over my EXTRA ADDED INGREDIENTS—PRE-SER-VA-TIVES and DE-FOAMING AGENTS! And I just love to make you—burp!

Chips: Hi ya, hi ya, hi ya! I'm Chips, your favorite snackie, by cracky! Betcha can't stop snacking on me! I'm loaded with grease and CAL-OR-IES. I just love to make you—FAT!

Candy: Hi ho kiddies! I'm Candy and I come in a cute little bar just chock full of gooey things to rot your teeth. When you're too busy to eat your dinner, grab me! I'll give you quick energy. I just love to make you rotten!

Cake: Hi kiddos, I'm the perfect end to a full-course junk meal. I'm Tummy Ache Chocolate Cake. Take a big chunk of me and I'll lay down—right on your stomach. I just love to give you a tummy ache!

Tooth: Ah, what a sweet sight you all are! I love you right down to my rotten old roots. And I am the True Hero of the Junk Food Junkies—my name is Sir Sweet Tooth. I zap your appetite! I spoil your dinner! I make you whine and beg and fuss! And I just love to turn you all into spoiled rotten brats!

All:
(To the tune of
"Hickory Dickory
Dock"

Junkory, junkory, junk!
We'll turn you into punks!
Just skip your lunch
And munch a bunch
Of junkory, junkory, junk.

Chips and fizzy pop,
Fill up to the top
Remember cake
For tummy aches!
Junkory, junkory, junk!

Tooth: Dandy, dandy, dandy!
Now, Junkies, here's the rotten plan!

Candy: Oh, goody. I just love rotten plans!

Pop Can: Quiet, marshmallow head!
Give the Tooth here a chance to jaw!

Candy:	Ah, shut up, Pop, or I'll pour you down the drain.
Tooth:	Ah, what sweet music to my ears. I love a good nasty fight! Now—let's get on with the plan. Pop, Chips, Candy, and Cake—line up.
All:	Ah, gee, do we hafta? We were just going to loaf around today.
Tooth:	Not on my sweet time you don't. Now, see here, the H Team has been exercising so they'll win the Race for Health and Happiness.
Candy:	Who could be happy with no candy bars?
Pop:	Quiet, Miss Goody Goody. Stop thinking of yourself for a change.
Tooth:	Thanks, Pop. Now, as I was saying so cleverly, the H Team thinks they can win the race. But, we are going to lick 'em!
Cake:	Yuck! I wouldn't lick any of those disgusting things!
Tooth:	Nobody asked you to lick 'em THAT way. Use your sweet head. (Looks out in audience.) I don't trust those kids out there. They don't look rotten enough. Come here, Junkies.

(They all crowd around Sweet Tooth who whispers to them. The Junkies then shout and punch each other.)

Candy:	That is a rotten plan, Toothie. Do ya think it'll work?
Tooth:	Trust me. The H Team won't know what hit 'em!
Pop:	I still think I should just pop 'em in the kisser.
Tooth:	Easy, Pop! Be cool. Remember, when the H Team jogs by, just give 'em some sweet talk. Chips and I will do the rest.

(The H Team jogs by sounding off 1—2—3—4. The Junkies tease them with such syrupy lines as ''Isn't he the cutest meatball you ever saw!'' ''Hi ya, Farrah, you're some peach!'' ''Vicky, I like the way you crunch!''

Tooth:	Ready, Chips?
Chips:	Ready!

(Chips throws a potato chip bag over Captain Mickey Milk and the Junk Food Junkies drag him off. The H Team falls down. Then, slowly, they help each other up.)

Victoria:	What happened? I feel like somebody just took something out of me!
Farrah:	I don't feel so good myself.
Hollywood:	Me, too. What's wrong with all of us?
Michael:	We've been tricked—and it's not even Halloween! Say, has anybody seen the Captain? He always keeps a cool head!
All:	He's gone!
Farrah:	The Junkies got him. I just know it!
Victoria:	Don't panic!
Hollywood:	But what'll we do? The race is tomorrow!
Michael:	The show must go on.
Farrah:	Michael's right.
Victoria:	Yeah, I haven't been shaping up all these weeks for nothing.
Hollywood:	I do hope the Captain's all right.
Michael:	Those Junkies are mean guys, but the Captain's strong. I'm sure he'll come through O.K. Now, team, sound off, 1—2—3—4!

(They all jog off. In the next scene, it's the day of the race. Mother Nature is holding center stage to announce the race.)

Mother:	Welcome to the Grand and Glorious Food Frolics—The Race for Health and Happiness. This is a race for your life. This year we have the all-time winners—The Health Team. The Health Team will run this year against the new upstarts, the Junk Food Junkies.

(Boos and cheers accompany her introduction.)

(Messenger Muscle runs in.)

Muscle:	Mother Nature, I have an important—maybe even crucial—announcement!
Mother:	Not now, please.
Muscle:	But Captain Milk has been kidnapped. And I strongly suspect that the Junk Food Junkies have spoiled him rotten!

Mother: Is that true? Sir Sweet Tooth, what do you have to say for yourself?

Tooth: Me? Why would such a sweet guy like me do such a nasty rotten thing?

Farrah: Because you ARE nasty and rotten!

Candy: Watch out, fruithead, or I'll turn you into a banana split! Besides, we don't want your old Captain. Why would we want milktoast when we can have all this jazzy energy?

Mother: Silence, please! The race is ready to begin—with Captain Milk or without Captain Milk. H Team, you'll just have to do your best. And may the best team win.

All right, teams in your places. Get back there, Candy. On the starting line. Cheaters never win—here!

Ready—set—grow! Oops, sorry.

Ready—set—go!

(She blows the whistle for the teams to start the race.)

Junkies: Push ahead,
(Chanting loudly)   We've got speed.
(They move out   Sugar helps us
   ahead)   Take the lead!

H Team: Slow but sure,
(chanting   Keep your pace.
   slower, but   Healthy eating
   with spirit)   Wins the race.

Junkies: Fading, sagging,
(running slower   Turning green,
   and slower as Now we're running
   they chant)   Out of steam.

S-s-s-s-s (They fall far behind).

Captain: Now, it's time for me to join the Real Winners!

(Captain Milk joins his team, pushes into the lead as the H Team steps across the finish line.)

Mother: Victory! The Health Team wins! I am bursting with happiness for you, my children! But, tell me, Captain Milk, what happened?

Captain: I hardly know where to begin.

Farrah:	Did they hurt you, Captain?
Captain:	They tried.
Hollywood:	The punks!
Captain:	They gave me a lot of sweet talk. They said nobody liked just plain old milk anymore. They said I should become ONE OF THEM. They said they wanted to make me into—CHOCOLATE MILK!
All:	Oh, No!
Hollywood:	Yeah, they just wanted to spoil you rotten.
Victoria:	We like you just the way you are.
Michael:	Good.
Farrah:	Pure.
Hollywood:	Wholesome.
Mother:	Congratulations on your strength, Captain. You've been an inspiration to us all.
	Now, children, let this be a lesson to all of you:
	Sweets will try to trick and treat, But healthy eating can't be beat!

(The Junk Food Junkies hold up a sign: "This is THE END!")

Puppets to Perform the H Team

One person can do all the puppet characters for this skit with two glove puppets.

Purchase a pair of garden gloves or dig out two old dress gloves.

Turn one glove into the five Junk Food Junkies and one glove into the five Health Team players. Pom pom balls and felt details glued on with tacky glue will make attractive finger puppets for each character. Give each finger puppet some distinctive feature such as a meatball head for Michael, apple cheeks for Farrah, etc. Make Captain Milk a separate, removable finger puppet. Heavy interfacing will work quite well. When the story requires that Captain Milk is kidnapped, simply slip off the Captain Milk finger puppet and slip him over one of the Junkies to show that he has temporarily become "one of them." Mother Nature and Messenger Muscle can be cut-out figures placed on a cardboard stand. Pick them up and move them as they make their brief appearances.

I Feel Good . . . I'm Growing Up

(To the tune of "London Bridge Is Falling Down")

Everyone knows that, in the song, London Bridge is falling down. (Even though it has been moved to Arizona!) Without good food, everyone starts to feel saggy. Just sing this new version of the song when you want to have plenty of pep.

You can sing this song without props, but you can also make it a lively and more graphic picture of good health if you divide children into the basic four food groups. Provide each group with cut-out pictures of the appropriate foods mounted on posterboard. Invite each group to wave its foods when you come to the verse about their food group. At the end of the song, tape pictures of foods to a large mirror (or foil-covered posterboard) and attach a sign to the top: "Look into a picture of good health!"

Leader: I feel good, I'm growing up,
                                        growing up,
                                        growing up.
                     I feel good, I'm growing up.
                     I eat healthy.

Group One: We eat fruits and vegetables,
              CORN AND PEAS! SQUASH AND BEANS!
              We eat oranges, pears, and please—
              PASS ME AN APPLE!

Group Two: We eat bread and cereal,
              WHOLE-WHEAT TOAST! CREAM OF WHEAT!
              We eat noodles, rice, and please—
              PASS ME SPAGHETTI!

Group Three: We like milk and lots of cheese,
              COTTAGE CHEESE! CHEDDAR CHEESE!
              We like yogurt anytime, and—
              MIX ME A MILKSHAKE!

Group Four: We eat meat and fish and nuts,
              HAMBURGER! TUNA FISH!
              We eat chicken, chops, and please—
              BLOB ON THE PEANUT BUTTER!

All: We feel good, we're growing up.
              We can skip, we can jump.
              We have pep to run and play.

Leader: Why?

All: WE EAT HEALTHY!

GAMES AND FROLICS FOR FOODS TO GROW ON

Healthy-Four Game

This game can be played with a small or large group. Just supply each child with a simple food tray—a rectangle of paper or stiff tagboard divided into four sections. Prepare a stack of playing cards by cutting out pictures of foods from magazines and seed catalogs and glue these to card stock the same size as each section in the food tray. The number of cards you will need depends on the size of your group. You will also need to prepare a few "junk cards"—cards of chips, pop, candy, etc. Now you are ready to play.

Give each player a food tray and place all the cards face down in the middle of the group. Explain to the children that a healthy diet needs to have at least one food from each food group. In order to win the healthy food game, a child will have to draw one each of the food groups to fill the tray. The first child draws a card and places it on the tray, the second child draws a card and does the same, and so on around the circle of children. If a child draws a duplicate food group, the card is placed in the discard pile (a "refrigerator" for safekeeping). Play continues until someone has a full and balanced tray. But beware of the junk cards! Anyone drawing one of these has to remove all healthy food cards from the tray and begin play all over.

Popcorn Bowl-Frolic

This is a game that invites everyone to participate as you end up having a full bowl of popped corn in the end. (We don't want any unpopped kernels, do we?)

Leader: What do we eat that smells and sounds as good as it tastes?

Popcorn! Let's make some.

First, we need a big round pan.
Can you make a circle?

Good, now everyone squat down low so you can be kernels in the pan. No jumping up until we're ready. We want a nice big bowl of popped corn.

Ready for the oil? (Pouring action.)

Oil's heating. Sizzles start—hotter and hotter and hotter.

NOW—you pop! (Point to first child who jumps up.) You pop (pointing to second child). You pop, you pop, and you pop (and so on until everyone has popped).

Everybody popped? Good! My, you smell good! (Sniff.)

I'll just add melted butter (pouring action around the circle) and a sprinkle of salt (sprinkle the group).

Now, I'll scoop you up (motion for children to come toward you) and put you in a bowl (motion for children to sit down).

Now, you're just right!

CRAFT EXPERIENCES TO GROW ON

Good Food Finger Puppet

Since puppets are an appealing way to teach nutrition, have children make finger puppets from penny wrappers (free from banks). Cut penny wrapper to about a 3-inch length. Then cut the wrapper at lengthwise seam so the plain inside can be turned inside out. Tape shut with clear tape down original seam. Tape one end shut but leave other open for finger. Glue or draw on pictures of good food.

You-Are-What-You-Eat Puppet

Cut out pictures of apples, corn, carrots, cabbage, milk, hamburgers, and other foods. Glue these on stiff paper or tagboard as the body of the puppet. Attach arms and legs with brad fasteners so they will move. Tape a craft stick or tongue depressor to the main body part so the puppet can be held easily. Move your puppet with lots of zest to show what good foods will do for you.

You Are What You Eat Puppet

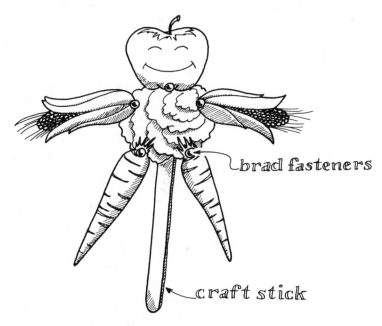

brad fasteners

craft stick

Apple Mac, the Puppet

Color a paper plate red and add a stem and face if you wish. Staple a rubber band tightly across the mouth area. Attach a string to the "lower lip." Now tape a craft stick or tongue depressor to the bottom of the plate. To make your puppet talk, pull the string to make the mouth move. Think of things an apple might say. "Crunch, crunch!" "An apple a day keeps the doctor away!" And so on. . . .

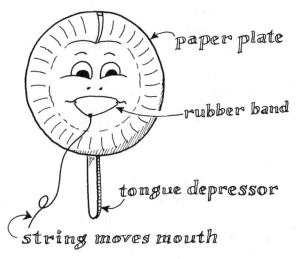

paper plate

rubber band

tongue depressor

string moves mouth

Apple Mac, the Puppet

A Well-Rounded Meal
Or, Look What's on My Plate!

Supply each child with a white paper plate that has been sectioned off into four pie-shaped wedges with a magic marker. Have four piles of food pictures representing the four food groups cut from magazines and seed catalogs ready to be glued on the plates. Children make choices from each group and glue the pictures on the plate. Write around the edge of the plate, "My Well-Rounded Meal."

COOKING AND TASTING EXPERIENCES THAT ARE "GOOD FOR YOU"

The Eating of the Green

This is a fun Saint Patrick's Day activity, but it's such a splendid way to get young children to try green vegetables that you'll want to try it anytime.

Arrange a platter of raw green veggies cut in small portions. Suggestions: celery, green pepper, broccoli flowerets, lettuce and cabbage wedges, cucumber and zucchini slices.

Mix up a bowl of Green Magic Dip (recipe follows). Tell the children that the recipe comes from the "wee folk" of Ireland and everyone knows they own secret treasures. This dip is just one of them. If you don't believe it, try some and watch the veggies disappear!

Green Magic Dip

Blend the following ingredients (use a blender if you want a nice, smooth consistency).

1 12-ounce carton cottage cheese
1 tablespoon lemon juice
1 teaspoon paprika
½ teaspoon garlic salt
dash pepper
few drops green food coloring (the magic ingredient)

Cedric Celery, the Garden Snake

Cut up celery into one-inch chunks and invite children to spread cream cheese, peanut butter, or a cheese spread on the ends of the sections. Now, assemble Cedric in a wavy shape on a platter, cookie sheet, or tray. After everyone has admired him, pass Cedric around for everyone to munch a section.

Cedric Celery, the Garden Snake

Right-Out-of-the-Garden Salad

Bring in a tray of garden vegetables that haven't been washed yet. Some good choices might be edible pea pods, carrots, lettuce, radishes, and green peppers. Let children wash veggies with scrub brushes and lots of water. Eat like bunnies—as is!

Garden Salad Open-Faced Sandwich

Take a slice of whole-wheat bread. Put on a slice of Muenster or Monterey Jack cheese for your "garden bed." Arrange the garden "cuttings"—lots of alfalfa sprouts. Then add the following: green pepper rings, tomato slices, cucumber slices, carrot curls. Top it off with a few sprouts. Drizzle a little light olive oil and vinegar dressing on top to moisten the greens and dress your salad sandwich. Eat your garden!

Catch-the-Sun Salad

This is a healthy salad with fruit and enough other goodies that it might make a whole lunch or light supper. It combines different food groups. Fill a peach half—either fresh or canned—with orange- or peach-flavored yogurt. Surround the center of the "sun" with different rays—banana strips, whole-wheat bread strips spread with cream cheese, thin strips of cheese. Don't you feel that healthy glow?

4.

FOR THE SWEET TOOTH

INTRODUCTION

Very young children often prefer sweets over other tastes. Some children simply crave sugar. It's as if they grew only one kind of tooth—a sweet tooth! With little encouragement, they dream of sugar plums and solid chocolate bunnies. So why have we included a program on sweets?

First, most of us know that TOO MUCH sugar will cause obesity and tooth decay, and has been related to hyperactivity. The clue here is "too much." If you feel strongly against children eating any kind of sugar, then you may want to skip this chapter. However, that may be sticking your head in the sand. Children DO eat sweets. And, not all sweets are bad for you. In fact, the body needs natural sweets in balance with other foods. Honey, a natural sweetener, is often used as a remedy for coughs and colds. You might use this chapter to talk about choosing ice cream, frozen yogurt, oatmeal cookies, and other "healthier" sweets over candy bars.

In this chapter you will find stories and songs, rhymes and games about ice cream, pie, cookies, donuts, and candy. Cakes appear in chapter 6, "Stir and Bake." Some sweets will also show up under "Holiday Foods," so if you are a confirmed sweet tooth, you will find other places in this book to indulge yourself.

The initiating activity song for the program can be sung while Lolly Pop, a stick-and-rod puppet (p. 68-69) tastes the children's fingers before the program begins. Some children's fingers will taste like chocolate, some like lemon, some grape or cherry. This get-acquainted technique is sure to win over even the shyest young child, and everyone will be more than eager to have a finger licked!

INITIATING ACTIVITY

The Big Sweet Tooth
(To the tune of "On Top of Old Smoky")

I have a big sweet tooth.
It likes to eat pie.
It likes any flavor,
My mommy will buy.

My tooth is so happy
When I eat a treat
Like ice cream and cookies
And anything sweet.

So if you have a sweet tooth,
Here in your head,
Just give it the brush off,
And send it to bed!

I spoil my big sweet tooth
With donuts and cake
My tooth is so rotten,
No wonder it aches.

LITERATURE-SHARING EXPERIENCES

Books about Ice Cream

Armitage, Ronda, and David Armitage. **Ice Creams for Rosie.** Andre Deutsch, 1981.
Rosie Posie sells the only ice cream on the island. One hot summer day, she runs out and has to devise an ingenious way to have the ice cream delivered to the island and distributed before it all melts.

Burgess, Anthony. **The Land Where the Ice Cream Grows.** Illustrated by Fulvio Testa. Doubleday, 1979.
Younger preschoolers may not be able to follow this adventure fully, but the journey to the land where the ice cream grows has plenty of appeal for special groups. Take a page-by-page picture excursion through the lollipop trees, the ice creamberg and the ice cream giants — even if you don't read all the words to the children.

Tether, Graham. **Fudge Dream Supreme.** Illustrated by Carl Knock. J. Philip O'Hara, 1975.
A boy whose father tells him he should be thinking what he'll be when he grows up declares he wants to make fudge bars! He proceeds to tell how: start with special cocoa from Bonga Boodad, add milk of the dangerous Jilk, and fill each bar with supreme fillings. His father is convinced and so is everyone else when the day comes to make Fudge Dream Supreme.

Related Activities about Ice Cream

The Ice Cream Super Scoopers
(A Flannel-board Story)

To prepare for this story, cut up to ten circles of felt for the ice cream as follows: green (lime), red (cherry), yellow (lemon), orange (orange), blue (blueberry), purple (grape), pink (strawberry), brown (chocolate), white (vanilla), and white with brown swirls (chocolate ripple). Cut one large yellow triangle for the cone.

Put the cone on a flannel board and hand out the circles to the children. Practice the word "slurp" with all the children so they can recite it at the appropriate time in the story when the child eats the ice cream.

Once there was a little boy who loved ice cream. Do any of you like ice cream? Good. This little boy liked the same kinds of ice cream you do. He liked chocolate. (Have child holding brown circle hold it up.) And he liked vanilla and grape and orange and chocolate ripple. . . . (Have the children hold up these flavors as they are named.)

Now one day his mother gave him money to get an ice cream cone. Oh, wow, thought the little boy. I can get any kind I want. And right away he picked strawberry. (The child holding the pink circle comes up and puts it on top of the cone.) That looked so good he took a big lick. (All SLURP!)

But then he looked again, and he saw lemon ice cream, and he decided to have that, too. (Child puts yellow circle above the pink.) The strawberry-lemon ice cream cone looked so good he took a big lick. (SLURP!)

But then he saw the chocolate ice cream, and he decided to have that, too. (Child puts brown circle above others.) And the strawberry-lemon-chocolate ice cream cone looked so good he took a big lick. (SLURP!) (Continue the story until all the circles are in place. Repeat description of the ice cream cone from the bottom each time and end with a "Slurp" from everyone.)

Now the boy was happy; he had a strawberry-lemon-chocolate-blueberry-cherry-grape-lime-chocolate ripple-vanilla-orange ice cream cone, and it looked so good he took a great big lick of the orange (remove the orange circle). (Slurp!) And he took a great big lick of the vanilla (remove white circle). (Slurp!) And a big lick of the chocolate ripple (remove ripple circle). (Slurp!)(Continue naming the flavors, removing the circles, and saying "Slurp".) And then he ate the cone and said, "Yum Yum! That was just the kind of ice cream I wanted!"

The Banana Split
(To the tune of "Mary Had a Little Lamb")

A banana split is a wonderful concoction, but it's usually too big for one child to finish. While you sing this song, you may construct a banana split. Then let the children construct their own concoctions to eat. Sing the song through first, then do the construction as you sing it again.

Let's all make banana splits,
Banana splits, banana splits.
Let's all make banana splits.
What do we need first?
    A BANANA!

Take off the banana peel,
Banana peel, banana peel.
Take off the banana peel.
What do we need next?
    ICE CREAM!

Scoop the ice cream, 1—2—3,
1—2—3, 1—2—3.
Scoop the ice cream, 1—2—3.
What do we need next?
    TOPPING!

Chocolate sauce and strawberry,
Strawberry, strawberry.
Chocolate sauce and strawberry.
What do we need next?
    WHIPPED CREAM!

Here comes whipped cream—squish, squish, squish,
Squish, squish squish—squish, squish, squish.
Here comes whipped cream—squish, squish, squish.
What do we need next?
    A CHERRY!

Add a cherry right on top,
Right on top, right on top.
Add a cherry right on top.
Now what do we do?
    EAT!

Ice Cream and Something to Go with It!

This is a "tell-and-do" story. Assemble ingredients: ice cream, dish, chocolate sauce, marshmallow creme, whipped cream, nuts, cherry, spoon. Begin telling story and add ingredients as the story indicates.

One day when I went out for dinner, I couldn't decide what to have for dessert, so I told the waiter to bring me something good to eat. He brought me a dish of ice cream. (Set out the dish of ice cream.)

"That's fine," I said. "But I need something to go with it."

"Of course," he said, and he brought out chocolate topping and poured it on. (Pour on chocolate sauce.)

"That's fine," I said, "but I need something to go with it."

"Of course," he said, and he brought out the marshmallow topping and put some on. (Put on marshmallow creme.)

"That's fine," I said, "but I need something to go with it."

"Of course," he said, and he brought out the whipped cream and put it on. (Put on the whipped cream.)

"That's fine," I said, "but I need something to go with it."

"Of course," he said, and he brought out the nuts and sprinkled some on. (Sprinkle on nuts.)

"That's fine," I said, "but I need something to go with it."

"Of course," he said, and brought out the cherries and put one on top. (Put on a cherry.)

"That's fine," I said, "but I need something to go with it!"

He shook his head. "You've got ice cream and chocolate and marshmallow creme and whipped cream and nuts and a cherry. What else could you possibly need?"

Do you boys and girls know what that was? Of course! A SPOON! (Hold up spoon, then take a big bite.)

And it was delicious.

How Do You Eat an Ice Cream Cone?

Everyone does appropriate actions as you read this poem.

Some folks taste it daintily,
Others gulp it down quick-ily.
Some lick around and around,
So it never, ever comes dripping
down.

Some shove the ice cream
Down with their tongue,
So at the bottom of the cone,
You're left with some.

But some lick in just one place
So it gets sort of sloppy,
And the top plops off
In a great big bloppy!

Books about Pie and Cookies

Douglass, Barbara. **The Chocolate Chip Cookie Contest.** Illustrated by Eric Jon Nones. Lothrop, Lee, and Shepard, 1985.
Cory and Kevin learn to make prize-winning chocolate chip cookies with a little help from a babysitter, relatives, and neighbors. The boys win first prize: two tickets to the circus. Their prize-winning chocolate chip pizza cookie recipe is included.

Grey, Judith. **Mud Pies.** Troll Associates, 1981.
A controlled vocabulary book explores the rich variety of pies from apple to cherry, to big and small, but the best pies of all are the ones a child makes—mud pies!

Lindgren, Barbro. **Sam's Cookie.** Morrow, 1982.
Sam's doggie takes Sam's cookie, but Mother makes the ending a happy one. This is a comforting story for young children who have cried over a lost cookie.

Lobel, Arnold. **Frog and Toad Together.** Harper & Row, 1972.

The story "Cookies" (pages 30-41) tests the will power of Frog and Toad to not eat any more cookies. Finally, to keep from nibbling, they give away the cookies. Frog's will power may be working, but Toad goes home to bake a cake.

Miller, Alice P. **The Mouse Family's Blueberry Pie.** Illustrated by Carol Bloch. Elsevier/Nelson, 1981.

When Father and Mother Mouse are away gathering nuts, their oldest, Steven, takes matters into his own hands and begins baking a blueberry pie. Upon their return, Father and Mother Mouse hail Steven as the new family cook!

Schatell, Brian. **Farmer Goff and His Turkey Sam.** Lippincott, 1982.

Farmer Goff's turkey, Sam, has been a blue-ribbon winner at the county fair, but he decides winning blue ribbons isn't any good if he can't eat the truckload of pies Farmer Goff's wife has brought to the fair. Sam runs away from the turkey competition, enters a pie-eating contest, and wins another blue ribbon after all.

Related Activities about Pie and Cookies

Who Put the Cookies in the Cookie Jar?
(A Flannel-board Chant)

In preparation for this activity, cut out a felt cookie jar and circles to represent cookies as follows: white for sugar, brown with lattice pattern drawn on for peanut butter, brown with small black dots for oatmeal, yellow for lemon, and plain brown for gingersnaps. Distribute the circles and, as each cookie is named, have the children place them on the felt cookie jar on the flannel board. Everyone gets to clap in the end.

Leader:	Well, who will put the cookies in the cookie jar?
Response:	We will put the cookies in the cookie jar!
Leader:	What kind did you make?
Response:	We made sugar! (Sugar cookie is placed on board.)
Leader:	What kind did you make?
Response:	We made peanut butter! (Peanut butter cookie is placed.)
Leader:	What kind did you make?
Response:	We made oatmeal! (Oatmeal cookie is placed.)
Leader:	What kind did you make?
Response:	We made lemon! (Lemon cookie is placed.)
Leader:	What kind did you make?

Response: We made gingersnap! (Gingersnap is placed.)

Leader: Let's all clap. (Clap, clap, clap.)

All: Let's all clap for gingersnaps!

A Song for Making Mud Pie
(To the tune of "Sing a Song of Sixpence")

Sing a song for mud pie,
It's my favorite brand.
Mix it til it's mooshey,
Squeeze it with your hand,
Put it in a tin pan,
Leave it in the sun.
Wait about an hour,
Then you know it will be done!

Hungry-for-Pie Song
(To the tune of "Sing a Song of Sixpence")

Let's make pie for dinner.
What shall it be?
Huckleberry, gooseberry,
Let's make two or three.
Cherry, Apple, Pumpkin,
Banana Cream, of course.
I can eat them all alone,
I'm hungry as a horse!

Easy as Pie

This is a good activity to get the wiggles out. It's easy because all children have to do is to sit down when you point to them. Everyone begins standing up, either in a circle or in a group in front of you. Go through the rhyme as many times as you need for all children to sit down. Now you are ready for the next activity.

Apple
Cherry
Boysenberry
Peach
Pumpkin
Round
Black bottom
Shoo fly
Now sit down!

Books about Donuts, Candy, and Other Sweet Treats

Balian, Lorna. **The Sweet Touch.** Abingdon, 1976.
> Penny finds a magic ring that makes a young genie appear. He grants her wish that everything she touches will turn into something sweet. Under her feet she finds chocolate, her jumping rope becomes a licorice whip, her bedposts, gingerbread. When she becomes stuck up in taffy quilts and sick to her stomach, she asks for help, but the young genie has to call on his mother to rescue them.

Milne, A. A. **The Hums of Pooh.** Methuen, 1972.
> Pooh's hums appear in other Pooh books as well. Whatever source you use, you'll want to sing or hum these favorites: "Isn't it funny/how a bear likes honey," "Cottleston Pie," and "Sing Ho! for the life of a bear"—all sweet-related songs.

Moskowitz, Stewart. **Too-Loose the Chocolate Moose.** Simon and Schuster, 1982.
> Momma and Poppa Moose's favorite food is chocolate, so the baby moose they get is, of course, a chocolate moose!

Stamaty, Mark. **Who Needs Donuts?** Dial, 1973.
> A little boy goes out looking for donuts, meets a man who collects them, and saves a woman from drowning in a flood of coffee with his donuts.

Related Activities about Donuts, Candy, and Other Sweet Treats

The Disappearing D-O-N-U-T
(A Flannel-board Song)

Almost every child loves the popular B-I-N-G-O song. It's fun to clap and try to remember to leave out the letters as you proceed through the song. This new version is about donuts and even reinforces the idea with a flannel-board donut cut into sections.

In preparation, make a large donut shape from felt, cutting the donut into five sections. Glue the letters D-O-N-U-T on the sections. Assemble these on a flannel board to begin the activity. You may want to serve donuts after the activity.

I know a treat that has a hole
As you can plainly see.
D-O-N-U-T
D-O-N-U-T   (Leader: point to letters as you sing.)
D-O-N-U-T
Save a bite for me!
CHOMP!   (Remove D section.)

I know a treat that has a hole
As you can plainly see,
(Clap) O-N-U-T   (Point to blank space, then letters.)
(Clap) O-N-U-T
(Clap) O-N-U-T
Save a bite for me!
CHOMP!   (Remove O piece.)

(Continue song clapping for each section of disappearing donut, pointing to blank spaces and remaining letters until the donut is all gone.)

I know a treat that has a hole,
But now where could it be?
(Clap-clap-clap-clap-clap
Clap-clap-clap-clap-clap
Clap-clap-clap-clap-clap)
And there's none left for me!

Dippy Donut Song
(To the tune of "Baa Baa Black Sheep")

Yum, yum, Donuts.
Chocolate iced,
Glazed and twisted,
Warm and nice.
Cream filled,
Peanuts on the top.
Long John! Jelly!
I can't stop!
Better than a sticky roll,
Eat them right down to the hole!

The Fudge Song
(To the tune of "Home on the Range")

Oh give me a pan,
And a spoon if you can,
Pour some milk and sugar right in.
Then add choc-o-lot
And good stuff you've got,
Now you know how to begin.

Stir, stir round and round.
Sneak a lick whenever you can.
Oh give me a taste,
But try not to waste
My fudge that's stuck in the pan.

Chorus:
Fudge, fudge is the best.
I eat it whenever I can.
Now caramel's O.K.
But I'd vote any day,
To lick the fudge out of the pan!

Gum Drop Sticky Teeth Rhyme

Gum drop, gum drop,
In a bowl,
How many gum drops
Can you hold?   (Leader pats tummy.)

(Mime eating one, hold one finger up.)

Grum drop, grum drop
In a bowl,
How many grum drops
Can you hold?   (Leader rubs tummy.)

(Mime eating two, hold two fingers up.)

Grum dum, grum dum
In a bowl,
How many grum dums
Can you hold?   (Leader rubs tummy.)

(Mime eating three, hold three fingers up.)

Gum dum, gum dum
In a bowl,
How many gum dums
Can you hold?   (Leader rubs tummy.)

(Mime eating four, hold four fingers up.)

Dum gum, dum gum
In a bowl,
How many dum gums
Can you hold?   (Leader rubs tummy.)

(Mime eating five, hold five fingers up.)

Dum dum dum dum
Gum gum gum
Un uh, un uh,   (Say last two lines through
Uh Uh Uh!   stuck-together teeth!)

GAMES AND FROLICS FOR THE SWEET TOOTH

The Honey Bee Dance
(To the tune of "Skip to My Lou")

Children may be interested in knowing that a beekeeper has to leave some of the honey in a bee hive so the bees can continue making honey. The words to this song teach about the honey-making process.

Children, the "bees," form a circle around the leader who acts as the beekeeper for this frolic. Everyone sings and dances as follows:

Bees making honey in a hive,   (Skip to beekeeper.)
Bees making honey in a hive,   (Walk back to circle.)
Bees making honey in a hive,   (Skip to beekeeper.)
Everyone is sticky!   (Put up hands as if they are sticky.)

Beekeeper cleans the honeycomb,   (Walk back to circle.)
Beekeeper cleans the honeycomb,   (Walk to beekeeper.)
Beekeeper cleans the honeycomb,   (Walk back to circle.)
Leave enough for dinner.   (Rub tummies.)

Bees do a dance, the work is done.   (Join hands and go around in circle.)
Bees do a dance, the work is done.
Bees do a dance, the work is done.
All clap hands together!   (Drop hands and clap.)

Queen Bee—A Honey of a Game!

Children sit in a circle. The Queen Bee walks around the circle tapping children on the head and says, "Buzz, buzz, buzz" with each tap. Each child tapped gets out of the circle and follows the Queen around. When the Queen calls, "Go make honey!" those tapped—and the Queen Bee—run off to an empty space. The one left out gets a special role—the role of Queen Bee. Play continues several times.

Doin' the Chocolate Shake
(To the tune of "Hokey Pokey")

This simple little dance lets children make a chocolate shake with their bodies. Sing the song through three times, getting progressively faster as your "shake" mixes more thoroughly. Children will be ready to listen more quietly after this activity.

You squat right down,	(Squat.)
Up you stand.	(Stand up.)
Stamp your feet,	(Stamp.)
Shake your hands.	(Shake hands.)
Wiggle all over	(Wiggle.)
And mix real well.	(Roll hands over and over.)
Doin' the Chocolate Shake!	(Clap hands.)
YUM!	(Reach high.)

Cookie Muncher Game

One child is chosen the Cookie Muncher. This child covers his eyes while the leader takes one cookie from a cookie jar or bag, and hands it to a child in the group. All children hide their hands behind their backs and chant:

Cookie Muncher, Cookie Muncher,
Do you know
Who snatched your cookie
Where did it go?

Cookie Muncher opens eyes, has three guesses to identify the snatcher. If the child guesses successfully, she or he gets the cookie (and saves it for the cookie munching part at the end). If the Cookie Muncher is unsuccessful, the child holding the cookie gets to keep it. Another child is chosen Cookie Muncher and the game proceeds. At the end, enough cookies are passed out so everyone can be a REAL Cookie Muncher!

CRAFT EXPERIENCES FOR THE SWEET TOOTH

An Incredible Everything-You-Want-in-One Pie

It's always hard to decide what kind of pie you want when there are so many delicious kinds. Help make this decision easier by giving children the opportunity to make an everything-you-want-in-one pie.

Each child needs a white paper plate—the kind with fluted edges is perfect. Provide a number of pie wedges—colored construction paper cut into eighths will work nicely. (If you are preparing the wedges ahead of time, trace the plate onto colored paper, fold circle into half three times, then cut to make eight equal sections. You can cut out lots of wedges this way.)

Children can choose what "flavors" they want. Some suggestions for colors and flavors might be: red for cherry, yellow for banana or lemon, green for mint or lime, blue for blueberry, orange for orange, purple for grape, pink for strawberry, and brown for chocolate. Glue the pie wedges down on the plate in any order you wish. You'll have lots of fun calling off the name of your pie. I have a banana-chocolate-cherry-strawberry-grape-orange-blueberry-mint pie. What's the name of your pie?

An Incredible Everything-You-Want-in-One Pie

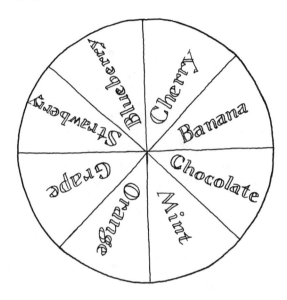

Double Scooper Ice Cream Cone

For this craft you can use the same colors of construction paper as the project above, but children will have to choose their two favorite flavors to make a double scoop ice cream cone. Use the same size pie wedges you've already cut (squaring off the rounded edge) for the ice cream cones. Now cut circles of brightly colored construction paper—approximately 3½ inches in diameter. Let children choose their two favorite flavors and glue to the ice cream cone. This is an excellent opportunity to talk about shapes (round and triangle) and colors, too.

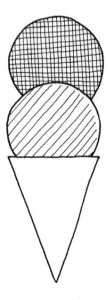

Pooh's Hunny Jar and the Bees' Bee Hive

Use a recipe for playdough that dries, or, if you want to be extra whimsical, use this peanut butter no-bake cookie playdough recipe.

Peanut Butter Cookie Play Dough

Mix 1 jar (18 ounces) creamy peanut butter
6 tablespoons honey (see how appropriate this is for the bee part of the craft?)
Nonfat dry milk—just enough so the dough will be pliable.

Now, make little "snakes" of your dough by rolling pieces of it back and forth with your hands on a board or clean paper-covered surface. When you have a pile of these long pieces, make them into coils and stack them on top of each other, working the dough with your hands so the coils will stick together. The coils should be slightly smaller at the top so the pot will look like a bee hive.

Pooh's Hunny Jar and the Bees' Bee Hive

Lolly Pop Puppet

Cut out a six-inch circle from posterboard and fasten a craft stick or a ¼-inch dowel 12 inches long to the back with strapping tape or masking tape. Cut a slit in the mouth area and insert strip of pink construction paper (about 1½-inch wide x 5 inches long) in the slit for the tongue. Slightly curl the end of the tongue by curling the paper around a pencil. Fasten another dowel or string to the end of the tongue so it can lick the children's fingers. Draw on features if you wish.

COOKING AND TASTING EXPERIENCES FOR THE SWEET TOOTH

Mud Pie

You may be surprised that this recipe does not call for mud. It *looks* like rich dark mud, but tastes—delicious. Be sure you don't overbake. The pie should be nice and soft.

Mix 6 heaping teaspoons cocoa, 1 cup sugar, ¼ cup flour, and dash of salt. Then add 2 eggs, slightly beaten, and ¼ cup melted margarine. Mix. Then add 1 teaspoon vanilla and mix in. Pour your mud concoction into a greased 9-inch pie pan. Bake 20 minutes at 350 degrees. Cut into *small* portions.

Chocolate Haystacks
(Or Butterscotch Haystacks)

Melt two packages of chocolate chips (or butterscotch chips) in a double boiler (or in a microwave oven). Stir in 1 can of chow mein noodles (and 1 cup peanuts if you like). Drop from teaspoon onto waxed paper and let set a bit.

Roll-the-Can Ice Cream

You can make ice cream without a commercial ice cream freezer, and the children will love the action!

Pour the following ingredients into a 1-pound coffee can:

1 cup heavy cream, 1 cup milk, 1 beaten egg, ½ cup sugar, and 1 teaspoon vanilla. Put lid on the can and place it inside a 3-pound coffee can. Add layers of crushed ice and rock or kosher salt around the smaller can. Put lid on larger can.

Now let the children roll the can briskly back and forth on a hard surface (like the playground) for about ten minutes. Open the larger can, dump the ice and water. Take out the smaller can, uncover, and stir down the contents from the sides of the can. Repack the larger can with fresh ice and salt. Return the smaller can, cover the larger can again, and roll again for another 5-10 minutes. The longer you roll, the firmer the ice cream will be!

Ice Cream Concoctions

Using the above ice cream recipe, play soda fountain by adding different juices. Almost as much fun as the making is the naming of your treats. Here are a few ideas:

Ice cream plus cranberry juice—a pink cow.
Ice cream plus orange juice—an orange cow.
Ice cream plus grape juice—a purple cow.
Ice cream plus limeade—a green cow.

5.
FUN AND FANTASY FOODS

INTRODUCTION

Most of the food in this chapter you will never eat. This is just for fun! And the fun is so outlandish that even very young children won't be tempted to try "Socks for Supper." But they will come up with their own hilarious menus.

Fun-food books range from the rollicking word play in *Pumpernickel Tickle and Mean Green Cheese* (p. 74) to the unlikely-sounding but tasty recipes in *How to Make Elephant Bread* (p. 73). We've added food-pun games and activities about shapes, sounds, and qualitites of food children find amusing. Wordplay comes so naturally to children as they learn language that you may want to write your own activities to add to this chapter and send them to us!

When we leave this everyday fun and enter a world where rain makes applesauce, meatballs come from the sky, and pickle creatures walk home from the supermarket, we have opened the pages of a fantasy-food book. Preschool-age children drift so easily into the make-believe world that these fantasy books are favorites. What child hasn't been told she would turn into a food she ate compulsively? "The Terrible Tale of Joshua Nickel" (p. 81) develops this familiar theme children will quickly recognize. And the theme of "Why Doesn't It Grow on Trees?" (p. 79) comes from the common wish that our favorite foods could grow from plentiful and unlikely places.

INITIATING ACTIVITY

Lick 'Em Up

Use any kind of talking-mouth puppet—preferably one with a long tongue—for this initiating play with children. The puppet's name is "Lick 'Em Up" and he resides in a big lunch bag. Write his name on the outside of the bag and tell the first children who come that you've brought along a guest. When Lick 'Em Up emerges, he can go around at first silently nibbling fingers and toes of the more curious children. His dialogue can go something like this:

"Hi ya! My name is Lick 'Em Up. I just love to lick silly food. Does anyone know something silly to eat?" (If children are shy, Lick 'Em can go around and lick the fingers of children and say things like "Where did you get that peanut butter thumb?" "Delicious! I just love sauerkraut juice fingers!" "Your big toe tastes just like limburger cheese!") Begin the activity when all the children have arrived.

Now, let's play a game. I'll name a silly food, and you show me what kind of animal eats it. O.K.?

Here's an easy one: carrot pie!
(Prompting: Can you wiggle your nose like a bunny?)

Now: peanut shell cookie!
(Prompting: O.K. Elephants, swing those trunks!)

This one is hard: Fly pie!
(Prompting: I know you can all hop like frogs!)

What about: mouse soup!
(Prompting: I can see a lot of cats out there!)

Hmmm: Let's try banana burgers!
(Prompting: Can you act like monkeys?)

Good. Very good. But before we get started, I'd like a little snack. Does anyone have a thumb? Show me your thumbs. Good. Could I just have a little lick? (Lick 'Em tastes a few thumbs and thanks children. He says things like: "Yours tastes like chocolate" and so on until all willing thumbs are licked.)

Well, I don't want to make a pig out of myself. I'd better curl up and take my "after-snack nap." See you all later! (Lick 'Em retires to his lunch bag.)

LITERATURE-SHARING EXPERIENCES

Books about Fun Foods

Ahlberg, Janet, and Allan Ahlberg. **Each Peach Pear Plum.** Viking, 1979.
Rhymed text and inviting illustrations ask the reader to join in a game of I-Spy-with-Mother-Goose characters in surprising situations. Everyone enjoys a plum pie picnic in the end.

Ahlberg, Janet, and Allan Ahlberg. **Yum Yum.** Viking Kestrel, 1984.
This "slot book" arrangement invites readers to feed animals and monsters with cutout removable portions of such foods as bowls of frogs, wiggle worms, coils, as well as more normal daily fare.

Aldridge, Josephine, and Richard Aldridge. **Reasons and Raisins.** Illustrated by John Larrecq. Parnassus, 1972.
Little fox swipes his mother's raisins and has many adventures before returning home. Among his encounters is a circus fat lady who recites "The Fat Poem." Finally, all ends well with his favorite dessert, raisin pudding.

Asch, Frank. **Mooncake.** Prentice-Hall, 1983.

Little Bear builds a rocket to the moon to see what the moon tastes like.

Asch, Frank. **Sand Cake.** Parents, 1978.

Baby Bear makes Papa a sand cake by drawing all the ingredients in the sand. Mama Bear answers the family's real hunger by making them a real cake.

Benedictus, Roger. **Fifty Million Sausages.** Illustrated by Kenneth Mahood. Andre Deutsch, 1975.

Aldo's father owns a large sausage factory in Italy, but Aldo is more interested in inventions than in sausage. But Aldo's super inventions end up helping his father in the sausage factory.

Brown, Marc. **Pickle Things.** Parents, 1980.

The verse in this fun book tells about things that pickles aren't—a pickle nose, pickle hair, pickle toes, pickle kite, pickle hat, and so on until you'll wonder what a pickle *is* good for—eating, of course!

Degen, Bruce. **Jamberry.** Harper & Row, 1983.

In romping rhythm, a bear discovers the joy of berries of all kinds. The illustrations are just as fun as the verse.

Dorros, Arthur. **Pretzels.** Greenwillow, 1981.

The first story, "How Pretzels Were Invented," explains how a ship cook uses hard biscuit dough for an anchor and the new invention turns into pretzels.

Eberts, Marjorie, and Margaret Gisler. **Pancakes, Crackers, and Pizza: A Book about Shapes.** Illustrated by Stephen Hayes. Childrens, 1984.

A controlled-vocabulary text explores round, square, and triangular foods that young children will love to eat.

Kent, Jack. **Socks for Supper.** Parents, 1978.

A poor couple get tired of eating turnips, so they trade socks for milk and cheese until they have no more socks or sweaters to trade.

Mandry, Kathy, and Joe Toto. **How to Make Elephant Bread.** Pantheon, 1971.

Fifteen incredible snacks with instructions for young children to make. The names are sillier than the actual snacks.

Noble, Trinka Hakes. **The Day Jimmy's Boa Ate the Wash.** Illustrated by Steven Kellogg. Dial, 1980.

The class trip to the farm is complicated by Jimmy's boa, whose presence upsets the chickens and begins a chain of events that includes egg-throwing and pigs on the bus.

Oxenbury, Helen. **Eating Out.** Dutton, 1983.

Eating out may not be as much fun for a young child and the family as they first think. Here's a humorously realistic picture young children should be able to identify with.

Patz, Nancy. **Pumpernickel Tickle and Mean Green Cheese.** Watts, 1978.

Benjamin and Elephant get caught up in a frenzy of fantastic food rhymes and puns on the way to the store. Anyone who has ever forgotten what was on the grocery list and loves to play with words will be delighted.

Rockwell, Thomas. **Oatmeal Is Not for Mustaches.** Illustrated by Ellen Christelow. Holt, Rinehart, 1984.

Two young children cavort through a day of play; many of their happy times concern food and cooking-utensil play.

Williams, Vera B. **The Great Giant Watermelon Birthday.** Greenwillow, 1980.

To celebrate the birth of their great grandchild, the owners of Fortuna Fruit Market give away watermelons to children who share the new baby's birthdate. The one hundred children and their relatives meet in the park with their watermelons to have a gigantic party complete with candles in the watermelons!

Zeifert, Harriet. **Munchety Munch.** Viking, 1984.

Tiny board book with clear photos treats the young child to food sounds.

Related Activities about Fun Foods

Silly, Silly Things to Eat
(To the tune of "Yankee Doodle")

Silly, silly things to eat
I bet you'd never try —
Groundhog burgers,
Skunk in stew,
Or porcupine pie.

Elephant or turtle leg,
That's too tough for me.
Caterpillar sandwiches
Would taste too wiggily!

A Square Meal
(A Flannel-board Story about Food Shapes)

In preparation for this story, make lots of waffle (square) shapes out of felt — at least three — for the sequence of three in each part that talks about Sarah's love for waffles. Also, prepare round shapes: a pizza, egg, and hamburger. Then cut out brown squares for the roast beef, green squares for the green beans, tan squares for the whole-wheat bread, and a red square for the cherry cobbler. Now, tell the story, putting the felt pieces on the board as the story refers to the various foods.

Sarah Sue wouldn't eat anything except waffles. Waffles with butter. Waffles with sugar or syrup or jam. Or just plain waffles. Waffles for breakfast. Waffles for lunch. Waffles for dinner. And leftover waffles before bed.

Sometimes for breakfast, her mother fixed her an egg. But Sarah Sue said, "How awful. I want waffles. Waffles with butter. Waffles with sugar or syrup or jam. Or just plain waffles."

Sometimes for lunch her mother gave her a hamburger. But Sarah Sue said, "How awful. I want waffles. Waffles with butter. Waffles with sugar or syrup or jam. Or just plain waffles."

And sometimes for dinner her mother made her a big round pizza. But you know what Sarah said!

"How awful. I want waffles. Waffles with butter. Waffles with sugar or syrup or jam. Or just plain waffles."

Finally, one day, Sarah Sue's grandmother came to dinner. Sarah Sue's mother fixed roast beef and gravy, green beans, whole-wheat bread, and cherry cobbler for dessert. Everyone ate and ate and ate. All except Sarah. And you know what she ate.

"Sarah," said her grandmother. "You should eat a good square meal."

"But I do, grandmother! Waffles are squares. Waffles with butter. Waffles with sugar or syrup or jam. Or just plain waffles. Waffles are my favorite square meal."

Sarah's grandmother laughed.

"Waffles are square. But they are not a square meal."

Then Grandmother took a clean plate and cut up little squares of roast beef and green beans. She took a slice of whole wheat bread and a square of cherry cobbler, and she gave it all to Sarah Sue and said, "*This* is a square meal. Try it."

And you know what? Sarah Sue ate every bite.

Now she tries other things in squares—like cheese and crackers. But she still likes waffles. After all, waffles are full of squares—even if they aren't a square meal!

Hello Jello
(An Action Poem)

Hello Jello!	
Are you cold	
Shaking in your	(Hug self and shiver.)
Fancy mold?	
Hello Jello!	
Did you sneeze	(Finger under nose.)
When they put you	
In to freeze?	
Hello Jello!	
You sure wiggle.	(Wiggle whole body.)
Bet they made you	
Out of giggles!	
Hello Jello!	
On my tongue.	(Stick out tongue.)
Slide right in	
My happy tum!	(Rub tummy!)

Ker Choo Ee!
(A Peppery Tale to Act Out)

Children can play the parts of the ants, the buttercups, the cattails, and the pepper. Give them face masks mounted on craft sticks. You as leader can be the anteater. If you wish, you may wear an anteater body costume like the one described in "The Very Hungry Bear" (p. 140-42). If you have a body suit, you will be able to let the children crawl underneath when you pretend to eat the ants. In any case, be sure to have the children practice sneezing before you begin the story. All children will get a chance to sneeze when you come to that part.

It was the spring of the year. An Anteater was looking for a hill of fresh ants to eat.

He came to a meadow. He looked around. But all he found were buttercups. (Give buttercups on sticks to three children.)

"You smell good," he said. "But I cannot eat buttercups." So Anteater walked on.

He came to a stream. He looked around. But all he found were cattails. (Give cattails on sticks to three children.)

"You look good," he said. "But I cannot eat cattails." So Anteater walked on.

Then he came to a hill of fresh ants. Just what he wanted! (Give ant masks to three children.)

"You smell and look and taste good," he said. And Anteater ate up the 1, 2, 3 fresh ants. (Ants crawl under Anteater's costume.) But Anteater was still hungry. So he walked on.

Soon Anteater came to another hill. A patch of pepper was growing on the hill. But Anteater didn't know it was pepper so he said,

"Ahhhh—more ants!" (Give pepper pictures to three children.) And Anteater ate up the pepper too. (Pepper children crawl under the Anteater costume.)

Well—Anteater's nose twitched. And Anteater's nose itched. Anteater's nose felt a great big sneeze down inside. It was trying to come out. Do you all know how that feels? Well, will you all help the sneeze come out? When I say "three," let's all help the sneeze come out.

1-2-3
A, A Choo
A, A Choo
A A Ker Choo Ee!

Thank you very much!

Anteater sneezed, and out came the pepper. (Peppers come out.) And out came the ants. (Ants come out.) Anteater felt so much better that he sat down to rest. But he rubbed his nose all day because it was sore from all that sneezing.

After that, he never ate pepper again. Would you?

Ker Choo EE!

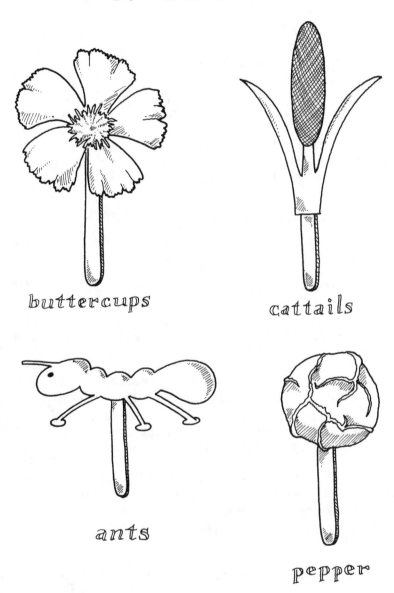

buttercups

cattails

ants

pepper

Oh Where, Oh Where Is My Peanut Butter?
(To the tune of "Oh Where, Oh Where Has My Little Dog Gone?")

Oh Where,
Oh Where,
Is my peanut butter?
It's stuck to my teeth and my gums.
But the place it likes best,
I bet you can guess—
It's up on the roof of my mouth!

(spoken) Now—what do we do?
(Children stand on their heads!)

Books about Fantasy Foods

Barrett, Judi. **Cloudy with a Chance of Meatballs.** Illustrated by Ron Barrett. Atheneum, 1982.
Grandpa's bedtime story takes us to a land where the food comes with weather. All is well when there is just a drizzle of orange juice, but a tomato tornado and other food catastrophes finally force the inhabitants to flee.

Benjamin, Alan. **Ribtickle Town.** Illustrated by Ann Schweninger. Four Winds, 1983.
This story in rhyme describes a young boy's dream of a fantastic town where gates are made of dinner plates, houses are teapots, and restaurants serve chocolate steak and spaghetti cake.

Koshland, Ellen. **The Magic Lollipop.** Knopf, 1971.
Reggie's magic lollipop makes fantastic things happen to him, and even when it's gone, the magic lives on—the stick turns into a banjo that Reggie can play.

Kroll, Steven. **Fat Magic.** Illustrated by Tomie de Paola. Holiday, 1978.
Prince Timothy finds himself under a fat curse that creates all kinds of disasters when he insults Edgar the Court Magician's feet. Determined to right the situation, he steals Edgar's magic shoes and ransoms them for a promise from his family to let him eat whatever he wants.

McGowen, Tom. **Dragon Stew.** Illustrated by Trina Schart Hyman. Follett, 1969.
King Chubby holds a contest to find a royal cook who can come up with the most unusual recipe. Klaus wins by letting the King do his own cooking. This works until a dragon is brought back to the castle for Klaus to turn into dragon stew. The dragon saves the day by making stew. Dragon stew is stew made *by* a dragon!

Pinkwater, Daniel. **Pickle Creature.** Four Winds, 1979.
Conrad likes to stay at his grandmother's because she bakes him oatmeal cookies, lets him stay up late, and sends him to the supermarket at night. On one of these trips, Conrad finds a pickle creature and takes it home. His grandmother instructs him on the proper care and feeding of pickle creatures.

Rees, Ennis. **Potato Talk.** Illustrated by Stanley Mack. Pantheon, 1969.
This preposterous tale of a man hearing potatoes talk seems to get sillier and sillier until it ends with a judge being the silliest of all.

Scheer, Julian, and Marvin Bileck. **Rain Makes Applesauce.** Holiday House, 1964.
A lyrical, nonsense series of images includes food and stars, and rain and a lot of fun. Each whimsical line ("the stars are made of lemon juice," "monkeys mumble in a jelly bean jungle," etc.) ends with the assertion "rain makes applesauce." Children love the silly talk and will chorus the last line, "But rain makes applesauce!"

Yaffe, Alan. **The Magic Meatballs.** Illustrated by Karen Barn Andersen. Dial, 1979.
On his way home from the store, Marvin is given magic chopped meat by a strange man. His family eats it by mistake and all turn into food.

Related Activities about Fantasy Foods

Why Doesn't It Grow on Trees?
(A Flannel-board Story)

This story recaptures the dream many children have about food growing from unlikely places, or unlikely food growing in their own backyards. For telling this story on a flannel-board, make felt cutouts (or paper pictures with felt on the back) of a wishbone, a small tree, a medium-sized tree, and a large tree, large and small pancakes, glasses of milk, a hot dog, a hot-dog bun, corn on the cob, pickles, chips, big meatballs, spaghetti, a cereal bowl, a soup bowl, and a turkey.

Now, you're ready to tell the story.

There was once a little girl named Jennifer. She was just about your age. And she had a wish. She wished that food could grow on trees. Not food like apples, but food like pancakes or spaghetti.

One night her mother fixed her fried chicken for dinner. Fried chicken was one of Jennifer's favorite foods, because she liked to get the wishbone and make a wish. (Put wishbone on board.)

Most of the time, Jennifer pulled the wishbone and got the short end. And her wishes didn't come true. But this time she pulled and pulled, and she got the big part of the wishbone. She made her wish: "I wish food would grow on trees." And she threw the wishbone out of the window. (Take wishbone off board.)

And that night a magic tree grew outside her window. (Put small tree on board.)

By the next morning it was just about this tall—the size of a bush.

There were little pancakes—no bigger than a penny—growing all over the tree. (Put pancakes on tree.)

"Oh goody!" said Jennifer. "I love pancakes!"

She reached out to pull just one pancake off the tree.

"Ouch," said the pancake. "I'm not ready yet. Can't you see we're not grown up enough yet?"

So Jennifer waited a few minutes until the pancakes grew as big as saucers. (Put larger pancakes over little ones.)

Jennifer reached out the window and pulled off a big pancake and popped it in her mouth. (Take off a big pancake.) It was delicious!

"I'm thirsty," she said. "I wish I had a big glass of milk."

And what do you know? The tree grew two glasses of milk. (Put milk glasses on flannel board.)

Jennifer carefully lifted off the glasses of milk and drank them both right down. (Take off the glasses.)

When Jennifer's mother called her for breakfast, she gave her a big bowl of cereal. (Put bowl cutout on another part of the flannel board.)

But Jennifer wasn't hungry. Jennifer's mother shook her head because Jennifer was always hungry for breakfast. You see, her mother didn't know about the magic tree.

"I'd just like to go outside and play," said Jennifer.

"All right," said her mother. "Maybe you'll be hungry for lunch."

Jennifer ran outside to see her magic tree a little closer. By this time it was nearly as big as she was. (Take off small tree and add medium-sized one.) The tree was starting to grow hot dogs. (Put on hot dog cutouts.)

"Oh, goody goody," said Jennifer. She loved hot dogs. But when she reached out to pull off a hot dog, it said, "Ouch! Can't you see I don't have my bun yet!"

So Jennifer waited another minute. The hot dog grew a nice fat bun. (Put bun on hot dog.)

Jennifer plucked the hot dog off the tree and took a big bite. And she ate it all up. (Take hot dog off board.)

That morning the magic tree grew corn on the cob, pickles, and potato chips. (Put these on board.) And Jennifer ate them all. (Take these off again.)

At lunch, her mother served Jennifer a bowl of vegetable soup. (Put bowl on board next to the cereal bowl.) But Jennifer wasn't hungry. You all know why, don't you?

Jennifer's mother started to worry. "Are you feeling all right, Jenny?" she asked.

"I think so," said Jennifer. (She really had eaten too many hot dogs and pickles and chips and corn on the cob.)

"Maybe you'd better take a nap," suggested her mother.

So Jennifer took a nap. She was sleepy after eating so much.

Now, when Jennifer woke up from her nap, she looked out of the window. The tree was almost as tall as the roof of her house. And it was growing meatballs and spaghetti. (Put large tree with meatballs and spaghetti on board.)

"Oh, goody goody goody," said Jennifer. "I love meatballs and spaghetti!"

By the time she got her shoes on and ran outside, the spaghetti was growing so big it looked like fire hoses. The giant spaghetti was reaching out and twisting itself around the house and starting to squeeze the chimney.

"Help!" shouted Jennifer. "Emergency!"

The neighbors looked out of their windows and saw the giant spaghetti coming. What if the spaghetti grew so big it choked the whole neighborhood?

The woman next door called the fire department. A big red truck came with ladders, and firemen got out their axes. They cut down the spaghetti and rolled it up like hoses. They chopped up the meatballs—they were the size of basketballs—and put them in firebuckets. And they hauled everything away.

Finally, Jennifer's mother heard all the noise and ran outside.

"You'd better cut down that monster tree," the fire chief said, "before it takes over the whole town!"

Jennifer's mother shook her head. "Jennifer," she said. "What did you do?"

So Jennifer told her the whole story about the wishbone and the magic tree. "We'll decide what to do when your father comes home," said her mother. "Maybe we'll have to call the tree trimmers."

But that night the tree began to shrink. And by the time Jennifer's father got home, it had disappeared. (Take tree off board.) No one knew why. Maybe the magic just got used up.

The next day Jennifer's mother fixed turkey for dinner. But this time, Jennifer didn't make a wish on the wishbone. After all, turkey wishbones are much bigger than chicken wishbones. And Jennifer didn't want the whole thing to start all over again.

The Terrible Tale of Joshua Nickel

If you read one of the silly pickle books in the book section, you will want to follow up with this poem story about a boy who turns into a pickle. For further drama, make a nickel-pickle puppet from socks. Simply sew two socks together at the tops—one green sock and one tan. Add felt features for Joshua (the tan sock) and green dots and bumps on the green pickle sock. Turn green sock inside tan sock. Pull the puppet on your hand with the tan Joshua side showing to begin the story, and slowly turn inside outside as Joshua becomes a pickle.

A small young boy
Named Joshua Nickel
Loved nothing so much
As eating a pickle.

Dill or sweet,
Bites or hunks,
Bread and butter,
Chips or chunks.

"You'd better be careful,"
His mother said,
"Don't eat too many,
You'll lose your head."

But Joshua kept on
Eating a bunch,
Sweet and sour,
Munch, crunch, munch!

One day his arms
Grew small green bumps,
And his nose became
A warty lump.

His mother cried,
"What shall I do?
A terrible thing
Has happened to you!

"He's got the pox,
Or is it mumps
Just look at his face—
It's full of bumps!"

But was he sorry?
Not Joshua Nickel!
He loved nothing more
Than BEING a pickle.

Joshua Nickel Pickle Puppet

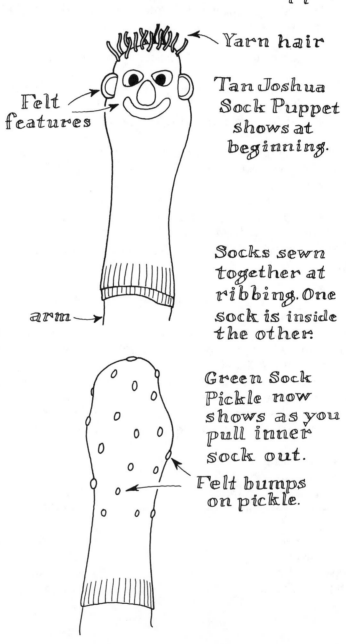

Yarn hair

Felt features

Tan Joshua Sock Puppet shows at beginning.

arm

Socks sewn together at ribbing. One sock is inside the other.

Green Sock Pickle now shows as you pull inner sock out.

Felt bumps on pickle.

Fantastic Food Dream

Last night it snowed cornflakes
And sugar outside.
So I took a crunchy,
Munchy slide.

Today it rained lemonade
And soda pop.
I filled our bathtub
This high up!

So when Mom and Dad told me,
"Bathtime—hurry and dash!"
I ran real fast
And took a SPLASH!

What a Cake!
(A Flannel-board Story)

In *Dragon Stew* (p. 78) the dragon makes a stew; in this case, the animals get inside the cake for silly fun. You can read this story or turn it into a flannel-board activity. In preparation, make a cake with a hole in the front so all the animals will be seen through the opening as you add them. You will need cutouts of a flea, butterfly, frog, snake, duck, and pig (see p. 85). Now, here goes!

Once there was a baker
Who baked a lovely cake.
Oh, what a cake he did make!

(Put cake on board.)

But when he wasn't looking,
A flea flew in
To the cake the baker baked.
Oh, what a cake THAT did make!

(Add flea.)

But when he wasn't looking,
A butterfly blew in
To where the flea flew
In the cake the baker baked.
Oh, what a cake THAT did make!

(Add butterfly.)

But when he wasn't looking,
A frog flipped in
To where the butterfly blew
And the flea flew
In the cake the baker baked.
Oh, what a cake THAT did make!

(Add frog.)

But when he wasn't looking,
A snake slipped in   (Add snake.)
To where the frog flipped
And the butterfly blew
And the flea flew
In the cake the baker baked.
Oh, what a cake THAT did make!

But when he wasn't looking,
A duck danced in   (Add duck.)
To where the snake slipped
And the frog flipped
And the butterfly blew
And the flea flew
In the cake the baker baked.
Oh what a cake THAT did make!

But when he wasn't looking,
A pig pranced in   (Add pig.)
To where the duck danced
And the snake slipped
And the frog flipped
And the butterfly blew
And the flea flew
In the cake the baker baked.
Oh, what a cake THAT did make!

But then the baker looked and
Said, "Enough!"
And out the pig pranced   (Remove each animal as it is named.)
And the duck danced
And the snake slipped
And the frog flipped
And the butterfly blew
And the flea flew
And they all shared the cake
the baker baked.
And what a cake he did make!

· · ·

What a Cake!

duck

frog

flea

cake with hole in front

butterfly

snake

pig

Nimble Noodleheads
(To the tune of "Did You Ever See a Lassie?")

Noodleheads are silly people—so silly that people think they have noodles where their brains should be. Here is a song to use anytime the sillies are in order—just after reading one of the fun or fantasy books. See p. 88-89 for instructions on making a noodlehead.

Did you ever see a noodlehead,	(Wiggle fingers behind ears.)
A noodlehead, a noodlehead,	
Did you ever see a noodlehead	
Do anything like this?	(Shake finger.)

Can you make a face?	(Make face.)
Can you run a race?	(Run in place.)
Can you make a face?	(Make face.)
Can you run a race?	(Run in place.)
Did you ever see a noodlehead	(Wiggle fingers behind ears.)
Do anything like this?	(Shake finger.)

Can you touch your toes?	(Touch toes.)
Can you hold your nose?	(Hold nose.)
Can you touch your toes?	(Touch toes.)
Can you hold your nose?	(Hold nose.)
Did you ever see a noodlehead	(Wiggle fingers behind ears.)
Do anything like this?	(Shake finger.)

GAMES AND FROLICS FOR FUN AND FANTASY FOODS

Crunch! Squirt! Squish!
(A Noisy Food Game)

Children love to make noises with food. In this game, they will have to think what makes noise. There aren't "right" or "wrong" answers—just lots of possibilities.

Children are seated in a circle. The leader takes a bite of an imaginary food and says, "Crunch," then passes the "food" to the child on her right. This child repeats the action and the sound. The last child in the circle names a crunch food. Potato chips? Celery? A frozen icicle? (You may need to prompt shy children at first.)

Next, the leader bites into a "squirt" and passes it on. Is it a grapefruit? A dill pickle? A bottle of pop?

Finally, try a "squish." What sounds "squish"? A ripe banana? Mashed potatoes? Mud pie?

Make up your own sounds and let children try their own!

Who Eats Worms?
(A Funny Food Chant to Act Out)

Children join in the chant by responding with the appropriate animal and action. (They may need prompting the first time you try this.)

Leader: Who eats worms?

Children: Birds do!

Leader: Let's all fly like birds!
Who eats flies?

Children:	Frogs do!
Leader:	Let's all hop like frogs! Who eats nut-and-berry pie?
Children:	Squirrels do!
Leader:	Let's shake our tails like squirrels! Who eats slop?
Children:	Pigs do!
Leader:	Let's all squeal like pigs! Who eats grass?
Children:	Cows do!
Leader:	Let's all moo like cows! Who likes peanut butter and jelly too?
Children:	We do! (Everyone points to self at end.)

Eat-Your-Words Game

Children probably won't know the expression "Eat your words," but they will joyfully pretend to eat their words if they play this game. For those children who are starting to read, the word recognition in this context is a great reading motivator. Even if children aren't reading on their own, the game is fun. After several times of play, some children may be able to "read" the words.

Write words on cards and paste a picture of the word on the opposite side. Here are some examples of real and "off-the-wall" foods you might use: pizza, hamburger, carrot, apple, hot dog, banana, egg, bread, peanut butter, cat, hat, socks, elephant, monkey, coat, can.

To play, seat children in a circle. Pronounce each word on each card, and lay the cards, word side up, around the circle. Children are instructed not to touch the cards or move until you say, "Eat your words!" When the words are said, children scramble for a card. Then go around the circle and see what each child has selected to eat. If they need a hint, they can turn cards over for a picture clue.

Children will want to play this activitiy again and again.

Body Food
(Just-a-Little-Wiggle Frolic)

Start this frolic slowly. Then, after a few times through, get faster and faster until everyone collapses in laughter.

Banana peel,	(Put arms above head, then lower to sides.)
Taffy pull,	(Clap and spread arms wide.)
Pretzel twist,	(Cross arms in front of chest.)
Jelly roll!	(Roll hands over each other.)

Funny Feeling Foods

Since food textures fascinate chidren, play a feeling game by passing around a grocery bag filled with funny-textured foods: artichokes, pineapple, pretzels, marshmallows, pickles, and so on.

First let the children feel the food and guess what it is. Next, close eyes, smell the food and guess. Then, if everyone is game, try tasting it.

CRAFT EXPERIENCES FOR FUN AND FANTASY FOODS

Mudluscious!

If you're daring, mix up some mud (the real thing) and glob it on pieces of posterboard for children to "draw" their own pictures with craft sticks. (Naturally, you will want children to wear old clothes.) If you're not so daring, mix up a big batch of chocolate pudding. Stretch out a long piece of shelf paper. Glob on the "mud pudding" and let children finger-paint to their heart's delight.

Chocolate Pudding Just for Fun

Please carefully instruct children that this delicious-looking pudding can NOT be eaten. But it makes a wonderful display! Since this "pudding" does not spoil, you can keep it in a display for weeks or months. You might explain that one difference between this "fake" pudding and the real thing is that real pudding would spoil if kept out of refrigeration. And, obviously, this pudding is not safe to eat!

Add a few drops of brown tempera paint to one cup of shortening. Stir until the color is well blended.

Put the mixture in a small margarine tub and stick in a plastic spoon to look like a real dish of pudding.

Nellie or Nathan Noodlehead

This craft will be a fine accompaniment to the "Nimble Noodlehead" song mentioned earlier in this chapter (p. 85). Simply draw a face on paper, or let children draw their own circle for a face, and add features. Provide uncooked pasta of different shapes to glue on for the hair.

Nellie Noodlehead

Super Spaghetti Cake

Restaurants in *Ribtickle Town* (p. 78) serve spaghetti cake, and here's a recipe for a wacky one!

Poke lots of holes in a paper cake pan (the microwave-safe kind) or a cardboard bowl (found with picnic supplies in stores) and pull pieces of fat white yarn or old shoelaces through the holes. Leave just a little on the outside. Now, wave your hands over the "cake" and say:

> Abracadabra,
> Gitchy gitchy goo.
> Spaghetti,
> I'm ready,
> Come wiggling through!

Now pull the spaghetti strings through the holes and laugh.

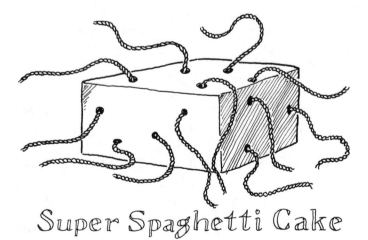

Super Spaghetti Cake

Paper Pickle Creature Puppet

If you read *Pickle Creature* (p. 78), send kids home with their own pickle-creature finger puppet. Simply tear green construction paper in an oval shape to fit the child's index finger. Now tear out another piece the same size (or tear out two at a time). Glue these together around the edges, add features and a few bumps.

Paper Pickle
Creature Puppet

Sand Cake

Frank Asch's book of the same name (p. 73) will inspire children to make their own sand cakes.

Draw an outline of a cake on paper. Brush on glue. Then give children sand (maybe in an oatmeal box with holes in the top for a shaker) to sprinkle on the cake cutout.

Sponge Cake

Please explain to children that sponge cake is not really made out of a sponge, but in this fun activity they will be making a cake from a sponge. Cut pieces of foam (available in bags in discount stores, or use packing foam) into round shapes like cakes. Provide children with glue and cotton balls, rickrack, ribbons, buttons—any notions you can find—to decorate their cakes.

COOKING AND TASTING EXPERIENCES FOR FUN AND FANTASY FOODS

Silly Jungle Dinner

The silly things mentioned in "Silly, Silly Things to Eat" (p. 74) would be the inspiration for a whole meal of silly jungle foods.

Here are just a few suggestions:

Tiger Stripes: cheddar cheese cut into long, thin strips
Monkey Tail: banana cut into long pieces
Leopard Spots: raisins
Elephant Ears: raw cauliflower flowerets
Hyena Juice: tropical punch with a little carbonated beverage to make you laugh like a hyena!

You can add your own inventions and give them names in the spirit of *How to Make Elephant Bread* (p. 73).

Peanut Butter Porcupines

Mix just enough non-fat dry milk with a jar of peanut butter so it isn't too sticky. Then roll the mixture into little balls. Sprinkle with coconut and add two raisin eyes.

Hello Jello Bars

Jello is a fun food to make with young children. This recipe is firm so it can be handled with fingers and adds extra nutrition with juice instead of water.

Sprinkle 3 envelopes of unflavored gelatin over 1 cup of fruit juice (orange, cranberry, apple, etc.) and let stand for one minute. Then stir this mixture over low heat until gelatin is dissolved, about 5 minutes. Add some food coloring if you wish. For extra flavor, stir in 3-4 tablespoons of honey. Pour into a 9-inch dish and chill until firm. Cut into bars (or squares and triangles if you wish to teach shapes). This jello treat can be served at room temperature.

Pickle Creature to Eat

This pickle creature is assembled on a plate so you don't have to attach the legs with toothpicks.

Use a small sweet pickle for the body. Make lots of legs from thin strips of carrot and celery (so the creature looks like a thousand legger!).

6.
STIR AND BAKE

INTRODUCTION

Along with the fruit of the vine, bread has been the staple in people's diets from earliest times. Our white sponge grocery-store variety seems a far cry indeed from that staple. Many young children have never stirred up a batch of yeast bread and watched it grow, let alone savored the aroma of a fresh homemade loaf. And cakes made at home quite often come from a prepared mix with frostings ready to spread from the can. Cooking from scratch seems more a thing of the past with so many convenience foods crowding our shelves and freezers.

Despite many young people's preferences for presliced white bread, the stories and activities in this chapter will introduce breads from tortillas to matzos. "The Happy Baker" (p. 93) still prefers his own bread to a crusty French loaf or a dark Russian rye, but Bembelman's bread of "every taste you wanted to taste" (p. 93) and Miss Tilly's whole-wheat brown sugar loaves (p. 93) will make children hungry for something new.

Holidays call for special breads and cakes throughout the world, so we have included some of these in this chapter instead of the holidays or many-lands chapters (chapters 10 and 9). The bread dolls Joey's grandmother makes in *Watch Out for the Chicken Feet in Your Soup* (p. 93) are favorite Easter treats in Italy. If you're ambitious, you might mix up a batch using de Paola's recipe in this delightful book for a tasty and memorable treat. Birthdays, almost every child's favorite holiday, are naturally linked with cakes, so birthday cake stories are also included here.

Even if you don't pull up your sleeves and knead bread with your preschoolers, perhaps you'll enjoy the stories and be inspired to squeeze a bread-dough sculpture from grocery-store bread (p. 109), "wake up a yeast giant" (p. 94), or visit a nearby bakery. You'll find lots of stirring experiences to recapture the fun of baking for young children.

INITIATING ACTIVITY

Baker, Baker
(A Clap-and-chant Rhyme)

Use this chant as children arrive, then do it again when you're ready for everyone to sit down and begin the storytime.

Baker, baker,
Are you awake?
Time to mix up
Bread and cake.

Pour in milk,
Two cups of flour,
Three brown eggs,
And paking powder.

Stir it, beat it,
Fast as you can.
Spoon it in
A shiny pan.

Bake it 'til
It's good and brown.
Baker, baker,
Now sit down!

(And let's eat!)

LITERATURE-SHARING EXPERIENCES

Books about Bread

De Paola, Tomie. **Watch Out for the Chicken Feet in Your Soup.** Prentice-Hall, 1974.
Eugene and Joey visit Joey's Italian grandmother who makes them a delicious meal, including special bread doll treats. De Paola's family recipe for bread dolls is included.

Galdone, Paul **Little Red Hen.** Seabury, 1973.
The resourceful little red hen makes bread from scratch without the help of three lazy barnyard animals. Children love the repetitive line "Not I" throughout this old favorite folktale that is illustrated in Galdone's familiar jaunty style.

Gibbons, Gail. **The Too-Great Bread Book.** Warne, 1980.
Miss Tilly is kept so busy baking bread for everyone in the valley that she sleeps fitfully. In her dream, the "yeastie beasties" in her dough grow so much that dough oozes out of her house and into the valley. The whole-wheat, brown-sugar recipe included in the book is delicious, and complete instructions for kneading are included.

Green, Melinda. **Bembelman's Bakery.** Illustrated by Barbara Seuling. Parents, 1978.
In the old country, Aaron and Sarah Bembelman leave their children with Saul, the eldest child, but when they return they discover bread coming out of the house. The boy hides, only to have his mother come begging him to return and show them how to make bread. Saul's bread "is . . . every taste you wanted to taste, all in each wonderful bite." The family sells enough of it to come to America and open a bakery.

Nobens, C. A. **The Happy Baker.** Carolrhoda, 1979.
Joseph, the happy baker, longs to see the world, so he sets off on a food journey to many lands. He loves the soups he tastes, but thinks his own bread is best. He returns to open a

bakery-and-soup shop. Despite the multicultural appreciation of the soup, the happy baker comes off a bit smug in his criticism of breads from other lands. Still, the story does introduce children to some foods they may not know about.

Stevens, Carla. **How to Make Possum's Honey Bread.** Illustrated by Jack Kent. Seabury, 1975. Possum shows his animal friends how to make honey bread, but Raccoon goes off to fish until the bread is done. Possum's recipe follows with variations for each animal friend.

Related Activities about Bread

Wake Up the Yeast Giant!

Yeast is a fascinating foodstuff for young children to watch in action and has inspired several stories. Miss Tilly (p. 93) uses "yeastie beasties" to make her bread rise, and Saul's bread (p. 93) grows to gigantic proportions.

Before you read one of these stories, pour some yeast granules in a bowl, add hot water, and let the action take place. At the end of the story, look at the change in the yeast.

Now, act out the yeast action with children as you read this little verse.

> Yeastie Beastie,
> Fast asleep.
> Pour on water,
> Out I creep.
> Bigger—
> Bigger—
> Here I come.
> Punch me down,
> Back I'll come.
> Resting—
> Growing—
> Watch me rise.
> I am now—a giant's size!

Little Red Hen
(A Puppet Story)

Tell this familiar story with glove puppets. Simply attach pompoms with cutout felt details to the tips of work gloves. Hold up the appropriate finger as the character appears in the story. On the left glove, use the little finger as the mouse, the index finger as the cat, and the thumb as the dog. On the right glove, the head of the hen is the thumb, tail feathers are fingers, the body is the palm, and the legs are on the wrist. This approach makes the little red hen the dominant character.

Little·Red·Hen Glove Puppets

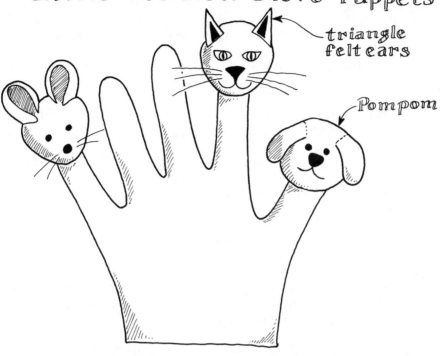

triangle
felt ears

Pompom

felt feathers

Can you say, "No, I won't"? (They can!)

I have three friends here who say, "No, I won't" all the time. My first friend is a mouse, and when he says "No, I won't" he says it in a high squeaky mouse voice: "No, I won't." (Say this in a high squeaky voice and have children imitate this.)

My next friend is a cat. He says it in a whispery soft voice: "No I won't." (Have children imitate this.)

And here is my big, old doggie friend. He says it in a big, old doggie voice: "No, I won't." (Children imitate this.)

That's fine. Now you are all ready to help me tell the story of the Little Red Hen.

One day when the little red hen was scratching around in the dirt, she came upon some grains of wheat.

"Oh, good," she cried. "I'll plant this grain and grow some wheat to make bread. Now who will help me plant the wheat?"

But the mouse said in his high squeaky mouse voice (Prompt children each time.), "No, I won't." And the cat said in his soft whispery cat voice, "No, I won't." And the dog said in his big, old doggie voice, "No, I won't!"

"Well," said the little red hen, "I'll have to do it myself." And she did.

She planted the seeds in the ground, and they grew and grew and grew until one day the little red hen said, "Now it is time to cut the wheat. Who will help me cut the wheat?"

But the mouse said, "No, I won't." And the cat said, "No, I won't." And the dog said, "No, I won't!"

"Well," said the little red hen. "I'll have to do it myself." And she did.

She cut that wheat down and put it all in a big bag to take to the miller's up the hill for him to grind into flour.

"Who will help me carry this bag of wheat to the miller's?" she asked.

But the lazy mouse still said, "No, I won't." And that cat still said, "No, I won't." And that dog still said, "No, I won't!"

"Well," said the little red hen, "I'll have to do it myself." And she did.

All the way up the hill, she carried that bag of wheat and waited while the miller ground it into flour; then she carried it all the way back down the hill.

Then she got out a big bowl and a big spoon, and she poured in the milk and sugar and the yeast and the flour. She stirred and stirred and stirred, and pretty soon she had a nice loaf of bread all ready to put in the oven.

"Now," she said, "Who will help me bake the bread?"

But do you know what that mouse said? "No, I won't." And what did the cat say? "No, I won't." And how about the dog? "No, I won't!"

"Oh, my," said the little red hen, "I'll have to do it myself." And she did.

She put that loaf of bread into the oven, and pretty soon the smell of fresh-baked bread filled the house. The mouse smelled it (sniff, sniff), and the cat smelled it (sniff, sniff), and that big, old dog smelled it (sniff, sniff).

When the little red hen took the bread out of the oven, she said, "Now who will help me eat the bread?" This time the mouse said, "Yes, I will." And the cat said, "Yes, I will." And that big, old dog said, "Yes, I will!"

"Now wait a minute," said the little red hen. "You didn't help me plant or cut or carry or bake. I'll let you each have one piece, but then I'll eat the rest myself."

And she did!

Pokey, Pokey, the Bread Song
(To the tune of "The Hokey Pokey")

You put some flour in,
You add some yeast and salt,
Then you add the shortening,
And you stir it all about.
Add warm milk 'til it feels just right.
What a funny sight!

You put your fingers in,
And you push the stuff
Around the table
'Til it starts to puff.
Flop the glop around
And punch it down,
Make a thumping sound.

You dump the dough down now
Into a great big bowl.
Then you wait awhile
Until it starts to grow.
You give your dough another punch
    or two.
That's what you have to do.

(Use appropriate hand actions as you
    sing this song.)

Now you roll it out
Like a skinny old snake,
And you put it in the oven
'Cause it's time to bake.
You watch the clock
Until it's good and done.
Now—call the gang to come! (Yum!)

The World's Great Bread Basket

Bread in Mexico is round and flat.
In France it's long and sometimes fat.
Pita in India is pocket bread.
Matzo in Israel is a cracker, instead.
But however you slice it,
Wherever you go,
There's a world full of goodness
In all kinds of dough!

As you recite this poem, show the various breads mentioned.

Books about Cake

Da Rif, Andrea. **The Blueberry Cake That Little Fox Baked.** Atheneum, 1981.

When little fox sees "B. Day" written on the calendar, he thinks it must be his mother's birthday, so he picks blueberries and makes her a cake. When his family returns from the blueberry festival, little fox learns that "B. Day" means "Blueberry Day," a special festival and he had forgot to go, but all is forgiven as the family takes his dessert to the festival.

Grey, Judith. **Yummy, Yummy.** Illustrated by Joan E. Goodman. Troll Associates, 1981.

The hungry hippo in this easy reader makes cakes: apple, carrot, honey, and chocolate. Then he makes them all into one super cake.

Krasilovsky, Phyllis. **The Man Who Entered a Contest.** Illustrated by Yuri Salzman. Doubleday, 1980.

A man who likes to bake cakes needs a new stove, so he enters a contest to win one. He mixes up the cake but falls asleep. The cat spills extra baking powder in the batter, and the cake ends up covering everything in the room. The judges award him the prize for his unusual cakes: curtain cake, sink cake, flowerpot cake, and oven cake. (See p. 110 for instructions to make a flowerpot cake.)

Parker, Nancy Winslow. **Love from Aunt Betty.** Dodd, Mead, 1983.

Aunt Betty sends Charlie a chocolate fudge cake recipe from Transylvania. Charlie follows the simple instructions that call for such unusual ingredients as a cobweb and tree-toad flakes. A monster emerges from the oven, Charlie smacks it with a pan, and a surprise emerges: a four-tiered chocolate cake complete with lighted candles!

Rice, Eve. **Benny Bakes a Cake.** Greenwillow, 1981.

Benny helps his mother bake his own birthday cake. They decorate it, and while they take a walk, the family dog eats it. Benny's tears stop when Papa brings home another cake — and party hats, too.

Sendak, Maurice. **In the Night Kitchen.** Harper & Row, 1970.

Mickey hears a racket in the night and goes down to join the bakers who bake cake. Mickey's frolics and the rhythmical language invite reading this modern classic aloud to young children. (See p. 109-110 to make Monster Mickey Bread.)

Worthington, Phoebe, and Selby Worthington. **Teddy Bear Baker.** Warne, 1979.

Teddy Bear Baker has a bake shop and a van for delivering the bread and cakes he bakes for birthday parties to appreciative customers. Young children will enjoy this account of his daily activities and join in as he thump, thumps the dough and clang, clangs his bell.

Zion, Gene. **Sugar Mouse Cake.** Scribners, 1964.

When the Chief Pastry Cook in the Royal Kitchen retires, Tom, the ninth assistant, enters his Sugar Mouse Cake in competition to become the new chief cook.

Related Activities about Cake

The Day Barnaby Bear Fell in the Batter Bowl
(A Story with Paper-Bag Masks)

All the children can participate in the action in this story. Some children are given grocery-bag masks that are rounded off at the shoulders and have a big face hole to expose the child's face.

In preparation, cut off grocery bags so they will fit over the children's shoulders. Cut a large face hole in the front of the bag. Decorate bags with ears, bright colored details (hairs, etc.). This story uses a bear, lion, monkey, pig, and rabbit, but you can use any animal characters.

Barnaby Bear Grocery Bag Masks

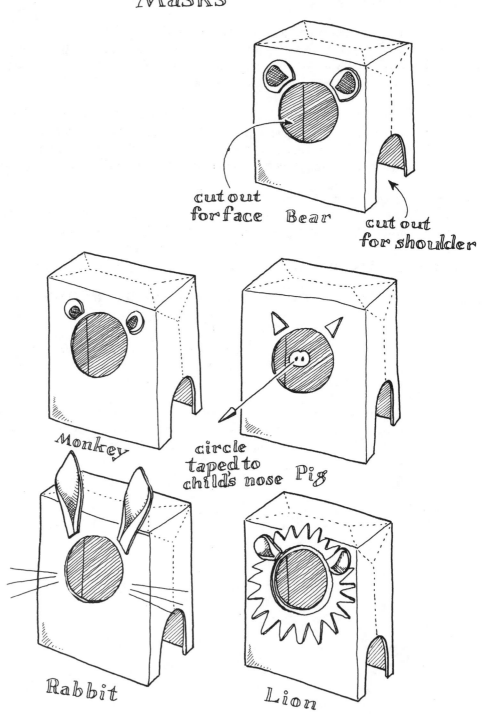

cut out for face   Bear   cut out for shoulder

Monkey

circle taped to child's nose   Pig

Rabbit   Lion

Select five children to stand in front of the group. Give these children the masks as each character is introduced in the story. Explain to the other children that they will get to pull, and practice a pulling action.

One morning Barnaby Bear woke up with a big smile. (Put Barnaby Bear mask on child.) That was because it was his birthday, and he was having a party for all his friends. Barnaby dusted and washed and polished his house. At last the house was all clean, and Barnaby said, "Now I need to make my birthday cake."

So Barnaby got out a little bowl like this. (Form hands into small circle. Have children do this action, too.)

"No," said Barnaby Bear. "I want a *big* birthday cake."

So Barnaby got out a bigger bowl. (Spread hands slightly.)

"No," said Barnaby Bear. "I want a big, *big,* birthday cake."

So Barnaby got out a bigger bowl. (Spread arms slightly.)

"No," said Barnaby Bear. "I want a big, big, *big* birthday cake."

So Barnaby got out the biggest bowl of all. (Spread arms wide.)

"Just right," said Barnaby Bear. And he put in the sugar and the flour and the milk and the eggs and the vanilla. Then he got out a big spoon and stirred and stirred and stirred.

Barnaby wanted to taste the cake batter. So he reached in the top of the bowl and took a taste.

"Mmmmmmm," said Barnaby Bear. He wanted another taste, so he reached into the middle of the bowl.

"Mmmmmmm," said Barnaby Bear. He wanted another taste, so he reached down, down, down to the very bottom of the big bowl, and—splash—Barnaby Bear fell right into the batter bowl. (Child wearing bear mask sits down on floor.)

Barnaby tried and tried, but he could not get out of that batter bowl. Finally, it was time for the party and the first one to arrive was Lion. (Put lion head on another child.)

"Oh, Lion," cried Barnaby. "I am so glad you are here. Help me out of this batter bowl."

So Lion took hold of Barnaby Bear (place hand of child wearing lion head on shoulder of child on floor), and he pulled and pulled and pulled (all children in audience do pulling motion). But it was no use. Barnaby Bear was stuck tight—stuck in the batter bowl.

Pretty soon up to Barnaby Bear's house came Monkey.

"Oh, Monkey," cried Barnaby Bear, "I'm so glad you are here. Help me out of this batter bowl." So Monkey took hold of Lion (place hand of child wearing monkey mask on Lion's shoulder), and Lion took hold of Barnaby Bear (put Lion's hand on bear's shoulders) and they all pulled and pulled and pulled (everyone pretends to pull), but it was no use. Barnaby Bear was stuck tight—stuck in the batter bowl.

Not much later Pig came to the party. (Put pig mask on a child.)

"Oh, Pig," cried Barnaby Bear, "I am so glad you are here. Help me out of this batter bowl."

So Pig took hold of Monkey (place each child's hands on other child's shoulders as before), and Monkey took hold of Lion, and Lion took hold of Barnaby Bear and they pulled and pulled and pulled—but it was no use. Barnaby Bear was stuck tight—stuck in the batter bowl.

Well, one more friend was coming to the party. Rabbit came up to Barnaby Bear's house. (Put rabbit mask on another child.) But when he said he could help, Pig and Monkey and Lion laughed and laughed.

"Don't be silly," they all said. "If we who are big and strong can't pull Barnaby out, how can you?"

But Rabbit really wanted to help, so he took hold of Pig (place each child's hands as before), and Pig took hold of Monkey, and Monkey took hold of Lion, and Lion took hold of Barnaby Bear, and they pulled and pulled and pulled, and all of a sudden—POP! (Lift child on floor under the arms and raise to feet.) Out of the batter bowl came Barnaby Bear.

And he and his friends had a very nice party after all.

My Birthday Action Rhyme

It's my birthday—	(Point to self.)
What a treat!	
I can pick what we all eat.	
YUM!	(Rub stomach.)
Should I ask for chicken legs?	(Point to leg.)
Or donuts?	(Touch fingertips to form circle.)
Or for scrambled eggs?	(Roll hands.)
Hmmmmmm!	(Scratch head.)
I know one thing	(Finger in the air.)
Without a doubt.	(Shake head.)
I want a cake	(Extend hands, palms up.)
To blow candles out!	
Poof!	(Blow.)

A Good Licken
(A Fingerplay)

I got to lick the batter bowl,   (Cup hands to form bowl.)
I licked just every place.   (Nod head.)
I licked it sloooow,   (Stick tongue out in slow circle.)
I licked it fast,   (Stick tongue out quickly several
                                     times.)

And now—it's on my face!   (Pat cheeks.)

Lighter-than-Air Cake
(A Flip-chart Story)

This unusual device can be made several ways. The easiest way is to use an 8½ x 11-inch five-ring binder. Cut several sheets of paper in half horizontally. Turn binder so rings are on top. Half of the paper is caught in half of the rings; the other half of the paper is caught in the other rings. On the right-hand half of the flip chart, draw the cake. In the first picture the cake is low on the sheet, and gets higher in successive pictures. On the left-hand half of the flip chart, draw the woman, pig, cow, bear, and bird. Show the pictures of the characters as they interact with the cake in the story.

Lighter-than-air-Cake

Flip-Chart Story

5-ring binder with pages divided in half

One day an old woman said to herself, "What a fine day it is today. It's a good day to bake a cake."

She found her cake pan and her bowl and spoon, but she couldn't find her recipe.

"Oh, well," said the old woman. "I have made this cake lots of times. I'll remember how to do it."

So she put in some flour and sugar and shortening and salt and vanilla. When it came time to put in the baking powder—and, that is the ingredient that makes the cake stand up tall rather than lay flat in the pan—well, she couldn't remember just how much to put in. So she put in a spoonful—but that didn't look like quite enough.

"Besides," said the old woman, "I don't want a flat cake. I want one lighter-than-air."

So she put in another spoonful and another and another and another.

"Now," she said, "my cake will be lighter-than-air."

And she was right! In fact, her cake was so light that when she took it out of the oven, it floated right out of her hands, out the door, and down the road.

"Come back, you lighter-than-air cake," called the old woman. "I want to eat you."

But the cake just rose higher and higher and called, "What a fine day it is today. What a fine day to fly away!" and it floated on down the road. The old woman couldn't catch it.

The cake hadn't floated far when it met a pig.

"Come here, lighter-than-air cake," said the pig. "I want to eat you."

But the cake just rose higher and higher and called, "What a fine day it is today. What a fine day to fly away!" And it floated even higher. The pig couldn't catch it.

Before long it met a cow.

"Come here, you lighter-than-air cake," called the cow. "I want to eat you."

But the cake just floated higher and higher and called, "What a fine day it is today. What a fine day to fly away," and floated on down the road. And the cow couldn't catch it.

Next it floated into the woods and met the bear.

"Come here, you lighter-than-air cake," called the bear. "I want to eat you."

But the cake just floated higher and higher and called, "What a fine day it is today. What a fine day to fly away," and floated on through the woods. And the bear couldn't catch it.

Higher and higher it floated until it met a little tiny bird perched on a tree branch.

"Come here, you lighter-than-air cake," called the bird. "I want to eat you." But the cake called back, "What a fine day it is today. What a fine day to fly away."

Now, down below on the ground, the old woman and the pig and the cow and the bear were laughing.

"Little bird, what makes you think you can catch that cake," called the woman. "You are just a little thing. We big strong ones couldn't do it." And they all laughed and laughed and laughed.

But the bird just smiled. She flew out of the tree and ate that lighter-than-air cake in one gulp (flip cake picture out of sight). Then the bird looked down at the others on the ground and called, "What a fine day it is today. What a fine day to fly away." And that's just what she did!

Come On and Do the Cake Walk
(To the tune of "She'll Be Comin' 'Round the Mountain")

Children love cake walks. Mothers, however, who have to bake the cakes may be less than excited. Since we are not terrific cake bakers, we'll share this story with you. One of our made-from-a-mix cakes was supposed to have a chocolate glaze on top, but it ended up on the bottom. If you wish to duplicate this sensation, just get a mix with a glaze and turn the whole thing upside down on the plate. That way, everyone will eat right to the bottom instead of licking the icing off the top! The following song celebrates just such an unusual cake.

Come on and do the cake walk round and round,
(Repeat line.)
Come on and do the cake walk,
(Repeat line.)
Come on and do the cake walk round and round.

If I'm lucky I will win a devil's food,
(Repeat line.)
If I'm lucky I will win,
(Repeat)
If I'm lucky I will win a devil's food,
                        round and round.

But the icing slid underneath the cake,
(Repeat)
But the icing slid under,
(Repeat)
But the icing slid down underneath the cake,
                        devil's food
                        round and round.

When the music stops I'll eat it upside down,
(Repeat)
When the music stops I'll eat it,
(Repeat)
When the music stops I'll eat it upside down,
                                        'neath the cake,
                                        devil's food,
                                        round and round.

Oh I'm now on number seven and I won,
(Repeat)
Oh I'm now on number seven,
(Repeat)
Oh I'm now on number seven and I won,
                                        upside down,
                                        'neath the cake,
                                        devil's food,
                                        round and round.

(Spoken): "But I'll share some with you too!"

GAMES AND FROLICS FOR BREAD AND CAKE

Colorful Cake Walk

Tape colored squares on chairs or around table. As the music plays, children walk past the squares and stop by the closest square when the music stops. The leader draws a colored square from a box, and the child standing by the matching colored square wins. This child goes to a box full of cupcakes to select the prize. The game continues until all children are winners and get cupcakes to eat.

Toast Pop-up Game
(The Best Thing since Sliced Bread)

Children love to jump up. This game invites them to become bread in a toaster.

Leader: What's better than sliced bread?
                 Toast!
                 Let's make some!
                 First we need a toaster. (Choose two children to put their
                     arms up and stand far enough apart that the other
                     children can get between.)
                 Now we need bread—a whole loaf.
                 (Line children up between the toaster children.)
                 What a good looking bread line!
                 Now, bread, we'll toast you two at a time.
                 Ready?

One slice, two slice,
Drop right down.
(Have children crouch down.)
Toaster's heating,
Nice and brown.

Ready? Set?
Toast, pop up!
You look so good—
I'll eat you up!

(The popped-up toast children sit down while the other children get their turns to be toasted and eaten. When everyone has been toasted, the next activity can begin.)

It's a Piece of Cake

Rhyme to begin action:

Roll a roll,	(Roll hands over one another.)
Stir the bowl,	(Make stirring action.)
Can you act like me?	(Point to self.)

(Here are suggestions for actions):

Make a face.	(Do appropriate action.)
It's a piece of cake!	(Make O.K. sign with hand.)

Touch your toes
    and stretch up high.
It's a piece of cake!

Rub tummy and pat head.
It's a piece of cake!

Continue with as many actions as you like, ending each one with the line, "It's a piece of cake!" Then, when all the actions are done, end with the stanza:

Roll a roll,
Stir the bowl,
You CAN act like me!

CRAFT EXPERIENCES FOR BREAD AND CAKE

Baker, Baker Doll

Have children make their own baker clothespin dolls with plain straight wooden clothespins. Glue on a cotton ball for the hat and draw two eyes with markers. Twist pipe cleaners around for arms. Wrap the baker with woolly white yarn around the bodice portion.

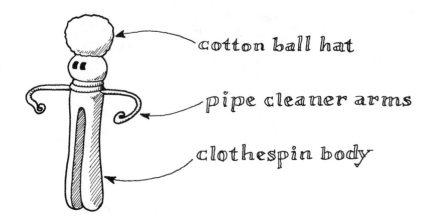

cotton ball hat

pipe cleaner arms

clothespin body

Baker, Baker

Eggbert the Baker

Draw facial features on hard-boiled eggs with crayons. Set the eggs in a circle of white paper for a collar. Make another circle of white paper for the hat band and stuff white tissue paper in this for the puffy part of the chef hat.

tissue

paper collar

Eggbert

Baker Hat for Children

Since you've read many stories about bread and cake that get big and puffy, you will want to make a puffy baker's hat for children to wear home. This easy-to-make project will not last long, but it's fun for a day.

Cut a strip of white paper about 20 inches long and staple the ends together for the band. Staple a piece of white tissue paper around the band and staple the sides and the top of the paper together. There will be lots of puffiness on the top that you can squash down.

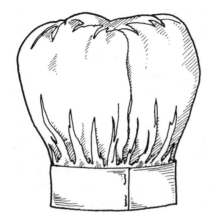

Baker Hat
for Children

Bread-and-Glue Dough

This bread dough uses the cheap white bread that squashes down easily. It also dries fairly quickly without having to be baked in a slow oven. You can even add a few drops of food coloring for fun. It is pliable and easy to sculpt.

Trim crusts from 8 slices of bread and tear into pieces. Pour ½ cup glue (plastic type is best) over bread and knead until smooth.

COOKING AND TASTING EXPERIENCES FOR BREAD AND CAKE

Depending upon your time and facilities, you can make bread and cake of some kind with children. If you really don't want to get into making a yeast bread or an angelfood, you can make a trip to the local bakery. Or, you could try a tasting experience by passing a bread basket for sampling varieties.

Breadbasket Sampler

Ask mothers to help by making different breads, or have children as part of their treat contribution for the day, bring different kinds of bread. Ethnic bakeries or delis will stock varieties of bread that some children may not have tried before. You might include pita bread, a Russian rye, French bread, San Francisco sourdough, and matzo crackers. Put small samples of the bread in breadbaskets and pass around for everyone to taste.

Monster Mickey Bread

This bread is named for Mickey in the book, *In the Night Kitchen* (p. 99). A variation of the popular "Monkey Bread," it is made on a cookie sheet rather than in a tube pan so you can form the bread into the letter "M." You can either make it with children or have a parent make the bread and bring it for the day's treat.

You will need: 3 tubes of biscuits
½ teaspoon cinnamon
⅓ cup sugar
nuts, just enough to sprinkle on bottom of cookie sheet
1½ sticks margarine
1 teaspoon cinnamon
1 cup brown sugar

Cut each biscuit into 4 pieces and roll each piece in the sugar/cinnamon mixture. Grease a cookie sheet with shortening and sprinkle nuts in a big "M" shape. Then place biscuit pieces on top of the nuts. Combine margarine, the remaining cinnamon, and brown sugar and boil for 2-3 minutes. Pour over the biscuits. Bake at 350 degrees for 25 minutes. Cool. (These are delicious, but rich and messy, so have napkins on hand!)

Birthday Cakes in a Cup

Make packaged cake mix according to directions, but instead of baking in a pan or cupcake tins, pour batter into flat-bottom ice cream cones and bake. For extra fun, tint the cake batter. Add candles, too!

Flower Pot Cakes

Prepare a packaged cake mix, but bake in earthenware flower pots that have been prepared by greasing and flouring. This tasty project will be perfect to use if you read *The Man Who Entered a Contest* (p. 98)!

7.
SOUP'S ON!

INTRODUCTION

The familiar cry, "Soup's On!" has brought people to the dinner table down through the ages. Made from what was left in the larder, soup became the meal. Just think of the varieties—shark's fin, bird's nest, bouillabaise, vichyssoise—not to mention the ever-popular vegetable, tomato, and chicken noodle! Here is an opportunity to let children create their own recipes—almost anything will be a success. And stories in the Stone Soup—Nail Broth tradition prove that a delicious brew can be made from almost no ingredients at all!

Let your imagination go into full swing as you use the activities in this chapter. Eating soup with a noisy slurp may be frowned upon at the table, but kids can indulge themselves by singing the "Alphabet Soup Song" (p. 114) with a "slurp, slurp, lick, lick, wipe it off your chin." And who hasn't stirred up ice cream and chocolate sauce until it becomes chocolate soup! (p. 122).

Even leftovers—possibly the most rejected food of all—can become fun when children see them as another chance to concoct their own dishes. Along this vein, leftovers become recycled makeovers, and children may even become leftover lovers.

INITIATING ACTIVITY

Clean the Fridge

Soup can be made out of almost any kind of leftovers. Clean out the fridge with this activity.

Two children are chosen to be the refrigerator. They hold up their arms in an arch and sway back and forth as the doors of the fridge swing.

Other children move through the doors in a line. When you get to the last line of the song and name a food, the child that is caught between the doors goes to a corner of the room that is called the "Soup Pot." When they are all in the Soup Pot, everyone sings the final stanza.

Clean-the-Fridge Song
(To the tune of "London Bridge")

Clean the fridge—
What's inside?
What's inside?
What's inside?
Clean the fridge—
What's inside?
Here's a _____!

(Name your own foods—cabbage, carrot, hot dog, chicken, etc.)

(When all children are caught and put in the soup pot, everyone sings):

Cook them in a big soup pot,
        big soup pot,
        big soup pot.
Cook them in a big soup pot—
Love those leftovers!

LITERATURE-SHARING EXPERIENCES

Books about Soup

Brown, Marcia. **Stone Soup.** Scribners, 1947.
This French folktale retold has become a modern classic about three soldiers who teach villagers how to make soup out of stones. Even young children will understand the humorous trickery.

De Paola, Tomie. **Watch Out for the Chicken Feet in Your Soup.** Prentice-Hall, 1974.
Eugene helps Joey's Italian grandmother make bread dolls. The boys enjoy a wonderful meal including chicken soup. De Paola's own recipe for bread dolls is included.

Hale, Linda. **The Glorious Christmas Soup Party.** Viking, 1962.
The Mouse family faces an unhappy Christmas ahead with nothing to eat but tea until their friends come to dine. Dog, pig, hen, rooster, rabbit, goose, duck, and cat all bring food presents to drop in the soup pot. They all celebrate with the most glorious soup for Christmas—ever!

Lasker, Joe. **Lentil Soup.** Whitman, 1977.
Matt and his young wife, Meg, sit down to a good stew that reminds Matt of his mother's lentil soup. Meg tries to make her own lentil soup, and though Matt likes it, it's not like his mother's. Finally, after a week of trials, Meg burns the soup. Matt declares it a success. Meg pours it on his head, and they laugh at the joke.

Marshall, James. **George and Martha.** Houghton Mifflin, 1972.

In the first story, "Split Pea Soup," Martha makes lots of soup because she loves to make it. Only when she catches George pouring it in his shoes does she realize that he has had his fill.

Sendak, Maurice. **Chicken Soup with Rice.** Harper & Row, 1962.

All twelve months of the year are nice for sipping chicken soup with rice as this favorite book in rhyme will attest to.

Stevenson, James. **Yuck!** Greenwillow, 1984.

Little Emma Witch is scorned by two older witches who are busy making magic potions. Aided by her animal friends, Emma cooks up a batch of her own brew, fools the old crones, but serves up the most delicious vegetable soup with an added magic ingredient—friendship.

Ventura, Piero, and Marisa Ventura. **The Painter's Trick.** Random House, 1977.

The monks have the last laugh on the painter as he tries to appeal to their vanity. By promising each that he will be the face of Saint George in the new painting, the painter avoids eating the monastery soup until he reveals the painting—with himself as Saint George. The monks celebrate with a feast—of soup!

Zemach, Harve. **Nail Soup.** Illustrated by Margot Zemach. Follett, 1964.

A tramp cannot beg any food from the old woman until he teaches her to make soup from a nail. The trick, of course, is to add something good—meat, potatoes, milk, and so on—until the nail soup is fit for a king.

Related Activities about Soup

Kid Soup
(A Peppy Chant to Get Acquainted)

Leader has children make a circle.

Leader:	Let's make soup!	(Snap fingers to set rhythm.)
Children:	Let's make soup!	
Leader:	What d' we need?	
Children:	What d' we need?	
Leader:	Kids like you.	
Children:	Kids like you.	
Leader:	Kids like me.	
Children:	Kids like me.	
Leader:	Souper Dooper, 1-2-3,	(Clap three times on the 1-2-3.)
	Can you say your name for me?	
	(Points to a child who gives name; e.g., "Sarah.")	
	Can we say it? SA-RAH!	(Clap twice)
Children:	SA-RAH!	
Leader:	Souper Dooper, 1-2-3,	
	Can you say your name for me?	
	(Points to another child who says name; e.g., "Jennifer.")	
	Can we say it? JENN-IFER! (Clap twice. The name should be pronounced so you come out with two beats to go along with the two claps.)	

Children:	JENN-IFER!
Leader:	Souper Dooper, 1-2-3,
	Can you say your name for me?
	(Leader points to each child and repeats the above procedure. End with Souper Dooper 1-2-3 and then go on with the rest of the chant.)
Leader:	Pop them in the old soup pot!
Children:	Pop them in the old soup pot!
Leader:	Wiggle fingers.
Children:	Wiggle fingers.
Leader:	Touch your nose.
Children:	Touch your nose.
Leader:	All clap hands.
Children:	All clap hands.
Leader:	All touch toes.
Children:	All touch toes.
Leader:	Happy faces.
Children:	Happy faces.
Leader:	Smile real big.
Children:	Smile real big.
Leader:	We are Souper Dooper Kids!
Children:	We are Souper Dooper Kids!

The Alphabet Soup Song
(To the tune of "This Old Man")

You may sing this song by itself or use flannel-board letters and point to each letter as appropriate.

Alphabet Soup,
Eat it up,
In a bowl or in a cup,
With a slurp, slurp,
        lick, lick,
Wipe it off your chin.
This is how it all begins.

Alphabet Soup,
Start with "A,"
Asparagus, broccoli,
Eat 'em every day,
Add a carrot, dumpling,
Drop 'em in the pot.
Get your soup now while it's hot.

Alphabet Soup,
Then comes "E,"
Escarole and fettucini,
Add a gooseberry, hot dog,
Drop 'em in the pot.
Get your soup now while it's hot.

Alphabet Soup,
Now comes "I,"
Ice cream, jelly,
Try it on the side,
With a slurp, slurp,
          lick, lick,
Wipe it off your chin.
Let's go on to K, L, M.

Alphabet Soup,
Kiwi fruit,
Lentils, mushrooms,
I don't give a hoot.
For nutmeg, okra,
Prunes and quinces too.
Now add R, S, T, and U.

Alphabet Soup,
Ready for "R,"
Rhutabaga,
Spinach in a jar.
Add a turnip, un-yun?   (Shake head)
I know! Ugli fruit—
This will make you want to root!

Alphabet Soup,
Almost through,
Vinegar, wax beans,
Feed it to a crew
With an X X, hug, hug,
Yams and zucchini,
SOUP IS SUPER STUFF FOR ME!

Too Many Cooks
(A Flannel-board Story)

In preparation, make a felt pot shape with a hole cut out of the center. Make enough felt carrots for every child to have one. You will also need one small felt carrot. You could use a rabbit puppet to help tell the story if you wish. Pass out the larger carrots to the children before you begin telling the following story.

Too-Many-Cooks Flannelboard

cut out hole

felt carrots

Benjamin's carrot

One fine day, Mr. Rabbit put his big pot on the fire to make carrot soup. (Place pot on board.) He put in water and three carrots. (Select three children to place their carrots on the board in the hole in the pot.) Then he stirred and stirred and stirred. How good that soup smelled!

Just then, Mrs. Rabbit came home. She looked at the pot of carrot soup and thought—if three carrots are good, three more will be better. So she put three more carrots in the pot. (Three more children put carrots in the pot.) One, two three carrots, and she stirred and stirred and stirred. How good that soup smelled!

(Continue in same manner with grandpa, sister, brother, grandma, cousin—until all carrots have been placed in pot. They will overlap and fill hole in pot.)

Last of all came little Benjamin Bunny. He was too short to see how many carrots were already in the pot, so he just reached up with his little tiny carrot and put it in the pot. (Add small carrot.) Crash! The whole pot tipped over (pull pot and carrots off board), and all the carrots spilled out. Benjamin got out of the way just in time!

Well, Mr. Rabbit came in and cleaned up all the carrots. He set the pot back up with 1, 2, 3 carrots and little Benjamin's carrot in the pot (place pot and carrots back on board) to make carrot soup. And that night at dinner, everyone agreed it was the best soup ever—with just enough carrots! And little Benjamin ate three bowls!

All-Kinds-of-Soup Song
(To the tune of "Polly, Put the Kettle On")

Children, put the soup pot on,
Children, put the soup pot on,
Children, put the soup pot on,
What shall we make?

Vegetable or good old bean,
Celery with lots of cream,
Chowder made with corn or fish,
What do you wish?

Potato, Cabbage,
Or split pea,
Won ton,
Minestrone,
Chicken noodle,
Chicken rice,
Soup is nice!

Out-of-This-World Soup
(A Puppet Play)

We suggest that you use finger puppets on a glove to perform this play. Follow the directions for the puppets used with the play "The H Team vs. the Junk Food Junkies" (p.47) in chapter three. For this play you will need a space explorer and five space-creature puppets. For props, use cutouts of an onion, potato, meat slice, a bottle of milk, a carrot, and a ray gun. Use music to open the play, then a count down of 5-4-3-2-1 and a blast-off sound.

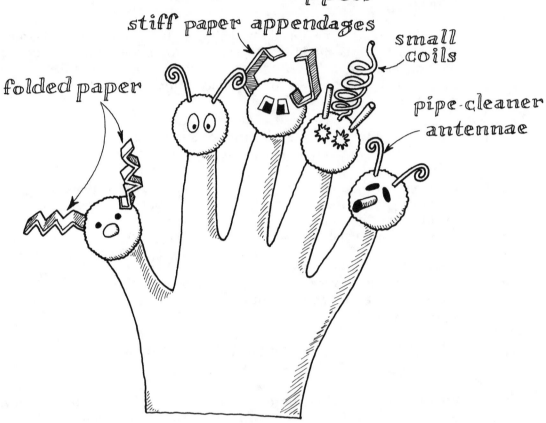

Space-Creature
Pom Pom Puppets

stiff paper appendages

small coils

folded paper

pipe-cleaner antennae

Space explorer:
(looks around)   Whew! What a trip. This planet isn't even on my space explorer's map! I'd better explore it, but first I need something to eat. All I have is some water and . . . (looks around) oh yes, my ray gun. Can't eat that! I'll look for something to eat. (He exits.)

(Play music as three creatures enter. Raise finger puppets.)

Space Creature 1:   Nert-nert-nert. Another of those pesky space explorers has landed. Now what shall we do?

Space Creature 2:   Twa-da, twa-da. I think we should do just like last time. He was delicious!

Space Creature 3:   Oooooooga. No, last time we fried him. This time let's boil him.

SC 2:   Twa-da, twa-da. Fried.

SC 3:   Oooooooga. Boiled!

SC 1:	Nert-nert-nert. Hold it, hold it! We have to catch him first. Then we'll decide.
SC 2:	Here he comes now!
SC 3:	He has a ray gun—hide! (All run off as SE enters.)
SE:	Well, that was a waste of energy. Not a potato or carrot or onion on this planet. I wonder if the natives would give me some of their food? (Calls) Hello! Hello? Does anyone live here?

(Music starts again as space creatures 4 and 5 enter.)

SC 4:	Puffin, puffin. Don't shoot. We are friendly. We like space explorers.
SC 5:	Twada ding ding. Especially stewed!
SE:	What?!
SC 4:	Puffin, puffin. Especially from the moon. Are you from the moon?
SE:	No, I am from. . . .
SC 5:	Dwada ding ding. Or on a bun.
SE:	(To audience): I don't like the way this is going.
SC 4:	Puffin, puffin. He means from the sun. Can you stay for dinner?
SE:	I'd love to. (To audience): That's more like it. (To creatures): What are you having?
SC 4 & 5:	Puffin puffin/dwada ding ding. You!
SE:	No, wait. I have a better idea. Will you promise not to eat me if I show you how to make a wonderful soup so you'll never go hungry again?
SC 4:	Puffin puffin. Maybe.
SC 5:	Dwada ding ding. Couldn't we just nibble a little of his hair while he cooks?
SE:	Touch one hair and I won't show you!
SC 4:	All right. What do we cook in?
SE:	Ah . . . ah . . . my space helmet. (Put space helmet on stage.)
SC 5:	And what do we make soup out of?

SE:	Well, er, that is . . . my ray gun! Then if you don't like it, you can eat me.
SC 4:	Puffin puffin. Agreed.
SC 5:	Dwada ding ding. I start fire. (They both exit.)
SE:	My ray gun! Why did I say I would make soup out of my ray gun? Well, I hope this works. (He takes helmet off and goes off, then returns with helmet and places it on the ground.) There, my helmet is all full of water. (Calls) Space creatures, I am ready to cook!

(Music begins as SC 1 enters.)

SC 1:	Nert-nert-nert. Let's see this soup.
SE:	Right here—water in the pot, and here goes my ray gun. (Puts gun in pot helmet.)
SC 1:	Nert-nert-nert. Doesn't look much like soup yet.
SE:	Well, it's still cooking. You'll like it. Of course, it could be much better.
SC 1:	Nert-nert-nert. How?
SE:	On my planet we have a food called onion and it makes soup much better.
SC 1:	Nert-nert-nert. We don't have onions, but I could get some poofle berries. (SC 1 goes out and returns with onion.) Will this help?
SE:	That will be fine. Put it in the pot.

(SC 1 puts onion in pot and exits. SC 2 enters.)

SC 2:	Twa-da, twa-da. That is a pot? That is soup? I think we should fry you now and get on with dinner!
SE:	Ah, hold on. This will be great soup—made from a ray gun. Of course it could be better.
SC 2:	Twa-da, twa-da. How?
SE:	On my planet we have a food called potato. It makes soup much better.
SC 2:	Twa-da, twa-da. No potatoes here, but I could get you some Martian grass. Would that help? (He goes out and brings back a potato.)
SE:	Perfect! Put it in the pot.

(SC 2 puts potato in pot and exits. SC 3 enters.)

SC 3:   Oooooga. I still say we should boil you.

SE: Wait till you taste the soup! Of course it could be better.

SC 3:   Oooooga. With you *in* the pot instead of cooking over it?

SE: Not exactly. On my planet we have a food called meat. A little of that makes a soup delicious!

SC 3:   Never heard of the stuff. Of course we do have some gooble flesh, and it is in season now. (He exits, gets meat, and enters.) Will this be any good in your soup?

SE: Just what I had in mind. Put it in the pot.

(SC 3 puts meat in pot helmet and exits. SC 4 enters.)

SC 4:   Puffin puffin. This better be good. I had a terrible time talking them out of eating you right off.

SE: Don't worry. It will be. Of course it could be better.

SC 4:   Puffin puffin. The last space explorer was too stringy. You look about right. The soup doesn't smell too bad. How could it be better?

SE: On my planet we have a drink called milk. I don't suppose you have any, but it really makes a soup much better.

SC 4:   Puffin, puffin. Nope, no milk. How about a jug of sparkling bingerclear. I could get that. (He exits, brings in milk.) How about this?

SE: Just what I need in ray-gun soup. Put it in the pot.

(SC 4 puts milk in helmet and exits. SC 5 enters.)

SC 5:   Dwada ding ding. I say we skip soup course and get to main entree—space explorer roast!

SE: Ah, not much longer now til the soup is ready. It smells good, but it could be better.

SC 5:   Dwada ding ding. It does smell good. What more do you need?

SE: On my planet we have a food called carrot. I wonder if you have anything like that.

SC 5:   Dwada ding ding. Grunips help? I get some. (He exits, brings carrot as he comes back.) Grunips, grunips. In pot?

SE: In pot! And now the soup is ready. Get your friends!

(All SC enter.)

SE: Come, try the soup.

(All SC make their own particular noises and jump in the pot.)

SE: Well, that is a new way to eat soup.

(All SC make their noises and jump out of pot.)

SC 1:   Nert-nert-nert. That was really good soup.

SC 2:   Twa-da, twa-da. Imagine, made out of a ray gun.

SC 3:   Ooooooga. I say the space explorer goes free.

SC 4:   Puffin, puffin. I told you it would work.

SC 5:   Dwada ding ding. Grunips! How about we just munch on a couple of his fingers for dessert.

SE: I think I better be going. I'll leave the ray gun for you so from now on you can have good soup whenever you want. (Exits quickly.)

(SC make their noises and look up in the sky as SE exits.)

SC 1:   Nert-nert-nert. That was one nice space explorer.

SC 2:   Twa-da, twa-da. They don't make them like that anymore.

(All SC make their noises and music ends the story.)

Chocolate Soup
(To the tune of "Twinkle, Twinkle, Little Star")

Dip some ice cream in a bowl,
Then add chocolate while it's cold.
Let it melt 'til it gets soft.
Lick your sticky fingers off.
Stir it, stir it, 'til it's goop—
Now you've made a chocolate soup!

Books about Leftovers

Barrett, Judi. **What's Left.** Atheneum, 1983.
  A simple concept-book answers questions such as "What's left after you've eaten your chocolate chip cookie?" (crumbs), and "What's left after you've licked up all of your lollipop?" (the stick).

Brierley, Louise. **King Lion and His Cooks.** Holt, Rinehart, and Winston, 1981.
  King Lion is such a glutton that he has five cooks to feed him during the week. On the weekend, the King eats leftovers. He decides that the cooks should make him a broth for

Saturday, but it's a disaster with too many cooks spoiling the broth until the King comes up with a solution.

Hogrogian, Nonny. **Apples.** Macmillan, 1972.

In this wordless picture book, children and animals toss away their apple cores and an orchard grows up. An apple seller picks the apples and moves his cart through the village.

Related Activities about Leftovers

The Best Part Is . . . What's Left

Read this poem to children, then read it again and let them make sounds and do actions. You might even serve "what's left" treats—cookie crumbs, donut holes, small bags of cereal with little prizes inside.

The end of a soda
I like the best,
'Cause you get to slurp
Down all the rest.

The best of a cake
Always comes,
When you get to lick
The sticky crumbs.

In a box of cereal
You have to eat,
The best part you know
Is always the treat.

And the best part of dinner
Is cleaning your plate,
Then comes dessert—
I can hardly wait!

Leftover Stew
(A Flannel-board Story)

Simplify this flannel-board story by cutting out pictures of food from magazines and mount pieces of felt on the back to attach to the flannel board. Include pictures of beef, peas, carrots, potatoes, onions.

Once there was a family who never ate everything the mother cooked for dinner. On Monday they had beef and potatoes and brussel sprouts. They ate all the potatoes and brussel sprouts, but there was some beef left. So the mother put the beef in a container in the refrigerator. (Put beef on board.)

On Tuesday, dinner was delicious. They had fried chicken, mashed potatoes, and peas. The family ate all the chicken and mashed potatoes, but there were some peas left. So the mother put them in the refrigerator with the beef. (Put peas on board.)

On Wednesday, they had hot dogs and baked beans and onions, but there were some onions left. So the mother put the onions in the refrigerator with the beef and peas. (Put onions on board.)

On Thursday, they had pork chops and corn and potatoes. They ate all the pork chops and corn, but there were potatoes left. So the mother put the potatoes in the refrigerator with the beef and peas and onions. (Put potato on board.)

Friday they had a wonderful meal of fish and rice and carrots. They ate all the fish and rice, but there were carrots left. So mother put the carrots in the refrigerator with the beef and peas and onions and potatoes. (Put carrots on board.)

Well, Saturday, when mother got ready to make dinner, there in the refrigerator was beef and onions and peas and potatoes and carrots. So mother got out a big pot and put all the leftovers inside.

That night for dinner they had delicious beef stew. And do you know what? They ate every bite!

Leftover Food, It Ain't What It Used to Be
(To the tune of "The Old Gray Mare")

Leftover food, it ain't what it used to be,
Ain't what it used to be,
Ain't what it used to be.
Leftover food, it ain't what it used to be.
Many long days ago.

The end of a ham,
And a wrinkled potato,
A handful of peas,
And a squashy tomato.
Leftover food, it ain't what it used to be,
Many long days ago.

Don't throw it out,
Be a leftover lover.
Put in a pot,
With a great big cover.
Leftover food, it ain't what it used to be,
Now you've got a stew!

The Casserole Roll

Tonight we're having leftovers,
We had no time to shop,
So let's look in the ice box,
And see what we have got!

Chicken!
We'll have chicken casserole!
Tonight!

(Stretch out that "role" syllable and roll hands over each other.)

Rice!
We'll have chicken-rice casserole   (Roll hands as before.)
Tonight!

Celery!
We'll have chicken-rice-celery
        casserole   (Roll again.)
Tonight!

Cheese!
We'll have chicken-rice-celery-
        cheese casserole   (Roll!)
Tonight!

Hamburger!
We'll have chicken-rice-celery
        cheese-hamburger casserole   (Roll!)
Tonight!

Chili!
We'll have chicken-rice-celery-
        cheese-hamburger-chili casserole   (Roll!)
Tonight!

Brussel sprouts!
We'll have chicken-rice-celery-
        cheese-hamburger-chili-brussel
        sprout casserole   (Roll!)
Tonight!

Chow mein!
We'll have chicken-rice-celery-
        cheese-hamburger-chili-brussel
        sprout-chow mein casserole   (Roll!)
Tonight!

Hot dog!
We'll have chicken-rice-celery-
        cheese-hamburger-chili-brussel
        sprout-chow mein-hot dog
        casserole   (Roll!)
Tonight!

Pickle!
We'll have chicken-rice-celery-
        cheese-hamburger-chili-brussel-
        sprouts-chow mein-hot dog-
        pickle casserole   (Roll!)
Tonight!

No, let's order out for pizza!

Hand-Me-Down Food
(A Count-Down Fingerplay)

Five leftover pizza pieces   (Hold up one hand.)
From the night before.
Dad came and ate one,
Gulp!
And then there were   (Lower one finger.)

Four leftover pizza pieces,
One with anchovies.
Mom came and ate one,
Gulp!
And then there were   (Lower another finger.)

Three leftover pizza pieces,
Cheese like sticky glue.
Brother came and ate one,
Gulp!
And then there were   (Lower another finger.)

Two leftover pizza pieces,
Not having any fun.
Sister came to take one,
Gulp!
And then there was   (Lower another finger.)

One leftover pizza piece,   (Hold one finger up.)
But I don't wanna be a hog,
So I went and got it,
And split it with the dog!   (Lower last finger.)
Arf!

Lost, Left, and All Gone
(A Tear-and-Tell Story)

Rather than cut with scissors, tear paper (diagram will help you do this) so the end result is even more effective!

Moja had a lot to carry. He had a jug of water and a basket of eggs and a bag of yams and three loaves of bread. As he walked down the path from the village to his house, he dropped one of the loaves of bread. (Hold up folded rectangle of paper.) But he didn't notice. He walked on home.

Now, in the jungle near this path lived an elephant. He saw Moja drop the bread, and he came over to it. He sniffed it (everyone sniff), and he licked it (everyone lick), and then he took a big elephant bite. (Tear #A: first corner of paper.)

Also in the jungle lived a hippo. He saw the elephant leave the bread, and he came over. He sniffed it (sniff), and he licked it (lick), and then he took a big hippo bite. (Tear #B: another corner). Then he walked on.

Now a lion was nearby in the jungle, and he saw the hippo leave the bread, so he came over. He sniffed it (sniff), and licked it (lick), and took a medium lion bite. (Tear #C: another corner.) Then he walked on.

Up in the trees there was a monkey. He saw the lion leave the bread, so he came over. He sniffed it (sniff), and licked it (lick), and took a medium monkey bite. (Tear #D: another corner.) Then he walked on.

In the tall grass was a little mouse. He saw the monkey leave the bread, so he came over. He sniffed it (sniff), and licked it (lick), and took a tiny mouse bite. (Tear #E: side of paper.) Then he ran away.

And the reason the mouse ran away was that he heard a noise. Moja was coming back. (Tear corners of one end of paper rounded to form a head.) He looked high and low, but the only thing he could find were a few crumbs and a worm (open paper) who sniffed (sniff) them, and licked (lick) them, and ate them all up.

Lost, Left, and All Gone

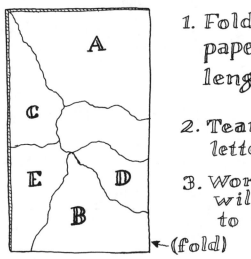

1. Fold 8½"x11" paper in half lengthwise.

2. Tear pieces in lettered order.

3. Worm section will be left to unfold.

←(fold)

Just My Dish

I ate all my salad,
And all of my rice.
I finished my ice cream,
It was cool and nice.
Bologna and brussel sprouts,
French fries and fish.
There are no leftovers,
What's left is my dish!

GAMES AND FROLICS FOR SOUP'S ON!

Alphabet Animal Soup

This variation of "I Unpacked My Grandmother's Trunk" asks children to add a different ingredient to the soup pot. To make the soup especially lively, have each child make the sound or do an action for each animal added. Seat children in a circle around the "soup pot"—the space in the middle.

Leader says, "We're going to make an animal soup, and I'm going to put an "A" animal in the soup—an anteater."

The next child repeats the sentence, and adds an anteater and a "B" animal (leader can prompt). Repeat until you go around the circle and finish the alphabet.

Camel Chowder

This circle game is a bit different from the previous one. Here the leader names a soup and the children say what kind of animal might eat it. (Have the soup and the animal begin with the same letter if you like.) You might hold up pictures of animals for children to get ideas.

Here's a list of soups to get you going:

Asparagus, alphabet, borscht, bean, broccoli, corn chowder, chicken noodle, egg drop, gumbo, jambalaya, lentil, mushroom, minestrone, noodle, onion, split pea, potato, tomato, shark's fin, bird's nest, vichyssoise.

Now, if you combine these soups with the kinds of animals that might eat them, you could come up with hilarious combinations: buzzard borscht, camel chowder, or newt noodle!

Soup-Can Roll—Just for Fun

Sit in a large circle. Give several children full cans of soup (unopened, of course!) and invite them to roll the can to someone across the circle. Cans roll easily on tile floors, and will roll with a little more gusto on rugs. Try to roll three cans across the circle at the same time without colliding.

Leftover Hopscotch

Draw a series of squares on a sidewalk, or, if inside, use squares drawn on a flat piece of cardboard box. The boxes could touch horizontally, vertically, or diagonally, but they need to make a path. On each box draw a food—an apple, carrot, chicken leg, or cookie—or write the word "leftovers." Each child selects a card from a stack of similar food pictures and has to hop on both feet from one box to another without touching the box with the picture of the card drawn. Leftover spots are always safe to step on.

CRAFT EXPERIENCES FOR SOUPER DOOPER KIDS

Make Your Own Soup Label

Let children use their imaginations to come up with their own kind of soup for this activity. Who wouldn't love lollipop soup or camel chowder?

Give children pieces of paper cut in 3 3/4 x 9-inch rectangles. Let them decorate the label with pictures or stickers. Help children write the name of their soup.

Tape labels to a soup can. Send soup cans home with the funny labels. No one will really know what to expect until the can is opened.

Make Your Own Soup Label

Alphabet Soup Bowl Just for Fun

Children won't eat this kind of alphabet soup, but they sure will have fun making it.

Give children paper bowls and alphabet soup letters (uncooked) or cereal alphabet letters. Glue the letters to the inside of the bowl. Children may color the inside of the bowl too. If you like, you may suggest they spell out their names.

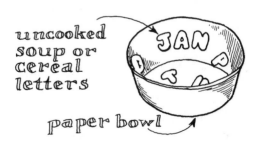

uncooked soup or cereal letters

paper bowl

Alphabet Soup Just for Fun

Garbage-Bag Bib

Cut bib shapes out of a single thickness of white garbage bags (about six bibs can be cut from one bag). Children can decorate bibs with cutout pictures glued on. Tie ends around child's neck for a super bib for eating soup!

This Bag is for the Dogs

Decorate lunch bags with dog faces and dog ears so the next time children eat out with their family, they will all be prepared. Write on the bag "This Bag is for the Dogs"—of course!

COOKING AND TASTING EXPERIENCES FOR SOUP'S ON!

You can make soup from many kinds of ingredients and in almost any kind of appliance, so this will be a creative time in the classroom or library. A Dutch oven or crockpot with its own electric plug works very well, but you can also use a popcorn popper or an electric wok.

Quick Alphabet Soup

Combine 3 cups water, one cup tomato juice, and three chicken bouillon cubes in pot and heat to boiling. Then add 1 cup alphabet pasta (most large supermarkets should stock these). For extra nutrition and taste, add 1 cup leftover vegetables. Cook about 5-8 minutes, stirring a bit as the soup macaroni alphabet cooks. Serve children small portions in little plastic cups that will hold hot liquids.

Easy Won Ton Soup

Combine 3 cups canned chicken broth and 1 tablespoon soy sauce and bring to boiling in pot. Add 1 10-ounce package of frozen Hawaiian- or Japanese-style vegetables. Reduce heat and simmer for 5 minutes. Add 2 egg roll skins (found in produce sections of large supermarkets) that have been cut into thin strips. Cover and simmer for 5 minutes. Ladle into little cups.

Make Your Own Soup Mix

Save money by making your own soup mix and use it anytime you like.

In a plastic bag or airtight container, combine ½ cup shell macaroni, ¼ cup dry lentils, 1 tablespoon instant chicken bouillon granules, ½ teaspoon dried oregano, 1 teaspoon dried parsley flakes, and a dash of garlic powder. Store tightly sealed until needed.

To cook your soup, add 3 cups water (or substitute some tomato juice for part of the water) to the mix in a 2-quart pan. Bring to boiling, reduce heat, cover and simmer about 30-40 minutes, stirring occasionally.

Soups Inspired by Books

Stone Soup
(See p. 112)

There's really no one recipe for a stone soup, but of course you'll want to add some stones—wash them well. Put the stones in a pot and add about 3 quarts of water. Now add meat—a soup bone with meat on it will do. Simmer this in the pot for about half an hour, then add chopped carrots, celery, potatoes, one small onion, and some chopped tomato (one can of tomatoes should be enough). Simmer until vegetables are tender, and serve in soup bowls or small paper cups.

Chicken Soup with Rice
(See p. 113)

Dilute 2 cans of canned chicken broth with 1 can of water and heat in a pot. Add 1 cup cooked rice and 1 cup chopped celery. Simmer this for about 10 minutes and serve in little cups.

8.
I'LL EAT YOU UP!

INTRODUCTION

Folklore is filled with food and stories about eating—often food that comes alive and rolls or runs away from hungry pursuers. "The Gingerbread Boy" may be the most familiar account, but its variants—"The Pancake," or "The Runaway Pancake," "The Bun," and Ruth Sawyer's modern tale, *Journey Cake, Ho!* (p. 134)—repeat an infectious line: "Run, run, fast as you can. You can't catch me———." Of course, in the end, the boastful cake or bun is eaten up.

Another type of eating story belongs in the Red-Riding-Hood tradition and involves a hungry beast (usually a wolf or troll) and succulent would-be victims—a little girl, pigs, or goats. In both types of stories there is something that is about to be eaten, but in the end, it may (and often does) escape!

Cultural historians have suggested reasons for the "food fixation" in these stories. Getting enough to eat was a major concern for common folk during the times many of these stories were created and passed on in the folk tradition. Also, peasant folk liked to tell stories about common characters who succeeded by their wits. Children still appreciate the theme of the weak overcoming the strong. Every generation of children will identify with the little pigs escaping the big, bad wolf and the Billy Goats Gruff overthrowing the troll.

Because dozens of good versions of these tales are easily available, the librarian or teacher probably has a favorite version and may already own puppets and flannel boards with the stock characters. Some ideas in this chapter—Three Pigs on a Tube (p. 139), the Gingerbread-Man masks (p. 135), and our own "The Very Hungry Bear" action story (p. 140-42)—will provide new twists to old tales.

INITIATING ACTIVITIES

I'll-Eat-You-Up Chant

Birds eat bugs,	(Clap throughout this part.)
Frogs eat flies,	
Cats eat canaries,	
Me—oh—my!	
Spoon, fork,	(Point to different children through-
Plate, cup.	out this part.)
I'll eat	
you up!	
(But not really!)	

Repeat this chant three times until everyone is eaten up.

Eat, Eat, Eat Your Food
(To the tune of "Row, Row, Row Your Boat")

Sing this as a round or simply sing three times to get children in the spirit of the program.

Eat, eat, eat your food,
Before it runs away,
Faster, faster, faster, faster,
Now go out to play!

LITERATURE-SHARING EXPERIENCES

Books about Food that Runs Away

Asbjornsen, P. C., and Jorgen Moe. **The Runaway Pancake.** Translated by Joan Tate. Illustrated by Otto Svend. Larousse and Co., 1980.

A mother makes a large pancake for her seven hungry children, but the pancake rolls away past a series of farm animals until Piggy Wiggy tricks it into sitting on his snout. The clever pig gulps the unsuspecting pancake.

Brown, Marcia. **The Bun.** Harcourt Brace Jovanovich, 1972.

A runaway bun escapes the old woman, old man, rabbit, wolf, and bear before the fox tricks the bun into singing a song from atop the fox's nose, then—SNAP!

Galdone, Paul. **The Gingerbread Boy.** Seabury, 1975.

A little old woman bakes a gingerbread boy for herself and her husband, but as she takes him from the oven, the boy runs away from them. He also escapes from a cow, a horse, some men threshing wheat, and a field of mowers. Finally, a sly fox persuades the gingerbread boy to climb on his back, his shoulder, and finally on his nose so they can cross the river. But the fox throws back his head and eats the gingerbread boy until he is all gone.

Lobel, Anita. **The Pancake.** Greenwillow, 1978.

A woman with seven hungry children cooks them a pancake. Just as she is to flip it, the pancake hears it is going to be eaten so it jumps out of the pan and rolls away. A merry chase of people and barnyard animals pursue the pancake, but the lucky eater this time is a pig.

Pomerantz, Charlotte. **Whiff, Sniff, Nibble and Chew: The Gingerbread Boy Retold.** Illustrated by Monica Incisa. Greenwillow, 1984.

In this verse variant of the familiar tale, a little old woman bakes a gingerbread boy for her brother, but the playful treat jumps from the oven and runs from a moo cow, an oink pig oink, and a fat cat fat. When the gingerbread boy returns home, the old man gobbles it down in one bite. But the gingerbread boy jumps back out of the man and runs away with the old woman.

Sawyer, Ruth. **Journey Cake, Ho!** Illustrated by Robert McCloskey. Viking, 1953.

When the farm falls on hard times, Johnny is sent on his way with a Johnny Cake. On the journey, the cake bounces out and gives Johnny a merry chase. A trail of farm animals follows them back to Johnny's farm to begin a new life.

Related Activities about Food that Runs Away

A Gingerbread-Man Story with Masks

This participatory story will involve children as characters in the story as you tell it. Prepare five masks from paper plates or face-sized cardboard circles and attach the masks to tongue depressors so the child can hold the mask in front of the face. Cut eye holes in masks.

Gingerbread-Man Masks

plate
mask

Old Woman

Cow

tongue
depressor

Rabbit

Pig

Fox

Make a gingerbread-man stick puppet out of posterboard with arms and legs cut out separately and joined to the body with brad fasteners. This will make him jump around as you move the stick up and down.

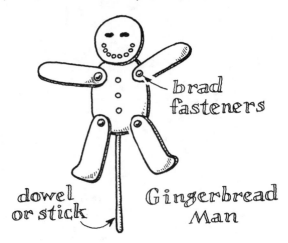

brad fasteners

dowel or stick

Gingerbread Man

Gingerbread-Man Stick Puppet

Before you tell the story, select five children to wear the masks and space them out far enough so you will have room between the characters. Teach the chant "Run, run, as fast as you can, you can't catch me, I'm the gingerbread man," to the other children.

One day an old woman baked a gingerbread man, but as soon as she opened the oven door, he jumped out and ran out the door and down the road. (Hold up gingerbread man puppet and make him run.)

The gingerbread man had not gone far when he met the old man coming home for lunch. (Give first child the old man mask.) "Stop!" cried the old man. "I want to eat you up!" But the gingerbread man looked at him and said: (All) "Run, run, as fast as you can, you can't catch me, I'm the gingerbread man!" And the gingerbread man ran away. (Walk past child wearing old man mask and on to next child.)

Before long the gingerbread man came to a pig in a pen. (Hand out pig mask to next child.) "Stop!" cried the pig. "I want to eat you up!" But the gingerbread man just looked at him and said: (All) "Run, run, as fast as you can, you can't catch me, I'm the gingerbread man!" And he ran away. (Walk on to the next child.)

In a little while, the gingerbread man came to a cow. (Give cow mask to the next child.) "Stop!" cried the cow. "I want to eat you up!" But the gingerbread man just said: (All) "Run, run, as fast as you can, you can't catch me, I'm the gingerbread man!" And he ran away. (Walk on to next child.)

Before long, the gingerbread man came to the forest, and there was a rabbit. (Give rabbit mask to next child.) "Stop!" cried the rabbit. "I want to eat you up!" But the gingerbread man just looked at him and said: (All) "Run, run, as fast as you can, you can't catch me, I'm the gingerbread man!" (Walk on to the next child.)

Now in the forest was a stream. When the gingerbread man came to it, he was afraid he would melt in the water. He stood by the stream—thinking what to do—when a fox came by (give last child the fox mask). "I was just going to swim across the stream," said the sly fox. "How about a ride on my back?" "All right," said the gingerbread man, so he jumped up on the fox's back. (Put gingerbread man on child's back.) But as they swam across the stream, the water got deeper. "Jump up on my shoulder," said the fox. And the gingerbread man did. (Move gingerbread man on child's shoulder.) And the water got deeper. "Jump up on my head," said the fox. (Move gingerbread man on child's head.) But when the gingerbread man got on the fox's head, the fox opened his mouth and ate the gingerbread man up! (Pull a bag from behind your back and drop the gingerbread man in it.) After all—that's what gingerbread men are for!

Gingerbread Boy in Verse

This version of the story can be acted out by everyone as you read this verse.

Oh, the gingerbread boy
Popped out of the pan,
Then he took off
Fast and ran.

He ran past a woman,
And a little old man.
Come and catch me
If you can!

He ran past a cow,
He ran past a cat,
He ran past some chickens,
And a big brown rat.

He ran past some men
Who were threshing wheat.
He ran right on
In the summer heat.

And all the time,
Calling as he ran,
Come and catch me
If you can!

But then he came
To a sly old fox,
And a big wide river
He couldn't cross.

The fox said, "Come on
My back, now, jump!"
But you know what happened—
He ate him up!

The Pancake Chase
(To the tune of "Pop Goes the Weasel")

All around the countryside,
The children chased a pancake.
The pancake rolled past everyone,
"Run, you can't catch me!"

Past a farmer and a goose,
A cat, a sheep, a goat.
Then it rolled up to the pig,
Gulp! In his tummy.   (Rub tummies.)

Books about I'll Eat You Up

Ambrus, Victor. **Grandma, Felix, and Mustapha Biscuit.** Morrow, 1982.

Grandma, Felix the Cat, and Long John Silver the Parrot live together. When Grandma brings home Mustapha Biscuit the Hamster, Felix tries to pick the lock in her cage. Mustapha, in turn, plucks his tail. Undeterred, Felix tries again but ends up in Long John's cage instead. Despite his wounds, Felix plots further revenge.

Brandenberg, Franz. **Fresh Cider and Pie.** Illustrated by Aliki. Macmillan, 1973.

In this rhymed story, a spider catches a fly and threatens to eat it up, but gives the fly one last wish. The crafty fly wishes for a dish of apple pie with a glass of cider. So the spider fetches the apples, bakes the pie, presses the cider. And the spider eats it all. The spider makes more. Fly eats it this time. Together they make more and the spider eats all. By the end of the day, the spider is too full to eat his prey.

De Regniers, Beatrice. **Little Red Riding Hood.** Atheneum, 1972.

Verse retelling of the traditional tale of the wolf's trickery and the hunter saving the day by cutting open the wolf to free Red Riding Hood and Grandma. De Regnier's verse is delightful to read aloud because of the unexpected rhyme and funny diction.

Flory, Jane. **We'll Have a Friend for Lunch.** Illustrated by Carolyn Croll. Houghton Mifflin, 1974.

Peaches the cat and her friends form a bird-watching club so they can have a "friend for lunch." The surprise in the end provides a twist to the "I'll-eat-you-up" theme.

Galdone, Paul. **Little Red Riding Hood.** McGraw-Hill, 1974.

Dressed in her hooded cape, the little girl is foiled by a hungry wolf who eats up the little girl and her grandmother. The hunter saves them in the end by cutting open the wolf and replacing the people with stones.

Maestro, Betsy and Guilio Maestro. **Lambs for Dinner.** Crown, 1978.

This story appears to be a retelling of the Wolf-and-Seven-Kids story with the wolf tricking his way into the lambs' house. But, when the mother comes to the rescue, she finds the wolf and the lambs playing games and having a dinner of soup and bread.

Rayner, Mary. **Garth Pig and the Ice Cream Lady.** Atheneum, 1977.

Garth Pig runs out to buy ice creams for all the little pigs from the ice cream lady in the Volfswagon. She invites him into the truck to see what's in her freezer, and he's kidnapped. The other little pigs pursue the wolf/ice cream lady, rescue Garth, get their ice cream, and dispose of the villain.

Three Little Pigs. Illustrated by William Pène du Bois. Viking, 1962.

This version of the classic tale is told in verse and adds some episodes to the wolf/pig trickery. The refrains and ending remain basically the same.

Related Activities about I'll Eat You Up

Three Pigs on a Tube

Pigs and the wolf flip up around a cardboard tube to help you tell the familiar story with a new visual trick.

Cut out the pigs and mount them on the appropriate kinds of houses: straw, stick, and brick. Attach the pigs and houses to cardboard rings that will slip over a cardboard tube. Prepare the wolf in the same manner. Now attach the characters to the tube, arranging them far enough apart that each will flip up easily.

Start telling the story with the figures all hanging below the tube.

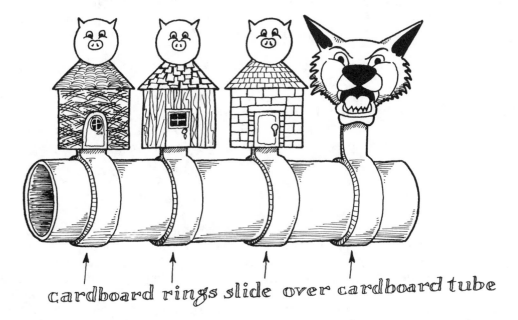

cardboard rings slide over cardboard tube

Once upon a time, there were one (flip up first pig), two (flip up second pig), three (flip up third pig) little pigs. Now one day, these pigs decided to build their own houses. So the first one built his house out of straw (point to the pigs as you mention them). The second built his house out of sticks, and the third built his house out of bricks.

Now, someone else lived in the forest besides the three pigs. (Flip down the pigs and flip up the wolf.) That was the big bad wolf. And the big bad wolf decided he wanted to eat pork chops for dinner. So he went to the house of the first little pig (flip up first pig) whose house was made of straw. The wolf knocked on the door (knock on table) and said, "Little pig, little pig, let me come in." But the little pig answered him, "Not by the hair of my chinny chin chin." Then the wolf said, "Then I'll huff and I'll puff and I'll blow your house in!" Let's all help the wolf blow. Blow, blow, blow. (Have everyone blow; flip house down.) The house blew down, and the first little pig ran away.

The wolf was still hungry, so he went to the house of the second little pig whose house was made of sticks. (Flip up second pig.) The wolf knocked on the door (knock on table) and said, "Little pig, little pig, let me come in." But the little pig said, "Not by the hair on my chinny chin chin." So the wolf said, "Then I'll huff and I'll puff and I'll blow your house in!" Can you all help the wolf again? Blow, blow, blow. (Flip house down.) The house blew down and the second little pig ran away.

The wolf was still hungry so he went to the house of the third little pig (flip up third pig). Remember what that house was made of? Right—bricks. Well, the old wolf knocked on the door (knock on table), and yelled out in a very loud voice, "LITTLE PIG, LITTLE PIG, LET ME COME IN!" But the little pig answered just like his brothers, "Not by the hair on my chinny chin chin." And the wolf said, "THEN I'LL HUFF AND I'LL PUFF AND I'LL BLOW YOUR HOUSE IN!" Everyone blow with the wolf. But the house did not blow in. Let's all try again. Blow, blow, blow. One more time. Blow, blow, blow. I don't think it's going to work this time.

In fact, that old wolf got so tired that he gave up and crawled out of the forest. He was never seen again. (Flip wolf down.) As for the little pigs, they came out of hiding and rebuilt their houses. The first little pig built a house out of straw (because he liked it that way) and the second little pig built his house out of sticks (he liked sticks) and the third little pig built his house out of bricks (bricks were his favorite). (Flip pigs back up as you tell this part.) And they all lived happily ever after.

The Very Hungry Bear

This action story in the Wolf-and-Seven-Kids tradition uses masks, but adds an extra touch—a sheet costume for the bear who is doing the eating up. To prepare for this story, make a casing on one end of a full-sized sheet and pull elastic through the casing. The elastic should be big enough to stretch comfortably over the leader's head and rest on the shoulders. Make paper-plate masks for the other characters—a dog, cat, mouse, duck, pig—as many animals as you wish to use. Cut out the eyes in the masks and attach a tongue depressor so children can hold the mask in front of the face. To begin the story, put sheet costume over your shoulders as you become the hungry bear. Give masks to the other children to hold and ask them to stand to the side. Ask other children if they can burp (all children love this part). Practice burping—on cue!

Very Hungry Bear Puppets

It was fall. Bear was getting ready for his long winter's nap. And he had to eat and eat and eat. He ate all his honey and berries in the cave, but he thought—I need more to eat before I sleep. So he went off to find more to eat.

Pretty soon he found a mouse. (Have child with the mouse mask come forward.) Bear said, "I need more to eat before I sleep. I am going to eat YOU!" And he ate the mouse. (Have mouse hide under the sheet.)

Pretty soon he met a cat. (Cat-mask child comes forward.) "I need more to eat before I sleep," said the bear, "And I am going to eat YOU!" And he ate the cat. (Hide cat under the sheet.)

(Continue with all the animals you choose to use for the story.)

By the time the bear had eaten all those animals, he was so full he could hardly move. And he knew he would never get to sleep until he had burped. So, he took a big breath and—

Everyone together—BURP!

Out came the mouse (mouse-mask child comes out), out came the cat (cat-mask child comes out), out came the dog (dog-mask child comes out), and so on until all the animals have been burped out.

And the bear went home to his cave and went right to sleep. (Everyone pretends to sleep.)

Did You Ever Eat . . .
(To the tune of "Did You Ever See a Lassie?")

Did you ever eat a hippo?
A hippo?
A hippo?
Did you ever eat a hippo?
Cause they taste just great!

Did you ever eat a lion?
A lion?
A lion?
Did you ever eat a lion?
Cause they taste just great!

Did you ever eat a rhino?
A rhino?
A rhino?
Did you ever eat a rhino?
Cause they taste just great!

I ate all the hippos and lions and rhinos,
I ate all the animals cause cookies taste great!

(You might substitute "crackers" for "cookies" in the last line if you plan to serve animal crackers.)

GAMES AND FROLICS FOR I'LL EAT YOU UP

You could repeat the "Piggy, Piggy" tag game from p. 8 of chapter one (Breakfast Starts the Day) for this program if you like, or choose these new games.

Gingerbread-Boy Treasure Hunt

This treasure-hunt game combines a traditional treasure hunt with a tasting experience in the end.

Hide seven to ten cutout cardboard or construction paper gingerbread boys around the room. Each gingerbread boy should contain a simple clue leading to the next clue. The first one might read, "Go look under the big round table." The second clue might read, "Look under a book cart." Follow the gingerbread boy trail to the end (perhaps in the card catalog) where everyone will find a package of—what else?—gingerbread boys for everyone to eat!

Spider and Fly
(To the tune of "London Bridge")

Sing this song and act it out the traditional way with children making a bridge with hands and catching a child as she or he goes through. Repeating the verses will allow several children to be caught.

Spider, spider
Catch a fly,
Catch a fly,
Catch a fly.
Spider, spider,
Catch a fly.
Here's my dinner.

Take the web
And wrap her (him) up,
Wrap her up,
Wrap her up,
Take the web
And wrap her up.
Here's my dinner.

CRAFT EXPERIENCES FOR I'LL EAT YOU UP

Several of the action stories in this section use paper-plate masks that you have prepared ahead. Children can make their own masks from paper plates to take home, too. Think of animals that get eaten up in the stories (or those that do the eating). Other paper-plate puppets or pictures are:

Hungry-Mouth Cat

Fold a paper plate in half. Draw on eyes, nose, and whiskers. Cut out two triangle ears and a long tongue from strips of colored construction paper. Staple these to the plate face. The long tongue is a nice, hungry touch.

Hungry-Mouth Cat

Paper-Plate Pig

Use the entire circle of a paper plate for a pig face. Draw a circle with two little circles inside for the snout. Draw two little eyes (even young children can manage this one). Glue two little pink triangle ears to the top. On the back write, "Pig Out on Good Food."

Paper-Plate Pig

Litter Eater

Cut a mouth out of one side of a brown lunch bag (or a grocery bag), fold down the top, and staple it shut. Draw funny eyes and nose on your bag. (You can make it as elaborate as you like.) Remember, litter eaters (or litter critters, whatever you like to call them) like to eat trash. So write on the bag, "Keep me happy! Feed me your litter." Take this litter eater along on car trips and keep one in the classroom or library.

cutout
mouth hole
for eating trash

Litter Eater

COOKING AND TASTING EXPERIENCES FOR I'LL EAT YOU UP

Pancakes that Might Run Away

Pancakes in chapter one, "Breakfast Starts the Day," aren't as daring as these. Make up the pancakes according to the basic recipe (p. 12), but add a few drops of food coloring to the batter. Put the batter in a ketchup or mustard squeeze container to control the flow. Squeeze pancakes out in the shapes of animals—bunnies, turtles, or monsters. Can they run away? Maybe into your mouth!

Food to Eat on the Run

We can run just as fast as the gingerbread boy and the little pigs did in the stories. When you want to eat like a pig, but are in too much of a hurry, just fix these quick snacks to "eat on the run."

Bumps on a Log

Spread peanut butter on a celery "log" and dot the top with raisins.

Porcupine Balls

Roll softened cream cheese in chopped peanuts, grated cheese, or chopped parsley. Add two olive eyes. This kind of porcupine won't stick you!

Hobo Bags

There's lots of fun in taking food with you in unusual containers. Johnny's sack in *Journey Cake, Ho!* (p. 134) can be made by simply filling large squares of bandana fabric (or any scrap material you can find) with snack foods such as sunflower seeds, raisins, peanuts, popcorn, or cereal mix. Tie the four corners in a knot to make the bag, then tie onto a stick (watch for sharp ends).

Any Food Kabob

Spear assorted fruits such as banana slices, melon chunks, apple slices, and cheese cubes (or ham cubes)—the list is endless—on toothpicks.

9.
MAGIC POTS COOKING 'ROUND THE WORLD

INTRODUCTION

Folktales from around the world abound with stories of magic cooking pots. In Germany, the pot holds porridge; in India, rice; and in Italy, pasta. The kind of food produced varies with the culture. But the cooking magic is usually the same. A witch or enchantress entrusts a magic vessel to a needy person, and all goes well until the vessel falls into the wrong hands. Porridge and pasta fill up entire villages as townspeople eat through the catastrophic results.

Many young children in a land of plenty will probably not recognize the dream of having more than enough to eat that prompted peasants in ages past to concoct these tall tales. But the broad humor and exaggerated results never fail to delight generations of young people. In our mechanized age, the cooking pot appears as a donut machine gone berserk in Robert McCloskey's modern classic for children, *Homer Price*. We have added a story about a more recent cooking wonder—the microwave (p. 150-53). Here a magic chant combines with the magnetron—a modern wonder in itself—to produce enough oatmeal for the neighborhood. Our stories, songs, and rhymes interpret the worldwide interest in magic pots through contemporary tall tales set in the United States. But the stories found in the suggested picture books come from Italy, India, Germany, and Russia.

Sharing food from all over the world is a focus of this chapter. What better way to promote understanding of different cultures than to introduce food from around the world! Children who read about the funny little woman who makes rice dumplings in Japan (p. 155) or the old woman who gets fat from eating curds and curry in the Indian tale *The Old Woman and the Red Pumpkin* (p. 154) may be more willing to try an unusual spice or an unfamiliar-sounding dish. This is a perfect opportunity to introduce a few words of another language. In addition to the foreign words in the food chants, we've included the words for "eat" in various languages. Good eating and *bon appétit*!

INITIATING ACTIVITY

Magic Pots Cooking in Many Lands

Bring children together to share food from all over the world with this beginning-circle poem. Stand in a circle, cross arms, and then join hands in a great, never-ending chain of friendship.

> Magic pots are cooking,
> In many different lands,
> From north to south, from east to west,
> Look, how many hands.
>
> All join in together,
> You and you and me,
> Sharing food together,
> The world's great family!

LITERATURE-SHARING EXPERIENCES

Books about Cooking Pots

De Paola, Tomie. **Strega Nona.** Prentice-Hall, 1975.
Strega Nona, Grandma Witch, warns Big Anthony, her helper, never to touch her magic pasta pot, but the moment she goes to visit a friend, he tries it out—much to the alarm of this small Italian town that becomes buried in pasta.

Galdone, Paul. **The Magic Porridge Pot.** Houghton Mifflin, 1976.
A poor girl is given a magic pot by an enchanted old woman who tells her the magic words to produce porridge. The girl and her mother live contentedly until the mother tries to use the magic but doesn't know the proper words to make the pot stop cooking.

Ginsburg, Mirra. **The Magic Stove.** Illustrated by Linda Heller. Coward McCann, 1983.
A poor man and his wife, with the aid of a rooster, find a magic stove that bakes them any kind of pie they want. When they invite the king to dinner, he steals the stove. The rooster is triumphant in the end as the stove is returned to the couple.

Towle, Faith M. **The Magic Cooking Pot.** Houghton Mifflin, 1975.
A poor man in India receives a magic cooking pot from the Goddess Durga, but it is stolen by a wicked innkeeper. The Goddess helps the man to regain his pot and live comfortably for the rest of his days.

Related Activities about Cooking Pots

Bubble, Bubble Pot

(To the tune of "Turkey in the Straw")

Oh, we skip round the pot,　　　　　(Form a circle and skip.)
And we look inside.
The pot is deep　　　　　　　　　　(Make hands indicate "deep,"
And the pot is wide.　　　　　　　　　"wide.")
The brew starts a boilin',　　　　　　(Roll hands over and over for
　　　　　　　　　　　　　　　　　　　　"boilin'.")

And the steam starts to rise.　　　　(Raise arms for "steam starts to
　　　　　　　　　　　　　　　　　　　　rise.")
Bubble, bubble, bubble, bubble,　　　(Roll hands for last two lines.)
Right before our eyes!

Happy Magic Pot

After you've read one of the magic cooking pot stories from another land, you may wish to try this flannel-board story set in the United States with familiar barnyard animals and a food familiar to children—popcorn.

In preparation, make felt pieces of Farmer Pete, his cooking pot, a cow, horse, cat, and rooster.

Farmer Pete had just finished picking the corn and beans and oats, but it had been a lean year. After everything was sent to market, all Pete had left was one handful of corn. (Put Pete on flannel board.)

Now every year after the harvest, Pete had a party for all the animal friends who had helped him all summer. Horse had pulled the plow. (Put horse on board.) Cow had given him cool, fresh milk to drink all summer when he was hot and thirsty. (Put cow on board.) Cat had chased all the mice from the barn. (Put cat on board.) Rooster had awakened Pete each morning with a cheerful "Cock-a-doodle-doo!" (Put rooster on board.)

All the animals looked at the one handful of corn Pete had.

"Oh, dear," sighed Horse. "We won't have a very big party this year. Look how little Farmer Pete has. I'm hungry as a horse!" (Point to horse.)

"Maybe Pete has something else in his pot for us," said Cow. (Point to cow.)

"Not unless that pot is magic," sniffed Cat. (Point to cat.)

"But Pete always seems to have enough magic to share," said Rooster, and he gave a cheery call: "Cock-a-doodle-doo! Here he comes now!" (Point to rooster.)

Pete came into the barnyard. In one hand he had the corn, and on his head he wore the pot. (Put pot on Pete's head and an ear of corn in his hand. Move figure closer to other animals.) "Ready for the party?" he asked.

"Some party," muttered Cat. "Where are the anchovies? Where's the tuna fish?" (Point to cat.)

"Yeah," said Cow. "Where's the alfalfa-sprout salad?" (Point to cow.)

"I don't see any apple tarts," said Horse. (Point to horse.)

"Well, it won't be much of a party without corn fritters," said rooster, "but let's see what Farmer Pete has in his pot." (Point to Rooster.)

And sure enough, Farmer Pete had put his big pot on the fire (take pot off Pete's head and place on background), and it was getting hot. He smiled and said to the animals, "What grows up tall, and now is small, but cooks up big to feed us all?"

"It's not anchovies," said Cat and went back into the barn. (Take cat off board.)

"Oh, crab apples—but they're not my favorite kind," sighed Horse. (Point to horse.)

Cow mooed and sat down near the fire. (Move cow close to pot.)

But Rooster crowed "Cock-a-doodle-doo!" because he knew the answer to Farmer Pete's riddle. (Point to Rooster.) And pretty soon they all knew because Farmer Pete put corn into the big pot, and POP—POP—POP!

Cow looked up. (Move cow up a bit.) Horse perked up his ears. (Move horse up a bit.) Cat came running from the barn. (Put cat back on board.) And Rooster called "Cock-a-doodle-doo!" again.

Do you know what Farmer Pete has in his pot that grows up tall, and now is small, but cooks up big to feed them all? Right! Popcorn!

When Farmer Pete took the lid off the pot (take lid off pot), it was full of hot, yummy popcorn—enough for everyone!

After all the popcorn was gone, there was something else left. It was a little bit of happy magic that friends feel when they have shared food and fun.

The Magic Microwave

After you've read *The Magic Stove,* (p. 148), a tale from Russia, you may want to tell this version that is closer to children's experiences with a modern kind of stove.

Have children practice the magic words, and then join in as you say them.

Once upon a time there was a little girl. She lived in a small house with her mother. They were very poor. One day, all they had left to eat was one box of oatmeal. The mother went to the kitchen, took the oatmeal off the shelf and began to boil some water to prepare their supper.

"Oh dear," she sighed. "When the oatmeal is gone, we shall go hungry. Whatever will we do?"

Just then the doorbell rang. The little girl ran to the door, opened it, and there—much to her surprise—stood a huge delivery man holding a big box.

"Sign here, please," said the man.

"But we didn't order anything," said the little girl.

"I know," he said. "I only bring good things to needy people who never order me around."

"Who are you?" the little girl asked.

"Just call me Mighty Magnetron. You will never be hungry again!"

"Wow! How?" asked the little girl.

Mighty Magnetron didn't say a word, but he set down the box just inside the door. Then he waved his mighty arms over the box and—presto—out rose a shiny new microwave oven with hundreds of dials and buttons.

"Wow!" said the little girl. "Mommy, Mommy, come see what Mighty Magnetron just brought!"

"Listen closely!" he warned. "This is a magic microwave, but only you shall know how it works."

"Wow! How?" asked the little girl.

"Just put in some food—anything will do. Close the door and repeat the magic words:

> Presto,
> Cook-o.
> Microwave,
> Cook me up
> The food I crave.

"Do I have to remember all those words?" she asked.

"Certainly," he said. "Even a magic microwave doesn't work all by itself."

So the little girl repeated the magic words. Can you remember them?

> Presto,
> Cook-o.
> Microwave,
> Cook me up
> The food I crave!

"Good," said Mighty Magnetron.

"But it didn't work."

"Well, you have to put some food in first."

The little girl started to run to the kitchen, but Mighty Magnetron said, "Wait, you must learn the important part. If you don't say the magic words, the magic microwave won't know when to stop, and that might be a disaster."

So he taught the little girl the magic words to stop the microwave. And those words were:

> Thank you, thank you,
> That's enough.
> Microwave,
> You've done your stuff!

And the little girl repeated these magic words. Let's all say them together:

> Thank you, thank you,
> That's enough.
> Microwave,
> You've done your stuff!

"Oh, thank you Mighty Magnetron. How can I ever repay you?" asked the little girl.

But when she turned around, the big man was gone. The little girl ran to the kitchen just as her mother was about to pour the last of the oatmeal into the pot of boiling water on the old stove.

"Mommy, Mommy, come see our wonderful surprise!"

The mother was so tired she didn't want to come, but the little girl begged and begged. At last the mother came. The little girl took the oatmeal and a big bowl, put them in the microwave, and whispered the magic words. Can you whisper the magic words with her?

> Presto,
> Cook-o.
> Microwave,
> Cook me up
> The food I crave!

And, presto! The bowl filled with delicious oatmeal. The mother was astounded! The little girl and her mother ate and ate all the oatmeal, but the magic microwave cooked up bowl after bowl. Finally when they had had their fill, the little girl whispered—can you whisper the magic words, too?

> Thank you, thank you,
> That's enough.
> Microwave,
> You've done your stuff!

And—just like magic—the oatmeal stopped.

Now, the little girl and her mother had all the good oatmeal that they wanted for weeks and weeks.

One day the little girl went to visit her friend next door. She was having such a good time that she didn't hear her mother call her for lunch. The mother had overheard the magic words—well, some of the magic words—and had started the magic microwave cooking. The microwave cooked and cooked oatmeal.

The mother began to worry. Oatmeal was starting to pour out of the bowl.

"Stop!" yelled the mother. But the magic microwave went right on cooking up more and more oatmeal. Soon, oatmeal spilled out of the door of the microwave all over the counter and floor.

The mother called the little girl, but there was no answer.

By this time, the oatmeal was filling up the kitchen and coming out of the house.

"Enough!" shouted the mother. But you all know those were not the magic words, so the magic microwave went right on cooking up the oatmeal.

Finally the little girl looked out of the window of her friend's house. And you can guess what she saw. Oatmeal!

Her backyard was so full of oatmeal that it looked like snow had fallen all night and day.

The little girl trudged home. It was very hard to run in all that oatmeal. And when she got to the door of the kitchen, she shouted out the magic words. Can you all help shout the magic words? Please! This is an emergency!

> Thank you, thank you,
> That's enough.
> Microwave,
> You've done your stuff!

And—presto—the magic microwave stopped. Just like that!

Well, there was so much oatmeal that the little girl and her mother invited all the neighbors to come for lunch. Everyone came and ate and ate—straight through until dinner. They ate and ate—straight up to the door. They even licked up the floor.

The next morning, only one big bowl of oatmeal was left for breakfast.

After that the mother let the little girl do all the cooking by herself because only the little girl knew how to use the magic microwave wisely.

Pot on the Stove

(An Action Rhyme)

This rhyme is a perfect accompaniment to a reading of *Strega Nona* (p. 148).

Pot on the stove goes	(Hold hands over head for lids.)
Bubble, bubble, s-s-s-s.	(Hold hands up, wiggle fingers.)
Smells reach my nose,	(Point to nose.)
Bubble, bubble, s-s-s-s!	(Hold hands up, wiggle fingers.)
I'll get my plate,	(Run in place.)
My tummy can't wait.	(Rub tummy.)
Bubble, bubble, s-s-s-s,	(Hold hands up, wiggle fingers.)
Bubble, bubble, s-s-s-s!	(Squat down while wiggling fingers.)
Spaghetti!	(Jump up.)
I'm ready!	(Sit down.)

Books about Many Lands

Bang, Betsy. **The Old Woman and the Red Pumpkin.** Illustrated by Molly Garrett Bang. Macmillan, 1975.

An old woman eludes a jackal, a tiger, and a bear on the way to her daughter's where she gets fat on curds and curry. On the way home, she hides in a red pumpkin. She is discovered, but she manages to trick the animals and returns home safely in the end.

Bang, Betsy. **The Old Woman and the Rice Thief.** Illustrated by Molly Garrett Bang. Greenwillow, 1978.

In this Indian tale, an old woman, with the assistance of a wood apple, a razor, a cowpat, and an alligator, catches the thief who has been stealing the old woman's muri (cold boiled rice).

Calhoun, Mary. **The Hungry Leprechaun.** Illustrated by Roger Duvoisin. Morrow, 1962.

A young Irish lad catches a leprechaun and orders him to turn the lad's dandelion soup into gold. The leprechaun is a bit out of practice and is not immediately successful, but the rocks that he comes up with become as valuable as gold—they are Irish potatoes!

De Brunhoff, Laurent. **Babar Learns to Cook.** Random House, 1978.

When Babar sees a cooking show on TV, he is determined to learn the art. All members of his family get involved and are rewarded with chef hats. There's definitely a French flavor to this colorful tale.

De Paola, Tomie. **Fin McCoul.** Holiday House, 1981.

In this retelling of an old Irish folk tale, Fin McCoul and his clever wife, Oonagh, outsmart the giant Cucullin. They trick him into eating Oonagh's bread with a surprise baked inside.

Domanska, Janina. **The Turnip.** Macmillan, 1969.

With the help of a chain of animals, Grandfather and Grandmother's great turnip is finally pulled up from the ground. After you read this favorite story, you might ask children what they would do with such an enormous vegetable.

Friedman, Ina R. **How My Parents Learned to Eat.** Illustrated by Allen Say. Houghton Mifflin, 1984.

A little girl tells how her father, who was an American sailor, met her mother, who was a Japanese schoolgirl, and how they learned each other's eating customs. In their house, then, it's natural for the family to eat with chopsticks on some days, and knives and forks on other days.

Galdone, Paul. **The Three Wishes.** Whittlesey House, 1961.

A man is granted three wishes by a magic spirit but foolishly wastes the first on wishing for a pudding (sausage). His wife wishes the pudding on his nose. The final wish removes the pudding. At least they enjoy a good meal in the end. Children may have to be told that, in this German folktale, a pudding is something like a sausage.

Mitchell, Barbara. **The Old Fasnacht.** Illustrated by Priscilla Kiedrowski. Carolrhoda, 1984.

Fasnachts (square donuts) are eaten on Fasnacht Day in this delightful story set in Pennsylvania-Dutch country in the 1850s. The illustrations and the speech patterns contribute to the flavor of a fun book.

Mosel, Arlene. **The Funny Little Woman.** Illustrated by Blair Lent. Dutton, 1972.

The funny little woman follows a rolling dumpling to the underworld where she stays to make rice dumplings for the wicked Oni. She escapes with a magic paddle and returns home where she makes enough rice dumplings to become the richest woman in Japan.

Related Activities about Many Lands

A World of Good Food to Share

Accompany this poem with some sample foods from around the world after you've read some of the books mentioned in the annotated bibliography. Since picture books about many of the places mentioned are not available, you may wish to talk about those places and point them out on a globe.

Food in India
Is full of spice.
In China
There's a lot of rice.
In England
Kids like Toad in the Hole.*
In Italy
Spaghetti is served in a bowl.
A torte in France
Is a fancy cake.

When feasting, Ethiopians
Use bread for a plate.
A taco in Mexico
May taste very hot,
But Eskimo food
Usually is not.
People eating
Everywhere
'Round the world,
Good food's to share!

---

*Toad in the Hole is a popular breakfast or supper dish consisting of a thick batter poured over sausage and baked.

A Pizza Pie to Perform

Clap out the rhythm of this catchy rhyme, then try it again using actions. Spread children out as if you are making a giant pizza. And teach children the world for "eat" in Italian—*mangia*!

Want to make a pizza?

Well—let's go!

Start with a crust, a crust,

Start with a crust.

Roll it,

Stretch it,

Toss it,

Up!

Catch, catch, catch, catch!

Smooth it,

Pat it,

Pull it,

All around.

Sauce!

The sauce—

Tomato sauce!

Can you stir it?

Pour it?

Spread it?

Good!

And sausage here,

Pepperoni there,

Hamburger, hot dog,

Everywhere.

Olives green

And olives black,

Sauerkraut,

Mushrooms,

Don't forget the cheese—

Swiss cheese,

Cheddar cheese,

Lots of Gouda cheese,

Pepper cheese,

Cream cheese?

Full of pimento cheese!

Mozzarella?

You betcha!

Ready?

Then, let's sit down—

'Cause I've got the Parmesan

To sprinkle all around.

(Everyone sits down on floor as

leader slowly draws out

last two lines.)

Oooooo, Joy!

The Pasta Song

(To the tune of "Clementine")

Be certain to show the children samples of some of the different pastas mentioned in the song. After a few times, children will be able to pronounce the words as easily as they do "spaghetti." At the very least, the song will limber up the tongue! "The Pasta Song" is a perfect accompaniment to *Strega Nona* (p. 148), the story of a magic pasta pot.

Fettucini, linguini,
Tortellini, fusilli,
Tagliati, manicotti,
Spaghettini, spaghetti!

First you sift it,
Then you mix it,
Then you knead it carefully.
Then you roll it,
Must control it,
Cut it up—1-2-3.

Pasta, pasta,
Mangia, mangia,
Eat your pasta skillfully.
Do not burp it,
Do not slurp it,
With your fork twirl daintily.

Mexican Fiesta

Begin this chant slowly, then do it several times faster and faster!

Enchilada,
Tostada,
Add a chile,
Whew!

Nacho,
Taco,
Muchas gracias!
Many thanks to you!

YUM!

Different and the Same
(A Fingerplay)

You use the chopsticks,	(Open and close two fingers on one hand.)
I use a fork.	(Hold up three fingers of other hand.)
You're not at all like me.	(Shake head.)
I eat my hot dog,	(Hold out hand in fist.)
You like rice.	(Cup other hand.)
You're not at all like me.	(Shake head.)
But your mom cooked your food for you,	(Point to other person.)
You eat it to grow tall,	(Touch head.)
My mom did the same for me.	(Point to self.)
We're not so different after all.	(Open hands, hold up shoulder high.)

Food from the U.S.A.
(To the tune of "My Country 'Tis of Thee")

My country smells of food,
And what I smell, smells good.
From East to West —
Cod caught in Cape Cod Bay,
Pork chops from Iow-ay,
Brown bread and beans baked all day —
From Boston, Mass.

Texas chili's hot,
But Baked Alaska's not.
From South to North —
Virginia ham is great,
Try Kansas City steaks —
I'll never get my fill of food
From the U.S.A.!

County Fair

(To the tune of "Old MacDonald")

When we go to the county fair,
How we love to eat.
When we go to the county fair,
Everything's a treat.   (Rub stomach.)
With a yum, yum, here,
And a yum, yum, there,
Here a yum,
There a yum,
Everywhere a yum, yum.
When we go to the county fair,
Everything's a treat.

When we go to the county fair,
Popcorn is a treat.
With a pop, pop, here,   (Hold hands shoulder high, open and
And a pop, pop, there,   close fingers.)
Here a pop,
There a pop,
Everywhere a pop, pop.
When we go to the county fair,
Popcorn is a treat.

When we go to the county fair,
Cotton candy's neat.
With a sticky, sticky, here,   (Touch finger tips, pull apart slowly.)
And a sticky, sticky, there,
Here a sticky,
There a sticky,
Everywhere a sticky, sticky.
When we go to the county fair,
Cotton candy's neat.

(Repeat the same pattern as above if you wish to go on and on with other favorite treats):

Snow Cone is a treat.
With a lick, lick, here . . .

Taffy is a treat.
With a chew, chew, here . . .

Lemonade's a treat.
With a slurp, slurp, here . . .

A Food Fair from Many Lands

Set up food booths around the room so children will get the idea of a food bazaar, the favorite way to shop for food in Nigeria as well as other lands. You might use large boxes and let the children decorate them with flags or pictures from the different countries. Here are some food chants to begin.

Mexico: Tacos, tacos,
Chiles hot,
Mexican—
Spicy hot!

China: Egg roll, egg roll,
Stir-fried rice,
Eat with chopsticks,
Chinese is nice!

Germany: Schnitzel, schnitzel,
On a plate—
Pass the noodles,
German's great!

England: Scones with butter,
Cream and jam,
English teatime's
Oh—so grand!

France: Cream puffs, French fries,
Good to eat,
Now in French,
Say *"bon appétit!"*

Nigeria: Paw paws, peanuts,
African treats,
Come to the market—
What fun to eat!

How to Say "Eat" in Different Languages

French—*manger* (mah´ jay)

Spanish—*comer* (cō mair´)

German—*essen* (es´ sen)

Italian—*mangiare* (mon jar´ ay)

Russian—*yest* (yĕst)

Yiddish—*essen* (es´ sen)

Hebrew—*achal* (a hol´)

Japanese—*kuu* (koo-o)

GAMES AND FROLICS ABOUT MANY LANDS

Mexican Jumping Bean

Pass out jelly beans and have everybody squat down. The leader says, "All yellow jumping beans, jump three times." Those with yellow jelly beans jump accordingly. Continue with all the colors, and vary the number of jumps just to keep things jumping. The last direction is, "All you jolly jumping beans, eat your jelly beans!"

Irish Potato Frolic

Pound out the rhythm of this frolic with your fist in your hand. Do it several times until children can repeat it with you.

One potato,
Two potato,
Three potato,
Four.
Baked potato,
Boiled potato,
Can you name some more?
Fried potato,
Mashed potato,
Tater chips galore!
One potato,
Two potato,
Three potato,
Four!

Egg Roll

Line children up in pairs. Join hands forming bridge. One child runs under bridge "rolling" hands (circle hands over each other close to body) to the end. She goes up either side on outside of bridge, tags any person currently part of the bridge, and says "egg roll." That person runs to the end of the bridge and starts rolling hands while the first takes her place as part of the bridge. This game takes little space and will get lots of wiggles out.

Fortunate Fortunes

Fortune cookies are such fun for young children. This game combines the idea with simple tricks for the children to perform.

Write tricks for children to perform—hop three times, tell a secret, wiggle your nose, etc.—on pieces of paper. Insert slips in "fortune cookies" made by folding squares of paper (thin paper works best).

First fold a square of paper to form a triangle. Then fold together lower corners. Overlap and staple them together. Each child chooses a fortune cookie and performs the indicated trick.

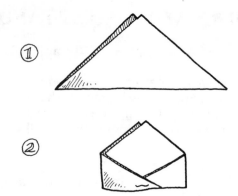

Fortunate Fortunes

CRAFT EXPERIENCES ABOUT MANY LANDS

Magic Cooking Pot

After you've read a cooking-pot tale, invite children to make their own magic cooking pots. Cut out a cooking-pot shape from construction paper and make slits in the bottom and in the top.

Now make a strip of paper to slide through the slits. Glue rice grains or pieces of pasta on the top of the strip.

When you say a magic chant—cook, pot, cook! for example—the strip can be raised to the top of the pot to show the rice or pasta coming out!

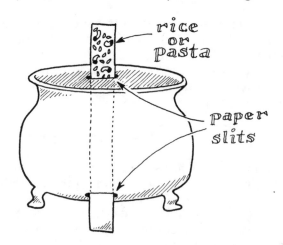

Magic Cooking Pot

Placemats from India

Give your preschoolers a taste of India by introducing a simple kind of Indian batik. Batik is a method of printing a design on fabric with wax and then dying the fabric. The wax resists the dye, so the design shows through.

Give each child a length of paper towel (commercial paper towel works better because it's smooth and sturdy). Draw on the towel with wax—ends of candles or crayons. Then dip the towel in tempera or water color paint and lay out your creations on newspaper or hang them on lines to dry. When the towels are dry, glue them on large pieces of construction paper and cover with clear Contac, if you wish, for a placemat that can be used again and again.

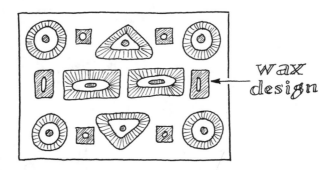

wax design

Placemat from India

Chinese New Year Tree Centerpiece

Chinese decorate tree branches with coins and small gifts for good luck during their New Year's celebrations.

Take a tree branch that has small branches on it and weight it in a container with rocks or sand. Have children hang gold-foil-wrapped candies (they look like coins!) on the branches. Use thread to hang the candy coins (sew on with needle). Leave this centerpiece in the room, or give each child a small branch to take home for luck!

Parrot Piñata

Fill sandwich bags or grocery bags with small food treats: candy, popcorn, etc. Tie or staple the top closed. Add a head, wings, and fantail. These parts may be made from construction paper, or use crepe paper fringed and stretched around and around for the feathers.

COOKING AND TASTING EXPERIENCES ABOUT MANY LANDS

Here is the perfect opportunity to draw upon community resources and parents' expertise in preparing ethnic foods. If you have an Italian or Chinese restaurant that will cooperate, plan a visit or invite a cook to come and bring along one of the restaurant's specialties. Or, try your hand at a few simple recipes.

Pasta Pig-Out

Most young children love pasta and Italian food. Invite someone who makes homemade pasta to bring along a pasta machine and demonstrate the process. Children can help knead the dough and turn the crank to make fettucini. A dutch oven with its own cooking unit will work nicely to cook the pasta. Have a batch of sauce cooking in an electric fry pan to serve over the pasta. Serve small portions in paper bowls. Be sure to tell everyone to "*mangia*" or "eat!"

Another way to pig-out on pasta is to bring in different kinds of pastas such as fettucini, tortellini, manicotti, and spaghetti. These can be cooked ahead and sampled at room temperature. A little butter and mild herbs and garlic will add to the taste experience. Try spinach pastas, too! They are attractive to look at and a delicious way to introduce young children to spinach. A little Parmesan cheese is a delicious accompaniment.

Either way you have your pasta pig-out, be sure to sing the "Pasta Song" (p. 157).

Taco Bar

Set up a taco sampling bar with taco shells (already prepared) and an assortment of fried meat (ground beef or chicken), grated cheese, shredded lettuce, and chopped tomatoes. If this is too expensive for your budget, have children bring the different ingredients. For a simplified treat, fry tortillas and serve in small pieces with a little cheese.

Chinese Noodle Pick-Up

Chopsticks are fun but frustrating for young children to use, especially to pick up single grains of rice! Practice a bit with chopsticks first, and if you're able to manipulate them at all, try picking up fried cellophane noodles. You can find these in oriental food stores or large supermarkets. They have a taste something like a very mild popcorn, and young children will love them. For a fun experience, fry a few for the children (but warn them to stand back from the hot grease). Break off a very small amount of the noodles and carefully lower them into hot grease. In a matter of seconds, the noodles expand almost like magic!

10.
HOLIDAYS TO CELEBRATE

INTRODUCTION

Holidays seem to be more associated with food than other times in our lives. Even in our fast-paced day, we make time to prepare and enjoy traditional foods together. There is even a ritualistic air as we gather to eat Aunt Jane's pumpkin pie or watch Grandpa carve the turkey. Holidays are family times extending beyond the nuclear family to include relatives, friends, and associates—the few days in our lives that become extended family gatherings. The holiday meal becomes an occasion for companionship, for feeling a sense of community centering around the feast laid before us. And those associations will linger long after we are no longer children.

Holidays included in this chapter are Halloween, Thanksgiving, Christmas, and Hanukkah. These holidays focus more on food than other times of the year, and this emphasis is reflected in the books available for children.

Children's interest in Halloween food centers on the trick-or-treat bag but also includes apple bobbing, jack-o'-lantern carving, and pumpkin decorating—all part of the fall harvest. The ultimate harvest celebration in this country is, of course, Thanksgiving. Probably more than any other holiday, Thanksgiving focuses on preparing, eating, and enjoying food. Holiday preparations and treats for Christmas last longer, even longer than the "Twelve Days of Christmas" would suggest. The associated foods of the Christmas season contribute to a festive holiday spirit. And beyond the Western Christian tradition, the Jewish Hanukkah (and even Chinese New Year), make use of special foods to celebrate and add to the season of conviviality.

The holiday subsections in this chapter can be used at the appropriate times or you may choose to have a program on holiday food at an unlikely time. "Christmas in July" or "Celebrate August" (when there is no recognized holiday) are a few possibilities.

INITIATING ACTIVITY

A Tree for All Reasons and Seasons to Celebrate

Children love to decorate trees for holidays, so this tree will let them celebrate all of those special times of the year at once. Place a tree branch in a pot weighted with sand and make decorations—paper turkeys, pumpkins, stars, dreidels—whatever you like. As children arrive, let them decorate the tree. Then read the following verse about holidays.

Special seasons
Smell so nice,
Turkey, gingerbread,
And spice.
Special seasons
Sparkle, glow,
A grinning pumpkin,
Sugar snow.
Special seasons,
Good to eat.
Each holiday
Is time to feast!

LITERATURE-SHARING EXPERIENCES

Books about Halloween

Asch, Frank. **Popcorn.** Parents, 1979.
> Sam Bear invites his friends to an impromptu Halloween party and asks them to bring a treat. They all bring popcorn and decide to pop more—so much that they eat themselves silly. Sam's parents return from their party and bring Sam a treat—popcorn!

Carlson, Nancy. **Harriet's Halloween Candy.** Carolrhoda, 1982.
> Harriet, reluctant to share her Halloween candy with her little brother, Walter, gives him a small piece, then hides the rest so she can eat it all. When she gets a stomach ache, she begins to see the value of sharing.

In the Witch's Kitchen: Poems for Halloween. Compiled by John E. Brewton, Lorraine A. Blackburn, George M. Blackburn III. Illustrated by Harriet Barton. Crowell, 1980.
> This collection of 46 poems by favorite authors deals with Halloween, and many are about Halloween foods. Children will squeal with delight at "Wicked Witch's Kitchen" full of corn on the cobweb, broomstick cakes, milkweed shakes, and toadstool stew; and the "Witches Menu" includes a lively variety of lizard concoctions.

Johnson, Tony. **The Vanishing Pumpkin.** Illustrated by Tomie de Paola. Putnams, 1983.
> An old woman and man meet with all sorts of strange creatures as they hunt for their missing pumpkin. Finally, they locate the wizard who has turned it into a jack-o'-lantern—and pumpkin pie.

Nicoll, Helen, and Jan Pienkowski. **Meg and Mog.** Atheneum, 1972.
Meg Witch cooks up several spells in this colorful story—one turns her friends into mice.

Related Activities about Halloween

Jack-O'-Lantern Pie
(A Draw-and-Tell Story-Poem)

Draw this jack-o'-lantern on a chalkboard or with magic markers on a large tablet as you tell this story-poem.

Take a pumpkin,
Cut two eyes.
Make them just about
This size.
Next a nose,
Long and thin,
Don't forget
A scary grin.
What about
What's left inside?
Make a
Jack-o'-lantern Pie!

Jack - O'- Lantern Pie

The Marshmallow Ghosts
(A Fingerplay)

On Halloween night
Five little ghosts
Went out to have
A marshmallow roast.

The first little ghost   (Hold up one finger.)
Picked up sticks.
The second little ghost   (Hold up two fingers.)
Played some tricks (Boo!)
The third little ghost   (Hold up three fingers.)
Built a fire.
The fourth little ghost   (Hold up four fingers.)
Made it go higher.
The fifth little ghost   (Hold up five fingers.)
Fixed the treat.
Then the five little ghosts
Sat down to eat.   (Everyone sits down.)

Children may be given marshmallow ghosts for treats. Simply place a tissue over a marshmallow and tie the head with a string. Add two stick-on black dot eyes.

Apple Bob
(An Action Rhyme)

Halloween apples,
Bobbing in a pan,   (Bob head.)
Grab 'em with your teeth,   (Snap teeth.)
Don't use your hands!   (Put hands behind back; shake head
                 "no.")

Brrr! The water's chilly.   (Put hands to arms and shiver.)
Oooo! My head is wet.   (Shake head like a dog shaking water
                 off.)

Watch! Here comes an apple, (Put finger up.)
And—I've got it!   (Bend down and come up with
                 apple in mouth.)

CHOMP!

Halloween Treat Song
(To the tune of "Yankee Doodle")

Happy, Happy Halloween!
Do you have things to eat?
I won't play a trick on you
If you give me a treat!

Cookies, apples, candy bars,
Wrapped in orange and black.
Gum and fudge and lollipops,
Just drop them in my sack!

Books about Thanksgiving

Balian, Lorna. **Sometimes It's Turkey, Sometimes It's Feathers.** Abingdon, 1973.
> Mrs. Gumm and her cat find a turkey egg, care for it until it hatches, then feed the young turkey so he'll be big for Thanksgiving dinner. She goes about the other Thanksgiving preparations, but when the day arrives, she doesn't prepare the turkey. She prepares instead, a holiday table for her cat and the turkey.

Devlin, Wende, and Harry Devlin. **Cranberry Thanksgiving.** Parents, 1971.
> Grandmother sets out to bake her famous, secret-recipe cranberry bread on Thanksgiving and invites a dapper guest, Mr. Horace. Her granddaughter invites Mr. Whiskers, a scruffy sea captain whom Grandmother distrusts. But the "proper" Mr. Horace tries to steal Grandmother's recipe. He is apprehended by the tart Mr. Whiskers, whom Grandmother appreciates in the end.

Janice. **Little Bear's Thanksgiving.** Illustrated by Mariana. Lothrop, Lee, and Shepard, 1967.
> On a hot summer's day, Little Bear's friends try to keep him awake so he won't miss Thanksgiving dinner at Goldie's house. He takes a nap in the fall, but they manage to wake him in time by whispering "Turkey with chestnut stuffing," "mashed sweet potatoes with marshmallow," and "pumpkin pie." Goldie invites all the animals to enjoy just that kind of feast.

Spinelli, Eileen. **Thanksgiving at the Tappletons.** Illustrated by Maryann Cocca-Leffler. Addison-Wesley, 1982.
> The Tappleton family's Thanksgiving dinner seems doomed. The turkey skids away and falls into a pond. Mr. Tappleton gets to the bakery too late to buy the pies. Kenny feeds the salad fixings to the class rabbits. Jenny forgets the potato mixer, and potatoes fly everywhere. The family takes solace in Grandmother's prayer: "But we're together, that's what matters—not what's served upon the platters." They all enjoy liverwurst sandwiches instead.

Related Activities about Thanksgiving

Piggy Pie
(A Flannel-board Story)

People often "eat like pigs" on Thanksgiving, but what about a pig who is almost forgotten amid the holiday bustle? Tell this story with felt cutouts of the appropriate foods—a jar of pickles, a turkey, a loaf of bread, three pumpkin pies, etc.—and don't forget a cutout of a pig—Palmeroy Pig.

Palmeroy Pig was feeling punk. (Put pig on flannel board.) It was Thanksgiving and no one had remembered him.

He had seen Aunt Sally bring a pint of pickles. (Put pickle jar on flannel board.)

He had seen Uncle Fred bring a big turkey. (Put turkey on flannel board.)

He had seen Cousin Thelma bring a loaf of bread. (Put bread on flannel board.)

And he saw Grandma Mollie bring three pumpkin pies! (Put pumpkin pies on flannel board.)

But no one had remembered to share any of it with Palmeroy.

He curled up in a corner of the barn and pouted. (Take pig off flannel board.)

Now inside the house, dinner was just over. And everyone was helping clear the table. (Take off all the food.)

"Oh, look," said Aunt Sally. "There are two pickles left." (Put two pickles on flannel board.)

"Nobody ate the turkey leg," said Uncle Fred. (Put turkey leg on flannel board.)

"Two slices of bread! What am I going to do with them?" asked Cousin Thelma. (Put two slices of bread on flannel board.)

Grandma Mollie found a big piece of pumpkin pie left in the pan. And she knew what to do! (Put pan with wedge of pumpkin pie on flannel board.)

She took the pickles and the turkey leg and the bread and put them in the pie pan with the pie. (Rearrange food in the pan.)

"Now," she said. "I know someone who hasn't had Thanksgiving dinner yet." And she went out to the barn and took all that good food straight to Palmeroy. (Put pig back on flannel board.) Palmeroy perked up his ears. His pout turned into a big grin. He licked his chops and sniffed the leftover food. Then you know what he did? Palmeroy made a big Thanksgiving pig out of himself!

The First Thanksgiving
(A Fingerplay)

Five little Pilgrims fish in the morn.	(Hold up right hand.)
Five little Indians help them plant corn.	(Hold up left hand.)
Pilgrims bring bread,	(Move right hand closer to center.)
Indians bring meat,	(Move left hand closer to center.)
Ten new friends sit down to eat.	(Fold hands together, place in lap.)

We're Fixing a Thanksgiving Dinner Feast
(To the tune of "She'll Be Comin' 'Round the Mountain")

Oh, we're fixing a Thanksgiving dinner feast. (Oh, boy!)
Oh, we're fixing a Thanksgiving dinner feast.
Oh, we're fixing a Thanksgiving,
Oh, we're fixing a Thanksgiving,
Oh, we're fixing a Thanksgiving dinner feast. (Oh, boy!)

Mom is baking tasty turkey golden brown. (Gobble, gobble.)
Mom is baking tasty turkey golden brown.
Mom is baking tasty turkey,
Mom is baking tasty turkey,
Mom is baking tasty turkey golden brown. (Gobble, gobble.)

Grandma's making good old golden pumpkin pie. (Yum, yum!)
Grandma's making good old golden pumpkin pie.
Grandma's making golden pumpkin,
Grandma's making golden pumpkin,
Grandma's making good old golden pumpkin pie. (Yum, yum!)

Brother's mashing boiled potatoes up and down. (Mash, mash.)
Brother's mashing boiled potatoes up and down.
Brother's mashing boiled potatoes,
Brother's mashing boiled potatoes,
Brother's mashing boiled potatoes up and down. (Mash, mash!)

Sister's stirring dark brown gravy round and round. (Slosh, slosh.)
Sister's stirring dark brown gravy round and round.
Sister's stirring dark brown gravy,
Sister's stirring dark brown gravy,
Sister's stirring dark brown gravy round and round. (Slosh, slosh.)

Grandpa's cracking home-grown walnuts for a treat. (Crack, crack!)
Grandpa's cracking home-grown walnuts for a treat.
Grandpa's cracking home-grown walnuts,
Grandpa's cracking home-grown walnuts,
Grandpa's cracking home-grown walnuts for a treat. (Crack, crack!)

Dad is carving golden turkey, you all come. (Come on in!)
Dad is carving golden turkey, you all come.
Dad is carving golden turkey,
Dad is carving golden turkey,
Dad is carving golden turkey, you all come! (Come on in!)

Frozen Thanksgiving Meal
(An Action Song to the tune of "Mary Had a Little Lamb")

Let's all be a turkey fat,   (Flap arms tucked like wings.)
Turkey fat, turkey fat.
Let's all be a turkey fat,
For Thanksgiving day.

FREEZE   (Everyone freezes in this position.)

Let's all be a jello mold,   (Wiggle all over.)
Jello mold, jello mold.
Let's all be a jello mold,
For Thanksgiving day.

FREEZE   (Freeze in the wiggle.)

Let's all be a dinner roll,
Dinner roll, dinner roll
Let's all be a dinner roll,
For Thanksgiving day.

(Squat on floor, grasp knees and
    rock back and forth.)

FREEZE

(Freeze in place.)

Let's all be a pumpkin pie,
Pumpkin pie, pumpkin pie.
Let's all be a pumpkin pie,
For Thanksgiving day.

(Circle face with hands,
    puff out cheeks.)

FREEZE

(Freeze in place.)

Books about Christmas

Brown, Marc. **Arthur's Christmas.** Little, Brown, 1984.

Arthur worries about what kind of treat to leave for Santa; then he sees Santa ordering a banana split. Later he sees Santa drinking diet root beer, and still later, he sees Santa eating sub gum chow goo at the Golden Chopstick. Arthur makes a concoction of all of Santa's favorite foods, but his little sister fears that Santa won't be as pleased as Arthur is.

Hoban, Lillian. **Arthur's Christmas Cookies.** Harper & Row, 1972.

The Saturday before Christmas, Mother and Father were shopping. Arthur tries to bake Christmas cookies, but they turn out hard and salty. He almost despairs until his friends suggest he turn the "cookies" into decorative clay Christmas ornaments.

Kahl, Virginia. **Plum Pudding for Christmas.** Scribners, 1956.

With the Duke away at battle, the Duchess invites the King to dine. He agrees if they serve plum pudding. But the baby eats the plums just as the King is approaching. In the nick of time, the Duke returns with plums so the festivities go on—plum pudding and all.

Kraus, Robert. **The Christmas Cookie Sprinkle Snitcher.** Windmill, 1969.

Nat tracks down the Christmas Cookie Sprinkle Snitcher in this story told in verse.

Seuss, Dr. **How the Grinch Stole Christmas.** Random House, 1957.

The notorious Grinch tries to keep Christmas from coming in Whoville by stealing all the goodies, but he has a change of heart and returns everything. The holiday is celebrated with the Grinch himself carving the roast beast.

Related Activities about Christmas

Bring It Right Here!
(To the tune of "We Wish You a Merry Christmas")

Most preschoolers know "We Wish You a Merry Christmas" and are intrigued by the second verse, "Bring us a figgy pudding" even if figgy pudding is not part of their holiday fare. This version still incorporates the command that eager young children love: "Bring it right here!"

We'll feast on fine food for Christmas,
We'll feast on fine food for Christmas,
We'll feast on fine food for Christmas,
So bring it right here!
YUM! YUM!   (Rub stomach.)

We'll gobble up a turkey gobbler,
We'll gobble up a turkey gobbler,
We'll gobble up a turkey gobbler,
So bring it right here!
GOBBLE! GOBBLE!   (Put hands under arm pits,
                                                   flap elbows.)

We'll stuff us with lots of stuffing,
We'll stuff us with lots of stuffing,
We'll stuff us with lots of stuffing,
So bring it right here!
STUFF! STUFF!   (Hit palm with fist.)

We'll pig out on good plum pudding,
We'll pig out on good plum pudding,
We'll pig out on good plum pudding,
So bring it right here!
OINK! OINK!   (Cup hands over mouth.)

Let's Make Christmas Pudding
(To the tune of "Sing a Song of Sixpence")

Plum pudding, though mentioned in Mother Goose rhymes, is not a familiar dessert in many American households. Explain that this tasty Christmas pudding is made from suet and other ingredients mentioned in the song. It is steamed and served with a hard sauce. Traditionally, little charms or coins are mixed in before it is placed in a mold to steam, and much of the fun at mealtime is discovering the treasures inside.

Let's make Christmas pudding,
Add a cup or two—
Flour, sugar, suet,
Stir it through and through.
Then add eggs and nutmeg,
Bread and lemon rind,
Don't forget the raisins,
And some treasures you will find.

Gingerbread Boy and Gingerbread Girl on a Tree
(An Action Rhyme)

I'm a little gingerbread boy.   (Boys bow.)
I'm a little gingerbread girl.   (Girls bow.)
I can jump,   (All jump.)
And I can twirl.   (All turn around.)

I have raisins   (Point to eyes.)
For my eyes,
And bright red buttons   (Point to buttons down chest.)
Just this size.

I have a mouth,
It looks like this.   (Point to smiling mouth.)
I can even
Blow a kiss.   (Blow a kiss.)

I'm warm and tasty,
But don't eat me.   (Shake head.)
Hang me on
Your Christmas tree!   (Put hands over head.)

Christmas Treats Good to Eat

Christmas treats,
Good to eat,   (Lick lips.)
Gingermen,
With chocolate feet.   (Lift one foot, then another.)

Cutout Santas,   (Step forward as if stepping out.)
Sugar stars,   (Raise arms, wiggle fingers.)
Yummy fudge,
And lemon bars.   (Rub tummy.)

Candy canes,   (Lick imaginary cane.)
And sugar plums.
Fill a stocking
With bubble gum.   (Chew.)

Cranberry sauce,
A turkey wing,   (Make wings with arms.)
Grandma's stuffing,
Apple rings.   (Make circle with arms over head.)

Christmas smells
Fill the air.   (Sniff.)
Christmas, Christmas,
Everywhere!   (Raise arms high over head, arms
                                          outstretched.)

Something for Santa

What does Santa like to eat,
That I can leave him for a treat?
After sleighing in the cold,
Some nice hot popcorn in a bowl?
A cup of cocoa?—Not too hot.

A glass of eggnog might hit the spot.
Some cookies or a candy cane?
A slice of pizza? Some chow mein?
I won't forget—cause I know *this* is right—
Carrots for reindeer on Christmas eve night!

Books about Hanukkah

Goffstein, M. B. **Laughing Latkes.** Farrar, 1980.

The "laughing latkes," humorous potato pancakes, introduce many of the fun traditions of the Hanukkah season. Why are they laughing? Because they are potatoes! Non-Jewish children will need an explanation for the names and events referred to in this droll little book.

Hirsch, Marilyn. **Potato Pancakes All Around.** Bonim, 1978.

In the "Stone Soup" tradition, a wandering peddlar teaches a village family how to make potato pancakes from only a crust of bread so they can have a happy Hanukkah. Hirsch's language reads well aloud, and the soft, brown-and-gold illustrations set a warm mood. The recipe for potato pancakes is delicious. Try it!

Related Activity for Hanukkah

Happy, Happy, Hanukkah
(A Chant-and-Clap Dance)

Chant several times, once clapping, another time holding hands and going around in a circle. When the latkes are done (be sure to make some!) everyone can sit down and enjoy this traditional Jewish food.

Happy, happy, Hanukkah,
Candles burning bright,
Happy, happy Hanukkah,
Festival of Light.

Spin the dreidel,
Light the lights,
Presents are such fun
Dance and sing,
Eight happy nights—
Are the latkes done?

GAMES AND FROLICS FOR HOLIDAYS

Treat-Bag Treasure Hunt

Conduct a safe alternative to community trick-or-treat night. After making bags or boxes to collect treats (see Crafts Section (p. 180) for some ideas), trick or treat in your library or school. Designate two or three stations where children can knock—the circulation desk, a shelf, a work room—and have someone prepared to distribute treats after children chant the familiar "Trick or treat!"

Pluck the Turkey and Do a Trick

Make a paper turkey with separate paper feathers that children can pluck off. On the back of these feathers, write simple commands such as "Clap three times," "Make a face," "Gobble." Each child chooses a feather, and you read the "trick" to do. Continue plucking the turkey until all feathers are gone.

Popcorn-Cranberry Chain

Select two teams by giving white tags to "popcorn" and red tags to "cranberry" children. The tags should be cut in circles, of course!

Line up popcorns on one side, cranberries on the other and sing the following song to the tune of "The Bear Went Over the Mountain."

> Cranberries and popcorn,
> Cranberries and popcorn,
> Cranberries and popcorn,
> To decorate the tree.

Keep singing while the first popcorn walks down the center followed by the first cranberry, followed by the next popcorn and the next cranberry until all children are in a line alternating red and white. In this formation, walk to the tree still singing where children can take off the tags and decorate the tree!

Christmas Stocking Relay

Assemble the following materials: 8 oranges, 2 sacks, 2 Christmas stockings. Line up two teams with a sack of four oranges for each team at one end of the line and a stocking at the other. The first child takes an orange from the bag and passes it down the row. The last child puts it in the stocking and yells "Merry Christmas!" Then the second orange is taken from the bag and passed. The team getting all four oranges in the stocking first wins. Older preschoolers may want to try this with one hand behind their backs.

Candy-Cane Capers Relay
(A Flannel-board Game)

This variation of "Pin the Tail on the Donkey" can be played two ways.

First, make a large tree shape out of felt and attach to a flannel board. Cut enough felt candy cane shapes for each child. Place these in a basket.

For the first game, blindfold the children and see if they can hang the canes on the tree.

For the second game, simply divide into two teams. (You may wish to have two trees.) Each team tries to decorate the tree first. Each child races up, in turn, and places a cane on the tree. The second child is able to run up only after she or he has been tagged by the first child. The winning team is the one out of canes first.

What's Inside Jack Horner's Pie?

Prepare three boxes: small, medium, and large. Fill the smallest box with little treats—hard candies would be a good choice. Wrap the small box and place inside a medium-sized box. Wrap this one and place it inside a larger box. Draw a picture of a pie on the biggest box and write on the outside "What's Inside Jack Horner's Pie?"

Now, chant this catchy verse as children pass the box unit around in a circle:

> Everyone sits
> In a great big circle.
> Pass the Christmas Pie.
> Quick! Quick!
> Is it a trick?
> Tell me
> What's inside?

When the chant stops, the child who is holding the box gets to open it. Now repeat the chant and pass the rest of the box unit. When the chant stops, child two gets to open box two. Repeat the chant the third time. When this chant ends, the third child gets to unwrap the last box and share what is inside. (Guess first!)

CRAFT EXPERIENCES FOR HOLIDAYS

Applecrafts through the Holidays

Apple Bob Monster for Halloween

After you bob for apples on Halloween, dry off the apples and turn them into spooky faces. Stick raisins on miniature marshmallows for eyes and attach to apple with toothpicks. Use two raisins for nostrils, and a line of raisins for the teeth of Apple Bob.

Apple Turkey

Use the apple for your turkey's body. Attach a head section made out of brown cardboard. Color the beak and gobbler red. Cut strips of orange, brown, and yellow construction paper and curl the ends over a pencil or with scissors so the strips will look like feathers. Glue these on the curve of the apple or poke them in with brad fasteners.

Apple Turkey

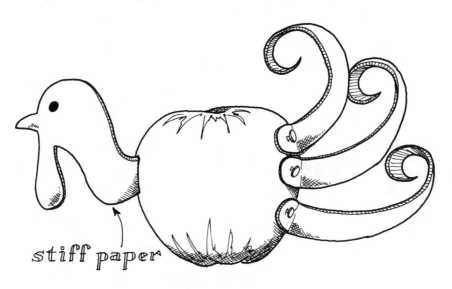

stiff paper

Apple Santa

An apple makes a nice red-cheeked Santa. Add a red paper cone hat, fat marshmallows and half marshmallows for the beard and moustache. Attach the marshmallows with toothpicks that are broken in half. Add raisin eyes and a line of raisins for the mouth.

Apple Menorah

The menorah is a candelabra with nine candles, four to the left of the shamus (or work candle that lights the others) and four to the right of the shamus. Poke small candles in eight apples for the eight candles representing the eight nights of Hanukkah, and poke a larger candle in a pineapple for the shamus candle. Line them up and you have an unusual Menorah to celebrate Hanukkah.

Haunted House Milk Carton

Turn half-gallon milk cartons into unusual Halloween trick-or-treat containers. Cover cartons with black adhesive-backed paper, or glue on black construction paper. Glue on a section of brown corrugated paper over the "A" frame part of the carton for the roof. Now, cut out doors and windows. Add a ghost or cat on the roof. Poke holes in the top of the roof and attach fat yarn for a handle. The treats can be put through the doors and windows.

Haunted House Milk Carton for Treats

Turkey Place Card for Thanksgiving

Fold an orange piece of construction paper in half and draw around a child's hand with the tops of fingers on the fold. Cut around the outline, leaving the three long fingers attached at the top so the turkey will stand up. Glue on a red triangle for the beak and a red oval for the gobbler. Add a black stick-on dot for the eye. Color feathers if you wish. Write the child's name on the turkey's body.

place this part on fold

AMY

Child-Safe Candles for the Tree

Cut out brightly colored candles from construction paper. Make flames from yellow paper. Glue these on pinch-type clothespins. Add a bow if you wish. (Older children may be able to tie a bow themselves.) Fat yarn or indoor-outdoor ribbon will work nicely. These candles won't burn, but they are a reminder of old-fashioned Christmas trees that were decorated with candles.

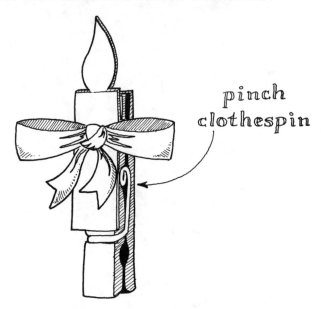

pinch clothespin

Sugar Snowperson

Have children draw three circles on dark blue construction paper for the snow man or woman shape. Light-colored crayons will work best for this. Spread glue lightly inside these shapes. Now sprinkle sugar over the shape so your snow figure will glisten. Red hots may be added for the mouth, and M & M's for the eyes.

Sugar Snowman

Arthur's Christmas Cookie Ornaments

Be sure to read Arthur's Christmas Cookies (p. 173) when you do this festive project.

Stir together 1 cup of cornstarch, 1 one-pound package of baking soda, and 1¼ cups of cold water. Stir over heat until the mixture looks like mashed potatoes. Turn out on a platter and cover with a damp cloth until it is cool enough to handle. The mixture may be stored in an air-tight container. Use when still pliable. The mixture may be modeled or rolled out and cut with cookie cutters. It will dry in about three hours at room temperature. Paint with tempera paints. If you wish to hang the ornaments on a tree, make a little hole in the top with a toothpick before it dries, and insert a piece of yarn.

COOKING AND TASTING EXPERIENCES FOR HOLIDAYS

Witch Brew

Heat together ½ gallon of apple cider, 2 cups of cranberry juice cocktail, and a "witch bag" of secret spices. The secret spices include 1 teaspoon of nails (cloves), 3-4 dragon bones (cinammon sticks), and ½ teaspoon newt eyes (allspice). Float a few orange full-moon slices on top. Heat your brew just until boiling. Remove from heat. Cackle a lot while the brew is cooling, and do a witch chant (Googlie, goolie, goolie, goolie, rem sem sem!) before drinking!

Jack-O'-Lantern Cake

Take a sharing lesson from Harriet in Harriet's Halloween Candy (p. 167), and give the cutout parts of the cake to someone else so you won't get a stomach ache.

Make a single-layer yellow cake, but tint the cake batter bright orange by adding yellow and red food coloring to the batter. Pour batter into a round cake pan and bake according to package instructions. When the cake is cool, cut out the eyes, nose, and mouth like this:

Jack- O'- Lantern Cake

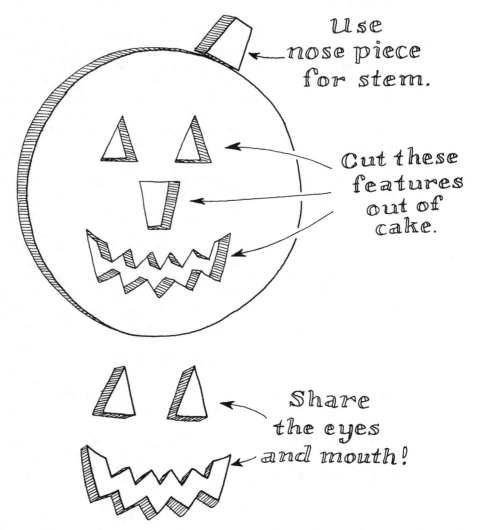

Use nose piece for stem.

Cut these features out of cake.

Share the eyes and mouth!

You can put the nose piece on top for a stem. But share the cutout eye and mouth sections. You can ice the cake with a canned orange frosting if you wish.

Gingerbread House on a Plate

Gingerbread houses are marvels, but constructing a three-dimensional house can be frustrating for young children. This house simply uses the "A" frame shape on a plate.

Provide children with a graham cracker for the house section and a graham cracker triangle for the roof section. The house is constructed, and taken home, on a paper plate. "Glue" sections together with icing and frost the roof with icing snow (recipe follows). Decorate by "gluing" on gumdrops, marshmallows, hard candies, and red hots.

Gingerbread House on a Plate

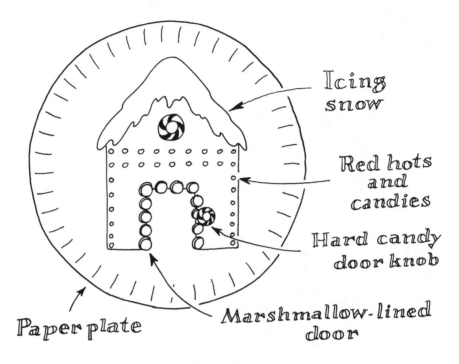

Icing Snow

Beat two egg whites with an electric mixer and add 2½ cups confectioners sugar, a little at a time, while beating. Beat until the icing is stiff and very white. This will dry quickly, so keep it covered with a damp towel when not in use. It may be stored overnight in the refrigerator.

Christmas Wreath Cookies

These no-bake cookies are beautiful to look at, and children love the taste.

Melt together ¼ cup margarine and 3 cups miniature marshmallows in a double boiler or in a microwave oven. Stir in 1-2 teaspoons of green food coloring. Stir in 4 cups of cornflakes. It doesn't matter if the cornflakes get broken up a bit. The idea is to mix the cornflakes until they are all a bright green color. Let the mixture cool until it is easy to handle, but not too long, or it will be difficult to shape. Put lots of margarine on the children's hands so they can work with the globby mixture. Spread out sheets of waxed paper that has been greased with a little margarine. Give children small globs of the mixture to pat into circles. Make a hole in the center of each wreath. Stick red hots all around for the holly berries. Let wreaths stand a few minutes until they are set.

Potato Pancakes (Latkes)

Peel and grate 4 potatoes and 1 small onion (or less) in a bowl. Add 1-2 eggs and 2 tablespoons of dried bread crumbs (finely grated). Add a little salt. Mix well and drop by large spoonfuls onto a hot, greased surface—an electric fry pan works well. Fry on both sides until golden brown. Serve hot with sour cream and/or applesauce.

11.
FUSSY AND
NOT-SO-FUSSY EATERS

INTRODUCTION

An overriding concern of today's parents is the picky eater. Young children, much to their parents' distress, often fix on a favorite few foods and refuse to try anything new. For the past twenty years *Bread and Jam for Frances* (p. 188) has been used by more preschool teachers, librarians, and parents than any other book to address this problem.

One purpose for sharing books about fussy and not-so-fussy eaters is to encourage children to think about eating habits. If children identify with Frances or Gregory, the terrible eater (p. 189), perhaps they might try "something new." And, if picky eating has become a family issue, books can help young children and their parents feel less isolated. Also, these stories convey hope that children often outgrow many food fixations. And, finally, the talented writers of these books have addressed children's eating problems with good humor so that we might laugh at ourselves. The related activities in this chapter are developed along this vein.

INITIATING ACTIVITIES

Food for Thought

This simple game can be played as children arrive. The directions are simple and the children will catch on right away.

Children stand in a circle. The leader in the center names lots of different foods. When the leader says the name of something that is *not* a food, children sit down. There are no winners or losers, but children need to listen closely. This game is a good introduction to *Gregory the Terrible Eater* (p. 189).

The Somewhat Inflated Story of J.S. and His Wife Nan

Jack Sprat and his wife are the prototypes of fussy and not-so-fussy eaters. Here is a modern version that graphically tells the story.

In preparation for the story, draw J.S.'s face on one balloon, and Nan's face on another balloon. Blow up the Nan balloon just until it stands up. Blow up the J.S. balloon fully. Do not knot the balloons, but hold them closed.

Once there was a man and his wife. He was called J.S., and she was called Nan. Now J.S. and Nan got along just fine for the simple reason that J.S. was fat and liked all kinds of food while Nan was thin and hardly liked to eat anything. What Nan didn't eat, J.S. did. So they got on very well.

One day a magic elf came to town and granted each of them a wish.

"Ah," sighed Nan, "I'd like to eat and gain some weight."

"Great!" said J.S., "I'd like to lose some of this fat."

"Well, Huff, Puff, Poof!" said the magic elf, and the wishes were granted.

J.S. began to lose weight (let a little air out of the J.S. balloon), and lose a little more (let out more air), and a little more (air should be about half gone). And Nan began to gain (blow up Nan balloon slightly), and gain (blow more), and gain (blow balloon about half full).

But the magic did not stop. J.S. got thinner (let more air out) and thinner (let more air out) and thinner (let out air so balloon barely stands). All the time Nan grew (blow balloon up more) and grew (blow more) and grew (blow balloon until it is fully expanded).

When the magic finally did stop, Nan was fat and J.S. was thin. But that was all right because then—

> Jack Sprat could eat no fat,
> His wife could eat no lean,
> And so between them both, you see,
> They licked the platters clean!

LITERATURE-SHARING EXPERIENCES

Books about Fussy Eaters

Gackenbush, Dick. **Mother Rabbit's Son Tom.** Harper & Row, 1977.
In the first story, "Hamburgers, Hamburgers," Mother Rabbit tries in vain to persuade Tom to eat "rabbity food"—tender dandelions, clover, nut and berry stew, but all Tom wants is a hamburger with onions and ketchup and pickles on a poppy-seed roll. The familiar warning, "You'll turn into a hamburger," seems to come true. Tom puts a giant hamburger with ears in his bed, then waits for everyone to enjoy the joke.

Hoban, Russell. **Bread and Jam for Frances.** Illustrated by Lillian Hoban. Harper & Row, 1964.
Frances only liked bread and jam, so her wise mother begins to feed her an exclusive diet of it. Finally, she begs for other things, and the picky eating syndrome is broken.

Paterson, Diane. **Eat!** Dial, 1975.
Because a fussy little girl won't eat ordinary food, her parents agree to get her anything she will eat. She asks for a frog. The surprise ending will delight children, especially those who have been nagged to "Eat!"

Rayner, Mary. **Mrs. Pig's Bulk Buy.** Atheneum, 1981.

Mrs. Pig gets a brainstorm when she goes shopping and brings home six jars of ketchup. Whatever she cooks, her ten little pigs always beg for ketchup to be poured on top. Mrs. Pig puts out dinner—a soup tureen of ketchup. At teatime she serves them ketchup. And for supper they get bowls of ketchup. Breakfast is half a bowl of cereal with ketchup. Lunch consists of ketchup sandwiches in their lunch pails. By dinner, the pigs beg for no more. From that day on, they eat ketchup only on ordinary things, but a strange thing has happened. All the pigs have turned pink from eating so much ketchup, and all pigs have been pink ever since.

Sharmat, Mitchell. **Gregory the Terrible Eater.** Illustrated by Jose Aruego and Ariane Dewey. Four Winds, 1980.

Gregory the Goat's parents worry about his terrible eating habits because he rejects tin cans, shoes, and shirts—usual goat fare. He prefers fruits, vegetables, eggs, fish, and bread. Dr. Ram advises them to slowly wean him by trying a new food each day. The experiment is such a success that Gregory eats everything in sight and gets a stomach ache. Finally, he settles down to a more balanced diet.

Van Witsen, Betty. "Cheese, Peas, and Chocolate Pudding," **Humpty Dumpty's Storybook.** Parents Magazine Press, 1966.

A little boy eats nothing but "cheese, peas, and chocolate pudding" in this story that uses the repeated line children will begin to recite along with the reader. One day, his older brother drops hamburger in his mouth, and he likes the change.

Williams, Barbara. **Jeremy Isn't Hungry.** Illustrated by Martha Alexander. Dutton, 1978.

Davey's mother is too busy to tend to Jeremy, who is crying, so Davey tries to feed him. Davey plays food games with Jeremy, but it's all in vain. In the end, Jeremy feeds himself—and the whole kitchen, too!

Related Activities about Fussy Eaters

Picky Paul
(A Flannel-board Story)

This story invites participation. Children are asked to repeat the line, "No, I won't," and they will respond enthusiastically. In preparation for telling the story, cut out felt pieces: tomato, green pepper, mushroom, cheese, and pizza. See p. 206 for a recipe for Picky Paul Pizza.

Paul was a little boy—just about your age—who was a picky eater. He picked at his food, especially if it looked different or smelled different, or if he'd never eaten it before.

"Won't you try one bite?" his father asked.

But Picky Paul always said, "No, I won't!"

One day his father said, "Paul, today I'm going to make something special—something you will like. Won't you try one bite?"

But Picky Paul still said, "No, I won't!"

"Well, come out to the kitchen with me anyway while I cook."

And Paul did.

In the kitchen, father got out a tomato (put tomato on board).

"Look," said father. "A nice red tomato. Won't you try just one bite?"

But Picky Paul said, "No, I won't!"

Next, father brought out mushrooms (put mushrooms on board).

"Here's something new," he said. "Mushrooms. Won't you try just one bite?"

But Picky Paul said, "No, I won't!"

Then father got out a green pepper.

"What a nice color," said father. "A green pepper. Won't you try one bite?"

But Picky Paul said, "No, I won't!"

Father went to the refrigerator and brought out the mozzarella cheese (put cheese on board).

"Mmmmm," he said. "That mozzarella cheese smells good. Won't you try just one bite?"

But still Paul said, "No, I won't!"

Then father got out a big bowl and stirred and stirred and stirred. And he got out a big round pan and he rolled and rolled. He put the tomato and the mushrooms and the green pepper and the cheese in the pan and put it in the oven. (Remove felt pieces from flannel board.)

Father and Picky Paul waited. And while they waited, the smell of something came out of that oven. Father sniffed it, and Paul sniffed it. And it smelled soooo good!

When it was all cooked, father took it out of the oven, and it was a nice warm pizza! (Put up felt pizza on board.)

Father said to Paul, "Here is our pizza. Won't you try just one bite?"

This time Paul said, "Yes, I will!"

And he not only ate one bite, he ate three whole pieces—all by himself!

Ketchup, Ketchup, Everywhere . . .
Only Six Jars to Spare

After you have read *Mrs. Pig's Bulk Buy* (p. 189), bring out six jugs or jars of ketchup and proceed with the following demonstration.

When Mrs. Pig goes shopping, she buys six jars of ketchup.

For dinner, she serves the little pigs a big soup bowl full of — — —. (Don't say the word "ketchup," just pour the first jar of ketchup into a soup tureen or large serving bowl.)

At teatime, the little pigs are hungry again, so Mrs. Pig gives them some cups of — — —. (Pour second jar of ketchup into teacups.)

By suppertime, the little pigs are starving. Mrs. Pig gives them nice bowls of — — —. (Pour third jar of ketchup in soup bowl.)

The next morning, the little pigs race downstairs and are delighted to find bowls with cereal inside. (Pull out a bowl of cornflakes—half full.) Mrs. Pig gives them each a helping of cereal with lots of — — —. (Pour ketchup on cornflakes and stir it around so its blobby!)

When the little pigs open their lunchboxes at school, they find sandwiches spread with — — —. (Open up lunch box with two pieces of bread, open the fifth jar of ketchup, pour plenty on the bread and make into a sandwich.)

By dinner, the little pigs are desperate. They beg their mama. "No more — — —!"

So—after that, she only keeps a little (pause, and everyone says "KETCHUP") on hand to eat with French fries. (Pour a little ketchup on a bowl of French fries and pass around for children to eat.)

The Fussy Eaters' Song
(To the tune of "Here We Go 'Round the Mulberry Bush")

This is how we eat our food,
        eat our food,
        eat our food.
This is how we eat our food, the fussy eater way.

Nibble, nibble,
Pick, pick, pick,
Nibble, nibble,
Pick, pick, pick,
Nibble, nibble,
Pick, pick, pick,
The fussy eater way.

Leave your crusts and drop your peas,
No more brussel sprouts with cheese,
Take that liver off my plate—
Fussy eaters hate—

Sauerkraut and stringy beans—
Casseroles with silly names,
Gristle, fat, and funny things,
I can't tell what they are!

Won't you please be nice to me
Give me time to try, you'll see.
I will clean my plate and say,

(spoken) "I'm hungry, Mom!"

(sung) What's to eat today?

How to Dump What You Won't Eat

(To the tune of "Skip to My Lou")

Children are ingenious at ways to get rid of food they don't want to eat. This song will probably not give them any ideas they don't already have. Everyone will get a good laugh and try something new in the end.

How to dump what you won't eat,
How to dump what you won't eat,
How to dump what you won't eat,
So you can leave the table.

Hide it underneath your plate,
Hide it underneath your plate,
Hide it underneath your plate,
So you can leave the table.

Tuck it in your jaws and cheek,
Tuck it in your jaws and cheek,
Tuck it in your jaws and cheek,
So you can leave the table.

Drop it on a dirty floor,
Drop it on a dirty floor,
Drop it on a dirty floor,
So you can leave the table.

Feed it to a puppy dog,
Feed it to a puppy dog,
Feed it to a puppy dog,
So you can leave the table.

Run to the trash when mom is out,
Run to the trash when mom is out,
Run to the trash when mom is out,
So you can leave the table.

Try one bite—it might be good,
Try one bite—it might be good,
Try one bite—it might be good,
Now you can leave the table!

Books about Not-So-Fussy Eaters

Carle, Eric. **The Very Hungry Caterpillar.** Philomel, 1970.
    A small, very hungry caterpillar eats through a chain of food each day of the week until he develops a stomach ache and eats a green leaf to feel better. He becomes a very fat caterpillar, builds a cocoon, and emerges as a butterfly. Die-cut eating holes in the pictures of brightly colored food will make everyone want to become a glutton.

Charlip, Remy, and Burton Supree. **Mother Mother I Feel Sick Send for the Doctor Quick Quick Quick.** Illustrated by Remy Charlip. Parents, 1966.

Told in silhouette drawings, the story tells of a boy who has eaten so much he has a stomach ache. The doctor extracts a green apple, a ball, a whole birthday cake, spaghetti on a plate, a flounder, a teapot, cup and saucer, cookies, a rabbit, a hat, galoshes, shoes, a bird and a tree, and a bicycle!

Cole, Joanna. **Golly Gump Swallowed a Fly.** Illustrated by Bari Weissman. Parents, 1981.

Golly Gump wins first prize at the fair as the best yawner, but when he goes home and yawns, he swallows a fly. Then he remembers that spiders eat flies, so he swallows a spider. The spider tickles him, so he swallows a bird, a cat, a dog, and a dog catcher. Then he threatens them that if they don't get out, he will swallow a grizzly bear. They're so scared, they all run out. And Golly learns to yawn with his mouth covered. The new version of the old lady who swallowed a fly will be welcomed by young children.

Dauer, Rosamond. **The 300 Pound Cat.** Illustrated by Skip Morrow. Holt, Rinehart and Winston, 1981.

As William Cat grows, he takes a fancy to unusual foods—turnips, typewriters, and boots. His worried parents take him to Dr. Cat, who recommends a diet to take off the excess baggage. William's alternative suggestions turn this funny story into a hilarious, if not improbable, tale.

Kent, Jack. **Fat Cat.** Parents, 1971.

In this Danish folktale, a cat eats a woman's gruel—and the pot, too, then goes on to eat the woman, Skihottentot, Skolinkenlot, birds, little girls, and a parson before a woodcutter opens him up. The repeated line, "And I'm going to also eat YOU!", will be happily chanted by children. This book could also be used with the "I'll Eat You Up" stories in this book (p. 138), but the fat cat is definitely a glutton, too!

Marshall, James. **Yummers.** Houghton Mifflin, 1973.

Emily Pig, upset that she is gaining weight, goes walking for exercise with her friend, Eugene Turtle. Along the way they stop for snacks—sandwiches from a vending machine, corn on the cob from a food stand, scones from Granner's tea room, Eskimo pies from an ice cream vendor, cookies from a Girl Scout, plus a malt, banana split and peach ice cream from the drug store. They sample free pizza at the supermarket and go to the park when Emily discovers she has a stomach ache and can't finish her pop and candy apple. Eugene suggests she recuperate in bed with plenty of good food, to which Emily replies, "Yummers!"

Nolan, Dennis. **Big Pig.** Prentice-Hall, 1976.

Simple text introduces large animals notorious for their large appetites.

Westcott, Nadine Bernard. **I Know an Old Lady Who Swallowed a Fly.** Little, Brown, 1980.

The popular cumulative rhyme of an old lady who swallows a fly, a spider, a bird, a cat, a dog, a goat, a cow, and a horse has been matched with humorously spirited illustrations. Music with guitar chords is included.

Related Activities about Not-So-Fussy Eaters

The Amazing Table
(A Shadow-Puppet Play)

Tell this story as a shadow-puppet play simply by making tagboard cutouts of the characters and props. Place these on an overhead projector to project your shadows on the screen or wall.

Once there was a poor but honest woodcutter, Hans, and his wife, Hannah, who by hard work managed to get just enough food to eat.

One day Hans was in the forest. He was just ready to chop down a tree when he heard a small cry.

"Save my tree!"

Looking about, he saw nothing. Once again he raised his ax. The voice said again, "Save my tree!"

Hans looked around again, but seeing nothing, raised his ax for the third time.

This time the voice said, "I am the spirit of the wood. Spare my tree and you shall lack nothing to eat!"

Hans wondered at this, but he did as he was told and returned home empty-handed. In his tiny cottage, there was Hannah with wonderful news.

"Husband," she said. "Come see the amazing table!"

There, in the middle of the room, sat a heavy table laden with all the foods they might ever dream of.

"But, how did this come about?" asked Hans.

"I know not," she replied, "but let us eat our fill. And there's more than enough for us, so let us invite our friends to dine with us."

The days passed and, as if by magic, the amazing table seemed to know the couple's needs before they even asked. In gratitude, Hans and Hannah took fine care of the table—brushing crumbs away and keeping it well polished. Friends and strangers alike were always welcome to share the food from the amazing table.

Now, Hans had a brother, Boris, who was as greedy and lazy as Hans was kind and generous. When Boris heard of the amazing table, he made plans to steal it and use it for himself alone. So he had a table made that looked exactly like the amazing table, and while Hans and Hannah were taking some of the food to their neighbors, Boris switched the tables and carried the magic one off for himself.

Boris placed the table in his own house, pounded his fist on it, and demanded, ''Feed me!''

Food appeared on the table, but Boris was not satisfied.

''Feed me!'' he shouted louder.

More food appeared, but still Boris kicked the table and yelled, ''Feed me!''

More and more food appeared until it spilled on the floor, and the table began to groan from the weight of the feast. With one last wallop, Boris shouted, ''More!'' and the table collapsed and sank through the floor. It sank into the earth—taking Boris with it. They were never seen or heard of again.

Hans and Hannah continued to work hard for the rest of their days, but even though they no longer possessed the amazing table, the wood spirit made certain they were never hungry.

The Old Lady Who Swallowed a Fly Told Two Ways

Even if you read a picture-book version of this story, make it graphically ''come alive'' one of these ways.

The Old Lady from a Bag

Turn a grocery bag into the body of the old lady. Glue on a separate head, arms, and long, skinny legs. Cut a large hole in the middle of the bag for her stomach and cover with clear acetate. Now, cut out the various creatures—the fly, spider, cat, dog, bird, goat, cow, and horse—from tagboard. ''Feed'' these characters into the neck slit in the top of the bag as you sing the song.

. . .

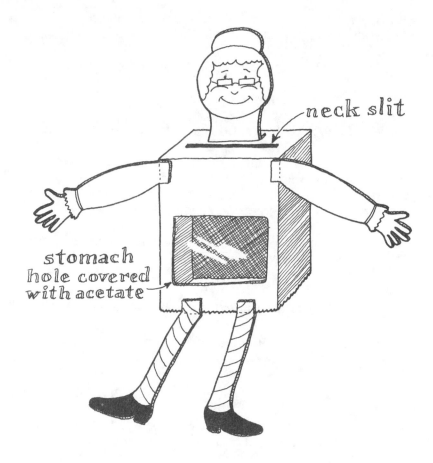

The Old Lady and the Fly:
A Jarring Experience

This version of the song may be more comforting to very young children who are concerned about the old lady dying in the end of the traditional version.

In preparation, make a large funny face without a mouth on paper or cardboard. Cut the face in half where the mouth would be. The cut should be a straight line. Put the top half of the drawing on the lid of a large jar and the bottom half on the jar. Cut out cardboard figures of a fly, spider, bird, cat, dog, cow, and horse.

top half
of face
on jar lid

bottom half
of face
on jar

As you sing the following song, lift off the lid and drop the animals in the jar as they are eaten. All the children can say "GULP" as the food is dropped in.

I know an old lady who swallowed a fly.
I don't know why she swallowed that fly—
I don't know why!

I know an old lady who swallowed a spider
That wiggled and jiggled and tickled inside her.
She swallowed the spider to catch the fly.
I don't know why she swallowed that fly—
I don't know why!

I know an old lady who swallowed a bird.
How absurd to swallow a bird.
Well, she swallowed the bird to catch the spider
That wiggled and jiggled and tickled inside her.
She swallowed the spider to catch the fly.
I don't know why she swallowed that fly—
I don't know why!

I know an old lady who swallowed a cat.
Fancy that, to swallow a cat!
She swallowed the cat to catch the bird.
She swallowed the bird to catch the spider
That wiggled and jiggled and tickled inside her.
She swallowed the spider to catch the fly.
I don't know why she swallowed that fly—
I don't know why!

I know an old lady who swallowed a dog.
What a hog to swallow a dog!
She swallowed the dog to catch the cat.
She swallowed the cat to catch the bird.

She swallowed the bird to catch the spider
That wiggled and jiggled and tickled inside her.
She swallowed the spider to catch the fly.
I don't know why she swallowed that fly—
I don't know why!

I know an old lady who swallowed a goat.
She opened her throat and swallowed a goat.
She swallowed the goat to catch the dog.
She swallowed the dog to catch the cat.
She swallowed the cat to catch the bird.
She swallowed the bird to catch the spider
That wiggled and jiggled and tickled inside her.
She swallowed the spider to catch the fly.
I don't know why she swallowed that fly—
I don't know why!

I know an old lady who swallowed a cow.
I don't know how she swallowed that cow, BUT (sing faster now)
She swallowed the cow to catch the goat.
She swallowed the goat to catch the dog.
She swallowed the dog to catch the cat.
She swallowed the cat to catch the bird.
She swallowed the bird to catch the spider
That wiggled and jiggled and tickled inside her.
She swallowed the spider to catch the fly.
I don't know why she swallowed the fly—
I don't know why!

I know an old lady who swallowed a horse—
Well—that's the end—of course!

Glutton Feast Song

(To the tune of "Farmer in the Dell")

When the glutton has a feast,
He eats just like a beast.
Gulp! Gulp! And it's all gone—
The glutton has a feast.

First he eats a batch of stew.
He doesn't even chew.
Gulp! Gulp! And it's all gone—
The glutton has a feast.

Then he eats up the spoon.
He looks around the room.
Gulp! Gulp! And it's all gone—
The glutton has a feast.

Then he eats the whole pot,
Even if it's hot.
Gulp! Gulp! And it's all gone—
The glutton has a feast.

Then he eats the table,
As fast as he is able.
Gulp! Gulp! And it's all gone—
The glutton has a feast.

Then he eats the floor,
And gnaws up to the door.
Gulp! Gulp! And it's all gone—
The glutton has a feast.

When the glutton has a feast,
He eats just like a beast.
Gulp! Gulp! And it's all gone—
The glutton has a feast!

Indigestion

Gluttons usually end up with a stomach ache and indigestion. Children will know the word indigestion from television commercials, and will enjoy this original song. Piano notes are included so you can play the song for the children.

   C   A G   A
Don't drink that pop—

   C   G   F   G
Don't eat that cake—

  C F   E   F
Unless you want

C E E^b E
A tummy ache.

C A G   A
If you pig out

C   G F G
On jelly beans

  C   F   E   F
Your face may turn

C E E^b E
A sickey green.

   C A   G   A
And you will know

C   G F G
Just what I mean

   C F   E   D
When people say—

  C F   A G F C   G F E C
I've got indigestion, indigestion,

   DD   E E   F F   G G
Flippy floppy oopsy doopsy

    A G F D
    indigestion,

D E F G A G F F
O O O O indigestion!

   C   A G A
Now go to bed

   C G F   G
And snuggle up.

   C F E   F
Sip chicken soup,

   C   E E^{b}E
Drink 7-Up.

  C   A G A
Tomorrow is

C G F   G
Another day.

C   F   E   F
By then you'll feel

D E F
A-O.K.!

The Groaning-Board Groan

In days of old, people feasted for days to celebrate special events. The heavily laden table was called a "groaning board" because the table wood almost groaned with the weight of so much food. (The people probably groaned too!)

Here's a groaning-board groan to do with children, and when you've acted out the groan, turn to the crafts section and make a groaning-board mural (p. 202).

On my table sits a big fat goose,	(Stretch out hands.)
A blackbird pie and a roasted moose.	(Lower hands as each "food" is named.)
A barrel of apples,	
And a pot of stew.	
Gulp it down,	
No time to chew!	
Ummmm Ahhh,	(Hold tummy and sway back and forth.)
Ummmm Ahhh,	
What a feast!	
Grunt! Groan! Grunt! Groan!	(Swing arms at sides.)
Let's be beasts!	(Jump up and down.)

GAMES AND FROLICS FOR FUSSY AND NOT-SO-FUSSY EATERS

Chicken Feed

On a drop cloth, sprinkle handfuls of corn kernels. Each child is given a bag which she or he has decorated with a picture of a chicken. At the signal, "Pick, Pick, Pick," each feeds the chicken bag by picking up corn with just two fingers. This feeding goes on a while; then, the leader says, "Eat, Eat, Eat!" The children may then scoop up corn with one hand to feed the chicken bag. Play can continue, alternating the "Pick, Pick, Pick" and "Eat, Eat, Eat" commands, until all the corn is picked up. The kernels are then put into a popcorn popper. Even "picky" eaters will be "not-so-fussy" with a bowl of popcorn!

Crumb Catcher

Select four children to form two arches by joining and raising hands. Sing the following song to the tune of "London Bridge."

> Crumbs are falling all around,
> All around, all around.
> Crumbs are falling all around—
> Ooops! We caught one!

On "oops" drop hands, and the two children caught then form another arch to catch more crumbs. On some rounds there will be an uneven number of children so an arch will not be formed. The extra child stands aside until another crumb is caught. Continue until all the "crumbs" are caught and the floor is clean!

Monster Messy Face

Use this variation of Pin the Tail on the Donkey by drawing a large monster face on a posterboard. Give your monster a large mouth opening. Each child receives a different kind of food cutout with a piece of masking tape on the back to feed the monster. Blindfold each child, spin him or her around, and watch where the food ends up—in the ear, the hair, on the chin. There is no real winner here. The object of the game is to see how messy you can make your monster's messy face!

Ogre Roar

Ogres, as everyone knows, love to eat—especially children. Keep this game lighthearted, and even shy children won't mind being eaten up!

Children form a circle, and the ogre leader stalks around the outside of the circle. Here is the chant for the ogre:

>Fee, Fie, Foo, Fum,
>I'm an ogre,
>Here I come!
>
>I am such
>A hungry beast,
>I'm ready for
>A giant feast!
>
>One, two—
>I pick you!

The ogre "snatches" someone and puts her or him in the middle of the circle—the stew pot.

Play continues with the chant. This time, the "count down" goes:

>One, two, three—
>I've got your knee!

The ogre snatches another child each time, and the play continues with the next count:

>One, two, three, four—
>I want more!

For the last count, you can say:

>One, two, three, four, five—
>Is anybody left alive?

When the rest of the children yell out (and they will!), the ogre chants:

>Fee, Fie, Foo, Fum.
>Dinner's ready,
>You all come!

Ogre then motions everyone to come sit together in the stew-pot circle.

Pachyderm Peanut Pitch

Decorate an ice cream tub with a picture of an elephant and label it, "I'm Patty Pachyderm. Pitch me a Peanut!" Children stand behind a line about two feet away from the tub and toss peanuts into the tub, one at a time. After Patty has been fed, she can share her peanuts with the children.

CRAFT EXPERIENCES FOR FUSSY AND NOT-SO-FUSSY EATERS

Groaning Board Mural

Draw BIG pictures of food (such as a turkey, fish, pies) on a long sheet of white paper. The bigger the pictures and the more fantastic the better! After everyone has finished, hold up the mural in front of children so they will look like they are gluttons at a fantastic banquet or a groaning board. Now, everyone groans like the groaning board and repeats the groaning board groan on p. 200.

Junk Food Rubby in the Tummy

Draw a fat goat on lightweight paper and place objects like coins, leaves, paper clips, and rubber bands under the paper where the goat's stomach is. Provide children with crayons to rub over the shapes so the objects will magically appear in the goat's stomach.

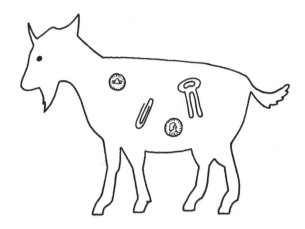

Junk Food Rubby

Why Pigs Are Pink

Pigs are usually portrayed as big eaters, but the piglets in *Mrs. Pig's Bulk Buy* (p. 189) are fussy eaters. In this hilarious story, the piglets eat so much ketchup that they turn bright pink. Have the children do the following activity after hearing the story.

Make pink pigs with your preschoolers by giving them a simple outline of a pig face drawn with black crayon on white paper.

Now give children paint brushes and jars of plain water.

Ask children to "paint" their pigs with water (to wash the face of the pig).

Go around with a paint brush full of red paint and tell the children that you are feeding their pigs plenty of ketchup.

Let the children spread the paint around with their brushes so the whole pig face turns bright pink. It's important to follow the directions in this order. If you apply the paint first and then add the water, the paint will stay in little dots, and the pigs will look like they have measles!

Why Pigs are Pink

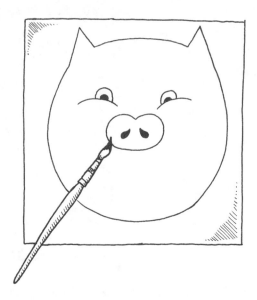

This Litter Piggy Went Home

Make a pig's face on the bottom of a grocery sack: small pink ears, a pink nose, and black eyes. Cut out a circle (about 6 inches in diameter) for the mouth. Children take home this "litter piggy" to place over a wastebasket. They won't have to be reminded to "put it in the wastebasket" if you say "Feed This Litter Piggy"!

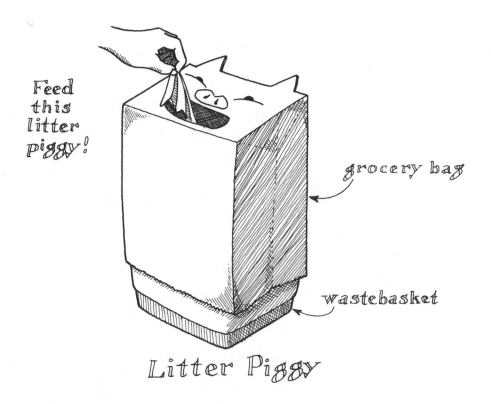

Feed this litter piggy!

grocery bag

wastebasket

Litter Piggy

COOKING AND TASTING EXPERIENCES FOR FUSSY EATERS

Pig Party
(Guaranteed to turn Picky Eaters into Pigs)

Most children will eat food if it is presented in an appealing way. Overly large portions discourage young children. Serve the following suggested treats in small portions. They are simple, and nutritious, too.

Bigfoot Sandwich

Young children love monster stories and will delight in putting this foot in their mouths! Either use foot-shaped cookie cutters or make your own cardboard pattern of a foot. Cut out foot-shaped pieces of bread. Spread feet with peanut butter or a spread of shredded cheese, pimento, and mayonnaise. Eat open-faced (or open-foot)!

Peanut Butter Letters

A sure-fire way to get children to eat is to make alphabet letters out of food. Use the edible play-dough recipe found on p. 68 in the "Sweet Tooth" chapter and make the dough into letter shapes. Ask children to make the first letter in their name.

Mouse Bites

Children love cheese as much as mice do. Serve tiny cubes of different cheeses and call them "mouse bites." If you ask children to each bring a small portion of different cheese, you will be able to serve a nice variety for tasting. Some favorites—cheddar and Swiss—might be included, along with Danish havarti and Gouda to give children new taste experiences. This is an especially effective experience if you read "Cheese, Peas, and Chocolate Pudding" (p. 189).

Pig Tails

Using a vegetable parer, cut carrots in thin strips, roll up and secure with toothpicks. Soak in ice water until the carrot strips curl like pig tails.

Picky Paul Pizza

Spread English muffin halves with tomato sauce, or prepared spaghetti or pizza sauce. Top with a slice of mozzarella cheese and chopped green pepper. Toast in toaster oven until bubbly. Serve each child one-fourth of the pizza. They will beg for more!

Be sure to tell the flannel-board story about Picky Paul (p. 189-90) when you serve this special treat.

12.
STUFFING MOTHER HUBBARD'S CUPBOARD

INTRODUCTION

Pantries, cellars, and cupboards (not to mention pie safes!), so familiar to our grandparents and great-grandparents, may seem like museum relics to young children accustomed to stainless steel kitchens filled with electric appliances. For today's busy family, "stocking the larder" probably means a weekly trip to the supermarket. Children today generally miss out on the drama of food gathering, marketing, and cooking known to past generations. Still, we can recapture some of the fun of country markets and food preparation so young children will begin to understand where food comes from — besides the shelves of a supermarket.

In addition to the supermarket activities included in this chapter are other experiences to introduce children to gardening, foraging for food, shopping at a country market, and helping in the kitchen. Young children can also help with meal preparation and kitchen activities if they are given instruction in simple tasks such as setting the table and arranging food on shelves. Taking turns stirring batter, kneading bread dough, and measuring ingredients for a recipe are all valuable lessons boys and girls will use throughout life. Use the "Kitchen Work Song" (p. 218-19) and games in this chapter, and everyone will discover that food preparation is no longer drudgery.

INITIATING ACTIVITIES

Old Mother Hubbard:
Three Ways to Stuff the Cupboard

The Traditional Tale

Recite the familiar Mother-Goose version of this popular rhyme with a dog puppet on your hand and an old-fashioned bonnet on your head. Or read Tomie de Paola's picture-book version for a light-hearted look at the traditional story.

De Paola, Tomie. **The Comic Adventures of Old Mother Hubbard and Her Dog.** Harcourt Brace Jovanovich, 1981.

In bright color with funny touches, Mother Hubbard and her dog search for food and clothing in the classic rhyme.

How Old Mother Hubbard's Dog Finally Got Dinner
(A Circle Story)

To make this "story wheel," cut two posterboard circles of the same size. On one circle (the bottom part of the wheel), paste pictures of the following: a bird, a worm, a frog, a fly, a pig, an ear of corn, a child, a pizza, a big dog, and a bone. On the other circle (the top part of the wheel), paste a picture of Mother Hubbard and her dog. Then cut a wedge from the top circle—about the size of a single picture on the bottom circle. Fasten the circles together in the center with a brad fastener. As you tell the story, turn the bottom wheel so that the appropriate picture shows in the wedge opening.

You all know that when Old Mother Hubbard went to the cupboard, there was nothing there for the poor dog. Of course Old Mother Hubbard went right out to the store to find something for the dog to eat. But on the way, she forgot what he wanted. Luckily she found some friends to give her advice.

The first friend she saw was a bird (turn wheel so bird shows).

"Oh, little bird," cried Old Mother Hubbard, "what shall I get for my little dog to eat?"

"That's easy," said little bird. "Little dogs like worms just like little birds do." (Turn wheel to show worm.)

"No," said Mother Hubbard, "I don't think he would like a worm."

The next friend Mother Hubbard asked was the frog. (Turn wheel so frog shows.)

"Little frog, what should I get my little dog to eat?" asked Mother Hubbard.

"That's easy," said little frog. "Little dogs like to eat flies just like little frogs do." (Show fly.)

"No, I do not think he would like a fly," said Mother Hubbard.

Then Mother Hubbard met a pig. (Show pig.)

"Oh, little pig, what shall I get for my little dog to eat?"

"That's easy," said little pig. "Little dogs like corn just like little pigs do." (Show corn.)

Old Mother Hubbard Circle Story

Top Circle with cut out wedge reveals picture on bottom circle

brad fastener

Bottom circle with pictures

"No," said Mother Hubbard, "I don't think he would like corn."

Next Mother Hubbard met a child. (Show child.)

"Oh, little child, what should I get my little dog to eat?"

"That's easy," said the little child. "Little dogs like pizza just like children do." (Show pizza.)

"No, I do not think he would like pizza," said Mother Hubbard.

Finally Mother Hubbard saw Mother Dog. (Show big dog.)

"Oh, Mother Dog, you must be the one to tell me. What should I get my little dog to eat?"

"That's easy," said Mother Dog. "Little dogs like to eat bones just like Mother Dogs do." (Show bone.)

And then Mother Hubbard remembered what she was supposed to buy at the store. So Old Mother Hubbard went to the store, got her dog a bone, took the bone home, and gave it to her little dog—who ate it all up.

For more fun at the end of the story, ask children to remember what animals Mother Hubbard met along the way and what foods they liked to eat. This is a good way to help children recall events of a story in order.

Old Mother Hubbard Retold
(A Finger Puppet Activity with Cupboard Puppet Stage)

Prepare a cupboard puppet stage from a piece of cardboard with side "wings" to stand up on a table top. Make three doors in the cupboard. Behind the first door, place a cardboard section with a wedge of cheese drawn on it and a big hole cut in the center. Use a mouse finger puppet to come out of this hole at the appropriate time. Behind the second door, place a cardboard section with an apple drawn on it and a hole cut for the worm finger puppet to come out of. Behind the third door, place a cardboard section with a front view of a frog with a big hole cut out for his mouth. Have raisins on hand to feed the frog at the appropriate time in the story. Now, you're ready for the fun!

Puppet Stage for
Old Mother Hubbard Retold

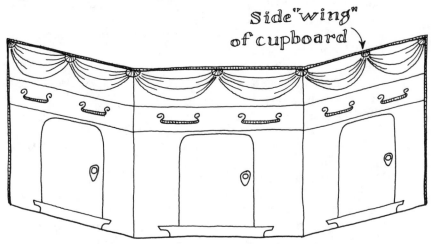

Side "wing" of cupboard

Simple Cardboard Stage
with doors closed

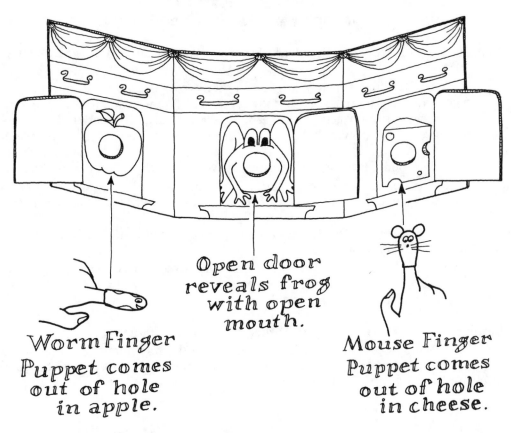

Open door reveals frog with open mouth.

Worm Finger Puppet comes out of hole in apple.

Mouse Finger Puppet comes out of hole in cheese.

Old Mother Hubbard
Went to the cupboard
To get a chunk of cheese.   (Open door one.)
But when she went there
She found a mouse   (Stick mouse puppet through hole.)
In a cottage-cheesy-house!

Old Mother Hubbard
Went to the cupboard
To get a delicious apple.   (Open door two.)
But when she went there
She found a worm   (Stick worm through hole.)
And did that apple squirm!

Old Mother Hubbard
Went to the cupboard
To get herself a pickle.   (Don't open door yet!)
But when she went there
She found a frog.   (Now, open door!)
Do you think he'd like some flies? (Feed raisin "flies" to frog; let
             children help, too.)

LITERATURE-SHARING EXPERIENCES

Books about Shopping and Selling Food

Allard, Harry. **I Will Not Go to Market Today.** Illustrated by James Marshall. Dial Press, 1971.

Fenimore B. Buttercrunch wakes up to find there is no jam for his morning toast. He decides to go to the market, but a blizzard is raging. A different excuse follows the next day—and the next. When he finally gets on the road, he is caught in a different kind of jam—a traffic jam, of course! More mishaps befall him before Fenimore makes it to the market to get his jam.

Asch, Frank. **Good Lemonade.** Illustrated by Marie Zimmerman. Watts, 1976.

Hank tries better advertising, fancy cups, prizes, and costumes to make his lemonade business a success. Finally a good friend suggests the answer—better lemonade. It works!

Black, Irma Simonton. **The Little Old Man Who Could Not Read.** Illustrated by Seymour Fleishman. Whitman, 1968.

When his wife goes on a visit, the old man has to do his own shopping at the supermarket. Since the man can't read, he ends up buying all the wrong things and gets very hungry before his wife returns to save the day.

Burningham, John. **The Shopping Basket.** Crowell, 1980.

Steven's mother sends him to the store, but on the way home he is threatened by a bear, a monkey, a kangaroo, a goat, a pig, and an elephant who try to take his food. His mother wonders why it takes him so long.

Gretz, Susanna. **Teddy Bears Go Shopping.** Four Winds, 1982.

The teddy bears discover they're out of essentials and have to go shopping. Their list becomes a rollicking song. The fun begins when the list gets lost. When they get home, the bears discover that they have forgotten things. Finally, one of the bears comes home with just the right thing for everyone—three kinds of ice cream.

Lobel, Arnold. **On Market Street.** Illustrated by Anita Lobel. Greenwillow, 1981.

A child wanders down Market Street buying wares from A to Z. Some of the delicious foods include apples, doughnuts, eggs, ice cream, lollipops, noodles, oranges, and vegetables.

Related Activities about Shopping

Shopping List for Porcupines and Other Peculiar Animals

Ask children to act out the animals with their unusual foods as you read this silly list:

Shopping for a porcupine?
Stick to something stick-ly,
Like pineapples or pears or things
That come with extra pricklies.

Get jelly beans for jellyfish,
Munch chips for chipmunks,
But only chocolate striped ice cream
Will suit your favorite skunk!

Armadillos eat artichokes,
Snakes slurp up spaghetti,
A snail will slip and slide around
In jars of rhubarb jelly.

Pick pocket bread for kangaroos,
Noodles for your newt,
Cocoa beans for koala bears
And one dozen kiwi fruit.

Now if you're running short on cash,
Be sure to save a nickel
To buy your frog his favorite brand
Of kosher dilly pickles.

I'm Going to the Market, Super-Dooper-Doo

For this action rhyme, wheel in a shopping cart and pantomime filling it with all the things described in the verse.

I'm going to the market,
    super-dooper-doo
I'm going to take my friends along,
You and you and you!

We'll take a cart and push it
Up and down the rows.
Whee! What super fun this is!
Ooops—better go slow.

Turn around the corner,
There are the cans
Of peas and beets and vegetables,
Will you give a hand?

Here is the cereal,
So many kinds.
Wheat and rice and corny stuff,
What shall we buy?

Where's the macaroni?
Next to the shelf
Of spaghetti and noodles.
Just help yourself!

Here's another counter
Where they keep the meat.
Chicken, bacon, sausage,
Wrapped up so neat.

Here's the cooler for the milk.
Can you find the cheese?
Can you reach the eggs?
Oooo, be careful if you please!

We're almost done, our cart is full.
It's time to get in line
So they can check us out,
And we'll get home in time.

Oh, we're going home together
To fix a great big lunch.
Shopping makes me hungry,
I'm glad we got so much!

After this rhyme, talk about how things are arranged in a supermarket—the canned goods, fruits, vegetables, the dairy case, etc. How does the arrangement help us find what we are looking for? Do you ever have trouble finding what you want?

A Country Market
(A Participatory Chant)

Grocery stores are a modern way to shop. The Country Market of days-gone-by offered a lot more than food. The street cries and songs of the food sellers made the marketing experience a lively interchange between the seller and buyer. In this chant, the leader begins the food cry and invites the children to repeat the last part of the line.

Leader:	Who will buy my eggs so white?
Response:	Eggs so white.
Leader:	Buy a dozen
	For your wife.
Response:	For your wife.
Leader:	Who will buy a purple plum?
Response:	A purple plum.
Leader:	Don't be shy
	Come sample one!
Response:	Come sample one!
Leader:	Who will buy a yellow peach?
Response:	A yellow peach.
Leader:	Selling now,
	Selling cheap!
Response:	Selling cheap!
Leader:	Who will buy this blueberry?
Response:	This blueberry.
Leader:	Take a bite,
	If you please.
Response;	If you please.
Leader:	Who will buy my apple core?
Response:	My apple core.
Leader:	I will even
	Sell you more!
Response:	Sell you more!
Leader:	Who will buy a pumpkin, fat?
Response:	A pumpkin, fat.

Leader:	I will even sell my cat.
Leader:	And that's SOME CAT!
	(Would you like to pet her?)

If you want to try a visual approach, make this chant into a country-market puppet presentation. Place a chunk of styrofoam in an old-fashioned market basket or a wooden peck basket. Make stick puppets of all the foods mentioned in the song by either cutting out pictures of food or drawing big colorful ones (note that a color is mentioned directly in most of the descriptions and implied in the rest) and attaching these pictures to tongue depressors. Poke each stick puppet into the foam as you do the chant. At the end of the verse, pull out a stuffed cat or a cat puppet, and stroke it dramatically.

Street Cries for Modern Children

Now that you've introduced a fairly traditional food market setting, try these appealing food cries that children might use if they were to sell food to one another today.

Lemonade, lemonade,
Made in the shade
With a dirty spade.

Ice cream bars,
Ice cream bars
From the Milky Way,
Made with stars!

Cool mud pie, cool mud pie,
Baked in the sun,
Solar dried.

Books about Finding and Growing Food

Barrett, Judith. **Old MacDonald Had an Apartment House.** Illustrated by Ron Barrett. Atheneum, 1969.
Old MacDonald and his wife and dog live in an apartment house owned by Mr. Wrental. The hedge outside makes their tomato plant droop, so Old MacDonald cuts it down. Encouraged by the plant's growth, he begins a garden in the apartment building and redecorates in "Late Vegetarian." The garden farm grows to such an extent that all the neighbors in the apartment house move out. Just when Mr. Wrental is about to evict the MacDonalds, he realizes the farm might be profitable, so they go into business.

Krasilovsky, Phyllis. **The Man Who Cooked for Himself.** Illustrated by Mamoru Funai. Parents, 1981.
A man who lives with his cat at the edge of a wood cooks for himself. When he eats up the supply of food he has bought, he begins to discover good food around him—fish in a stream, watercress along the bank, blackberries, apples, and acorns. The next year he plants a garden, too. After that he is never hungry again.

Lapp, Eleanor. **The Blueberry Bears.** Illustrated by Margot Apple. Albert Whitman, 1983.
Bessie Allen picks all the blueberries in the woods around her cabin. She freezes some, but also stuffs her kitchen and cupboards. Hungry bears follow the blueberry smell into the cabin and help themselves. Bessie decides that next time she'll leave some for the bears.

McCloskey, Robert. **Blueberries for Sal.** Viking, 1948.

Little Sal and her mother pick blueberries on Blueberry Hill to can for the winter just as Mother Bear and Little Bear set out on a parallel path. The mothers and children get all mixed up, but eventually find their ways home with plenty of blueberries. This Caldecott Honor book, a modern classic, has never lost its original appeal.

Moore, Inga. **The Vegetable Thieves.** Viking, 1983.

Des and Letty Mouse have an enormous garden they take great pains with. One night, thieves begin stealing from the garden. Des and Letty pursue the thieves only to discover they are orphans. They put the children to work, and in the end, they all become a big happy family.

Poulet, Virginia. **Blue Bug's Vegetable Garden.** Children's, 1973.

In this concept-book of *over, under, up,* and *down,* Blue Bug moves around big pictures of vegetables and ends with an interesting look at "underground" and "sunshine vegetables."

Rockwell, Anne, and Harlow Rockwell. **How My Garden Grew.** Macmillan, 1982.

Very simple text and clear pictures show a child planting, caring for, and harvesting a garden.

Related Activities about Finding and Growing Food

The Blueberry-Picking Song
(To the tune of "The Bear Went Over the Mountain")

After you've read the two blueberry books listed in this section (p.215-16), you can sing this blueberry song without the intervention of bears!

We're going to pick blueberries,	(March in place.)
We're going to pick blueberries,	
We're going to pick blueberries,	
Over on Blueberry Hill.	(Roll hands over and over.)
I'm going to take my bucket,	(Swing imaginary bucket.)
I'm going to take my bucket,	
I'm going to take my bucket,	
Over Blueberry Hill.	(Roll hands over and over.)
	(Stop and all mime picking blueberries.)
Now, I've got a bucketful.	(Swing bucket.)
Now, I've got a handful.	(Mime scooping.)
Now, I've got a mouthful.	(Mime eating.)
All on Blueberry Hill.	(Roll hands over and over.)
Let's go home and can some,	(March in place.)
Let's go home and freeze some,	
Let's make pie and jam some,	(Roll as if rolling piecrust.)
All from Blueberry Hill.	(Rolling hands over and over.)

We're Growing a Little Garden
(To the tune of "When Johnny Comes Marching Home Again")

Do this song-and-action play in a circle.

We're growing a little garden here,	(Extend arms, palms up.)
Dig in.	
Dig in.	
We're growing a little garden here,	
Dig in.	
Dig in.	
Oh, we'll dig the ground	(Make digging action.)
And then we'll hoe,	(Wipe brow.)
We'll plant the seeds	
In rows and rows.	(Wiggle fingers to plant seeds.)
Then we'll all clap hands	
To make our garden grow.	(Clap.)
We're growing a little garden here,	(Extend arms, palms up.)
Dig in.	(Dig with shovel.)
Dig in.	
We're growing a little garden here,	
Dig in.	
Dig in.	
Oh the corn will grow ears	(Point to ears.)
And the cabbage, heads,	(Point to head.)
Sweet potatoes root	
In their beds.	(Sleep on hands.)
And we'll all clap hands	
To make our garden grow.	(Clap.)
We're growing a little garden here,	(Extend arms, palms up.)
Dig in.	(Dig with shovel.)
Dig in.	
We're growing a little garden here,	
Dig in.	
Dig in.	
The beans will grow up	(Point up.)
And the turnips down,	(Point down.)
We'll eat our harvest	(Rub tummy.)
All year round	
And we'll clap our hands	(Clap.)
The day our garden grows.	

Where Does It Grow?
(A Fingerplay)

Corn grows tall,	(Reach high.)
Pumpkins crawl.	(Wave hands.)
Potatoes grow under the ground.	(Touch ground.)
Look high and you'll see	(Look up.)
Apples on a tree.	(Put arms up, hands open.)
Shake it—they all fall down.	(Shake hands, sit down.)

Books about Kitchen Help

Burningham, John. **The Cupboard.** Crowell, 1975.
> In this simple text, a young child plays with pots and pans in the cupboard despite his mother's frustrations.

Rockwell, Harlow. **My Kitchen.** Greenwillow, 1980.
> Through large pictures and simple text, we see the location of various foods and cooking utensils. The table is set, soup and sandwich prepared, and lunch is served.

Related Activities about the Kitchen and Helping

The Kitchen Band Song
(An Action Song to the tune of "Mary Had a Little Lamb")

Assemble 3 whisks, 3 small metal bowls, 14 wooden or plastic spoons, 7 oatmeal or macaroni boxes with rocks inside and ends taped shut, 3 pots. This will be enough equiment for 15-20 children.

(First verse, no props):
Let's all make a kitchen band,
Kitchen band,
Kitchen band.
Let's all make a kitchen band,
And we'll have lots of fun.

(Second verse, hand out whisks
and bowls):
We can play the whisk and bowl,
Whisk and bowl,
Whisk and bowl.
We can play the whisk and bowl,
And we'll have lots of fun.

(Third verse, hand out two spoons
to each of 7 children):
This is how we click our spoons,
Click our spoons,
Click our spoons.
This is how we click our spoons,
And we'll have lots of fun.

(Fourth verse, hand out boxes):
Hear our boxes shake, shake, shake,
Shake, shake, shake,
Shake, shake, shake.
Hear our boxes shake, shake, shake,
And we'll have lots of fun.

(Fifth verse, hand out pots to drum
with hands):
We can bang on lots of pots,
Lots of pots,
Lots of pots.
We can bang on lots of pots,
And we'll have lots of fun.

(Now repeat the first verse with ALL
the instruments playing!):
Let's all make a kitchen band,
Kitchen band,
Kitchen band.
Let's all make a kitchen band,
And we'll have lots of fun.

Kitchen Work Song
(To the tune of "Paw Paw Patch")
Act out all suggested actions as you hear them in the song.

Who can help us in the kitchen?
Who can help us in the kitchen?
Who can help us in the kitchen?
Let's work together, and we'll all
have fun!

I can beat a bowl of batter,
I can beat a bowl of batter,
I can beat a bowl of batter,
Let's work together, and we'll all
have fun!

I can learn to set the table,	I can wash and dry the dishes,
I can learn to set the table,	I can wash and dry the dishes,
I can learn to set the table,	I can wash and dry the dishes,
Let's work together, and we'll all	Let's work together, and we'll all
have fun!	have fun!

GAMES AND FROLICS FOR MOTHER HUBBARD'S CUPBOARD

Shopping Lists All Around

Have children sitting in a circle. Begin by saying, "We're going to make a shopping list together. I'm going to the store, and I will buy one apple." The next person adds two of something: "I am going to the store, and I will buy two eggs." Then see if everyone can repeat what the first person and the second person said: "One apple and two eggs." Continue around the circle. This new version of a traditional game works well in helping children remember what other people say. It's a good quiet game that also teaches listening skills.

A variation in the shopping-list game is to ask each child to put something on a shopping list that begins with the first letter of his or her name. Amy could buy apples, Beth could buy bananas, Charlie could buy cucumbers, David could buy dill pickles, and so on.

Children might like to make a list of things they like and things they don't like. Another list might be foods that are round, long, square, or foods that are red, yellow, white, blue, green, and so on.

If you wish, write down your list on a long piece of shelf paper and make a yard-long shopping list to put on the wall or bulletin board for a display.

Supermarket in the Library or Classroom

What child doesn't love to play store? Turn your room into a supermarket with big signs hung from the ceiling to designate different departments such as "Fruits," "Vegetables," "Breads," "Milk, Eggs, and Cheese," "Noodles and Rice," and so on. Cut out pictures of food. Label the food so children will begin to associate the name of the food with the picture.

Now haul in your "delivery truck" (a red wagon will do nicely).

Ask some children to be the store clerks, and give them paper hats. These children will arrange the foods in the appropriate departments.

Ask other children to be the shoppers and give them shopping baskets. Round up baskets with handles or use small boxes with yarn handles.

After the clerks have arranged the foods, invite the shoppers to find the following items:

Something round, something square, something triangular.

Something from each department.

Something red, something green, something yellow, etc.

Something that begins with A, B, C, etc.

You could be the check-out person and ask shoppers to line up and bag their "purchases."

Use the game as an opportunity to talk about how food is arranged in a store. Make the food cards on two sides of tagboard with the picture on one side and the name of the food on the other. These can be used as flash cards that children will be able to use on their own to practice "reading."

After the Shopping's Done

For a child, one of the best things about shopping is taking the food home and putting everything away on the shelves. Not all mothers and fathers find this fun, but it can be a marvelous teaching moment. Take advantage of the possibilities.

Bring an assortment of cans, food boxes, and containers. Give each child a pile of things to build towers, streets, whatever seems like fun. Then ask children to "arrange" shelves—a book cart or two will serve as the shelves. Put cans of soup in one place, cereal in another, and so on. This is an excellent opportunity to let children follow instructions and become good organizers.

CRAFT EXPERIENCES AND SOME THINGS TO GROW FOR MOTHER HUBBARD'S CUPBOARD

Utensil Art Prints

Go through your kitchen drawers and find utensils with interesting shapes to print. Potato mashers, gravy stirrers, flat-bottomed whisks and cookie cutters are perfect, but you can find more!

Fill paint trays or shallow disposable baking pans with paper towels or flat sponges that have been soaked with tempera paint. The towels act as a blotter and are less messy than paint poured directly in the tray.

Give children old shirts worn backwards to cover up their clothes. Have the children dip the utensils in paint and make patterns on white paper. These art prints make interesting murals or gift wrap.

How-to-Set-the-Table Placemat

Young children can learn to set the table, but getting things on the right or left may be confusing. This placemat will be a "pattern" that can be used at home again and again.

Give each child a large sheet of tagboard—approximately 12 x 18 inches. Write the child's name on the mat (or let him or her do it). The name could be written at the top or bottom, but leave enough room for the utensils.

Now give each child paper cutouts of a fork, knife, spoon, plate, and glass. These should be drawn approximately to scale.

Begin by asking children to put the plate in the middle of the mat. Then put the fork on the left, the knife on the right, and the spoon to the right of the knife. Place the glass just above the spoon. When everyone has the table set correctly, glue down the pieces and cover mats with clear Contac paper so it will be durable enough to send home and use for a long time.

How-to-Set-the-Table
Placemat

Gardens You Can Grow Inside
(A Resourceful Way to Stuff the Cupboard)

What a Sweet Potato You Are

Choose a "whiskery" sweet potato. Set the potato on the mouth of a jar so that the skinny end of the potato is in the jar and is covered with water. Keep in Mother Hubbard's cupboard (or any dark place) for several days until the potato starts to grow roots. Check water level regularly to make sure the end of the potato is sufficiently covered.

You may wish to make one ahead so children will see what's going to happen. Or just begin from scratch and let children discover the results. When the roots get long, plant the sweet potato in the garden (or just leave it to grow leaves and make a pretty plant for the room).

I'm Ready-for-Spring Garden

Plant vegetable seeds in the bottom of a cut-off milk container or paper cup with about 1-2 inches of soil in the bottom. Moisten the soil, but don't make a flood! (Children tend to get carried away with this step.) Put a plastic bag over the little garden so you have a greenhouse. Talk about moisture contained in the greenhouse and how it helps plants grow. Now put the greenhouse in a sunny window (living things all need sun). You may have to add a drop or two of water after a week. When little green shoots come out of the soil, send the I'm-Ready for-Spring Gardens home with children so they can begin their own gardens.

COOKING AND TASTING EXPERIENCES TO STUFF MOTHER HUBBARD'S CUPBOARD

The cooking experiences in this section will show children different ways food is prepared to set aside and keep for eating later.

Really Easy Strawberry Jam

This jam keeps in a refrigerator or food freezer. Send little containers of it home in margarine tubs to keep and enjoy later.

Crush one quart of strawberries. Add 4 cups of sugar. Mix together 1 package Sure Jell and ¾ cup water. Boil this mixture 1 minute. Mix with berries. Let stand outside refrigerator for 24 hours to set.

Freezer Fruits

The food freezer has made eating out-of-season fruits and vegetables a delicious reality. Young children can prepare fruits for the freezer. Strawberries are a good choice because they don't have to be put in a syrup. Wash the fruit and give children teaspoons to take out the hulls (safer and easier to use than knives). Pack berries in margarine tubs for children to take home and freeze.

Dried Apple Rings

Dried fruit may be completely unfamiliar to some children. The texture is quite different from fresh, but it still tastes good. Apples may be dried in the oven, but it takes a long time and isn't energy efficient because the oven door should remain open for ventilation. A more satisfactory method (and a fun one!) is to hang the apple rings on a string in the warmest part of a room—perhaps near a radiator. When children come back for the next class or program, check the results. When the apples are dry, cut the string, and all dive in.

RESOURCE BIBLIOGRAPHY

Ault, Roz. **Kids Are Natural Cooks.** Based on the ideas of Liz Uraneck. Illustrated by Lady McCrady. Houghton Mifflin, 1972.

Based on experiences at Parents' Nursery School, this cookbook begins with, and expands upon, familiar, everyday experiences. The recipes, which are organized by season, contain clear illustrations and captivating line illustrations that are full of child appeal. Guidelines for teachers and parents are included.

Bauer, Caroline Feller. **Handbook for Storytellers.** American Library Association, 1977.

This well-known handbook includes basic techniques for storytelling using a variety of methods and includes many bibliographies on food topics such as apples, popcorn, and gingerbread.

Bauer, Caroline Feller. **This Way to Books.** Wilson, 1983.

More ways to introduce books to children including booktalk and poem approaches with a focus on food. Some unusual recipes, such as dog cookies, are included.

Baxter, Kathleen M. **Come and Get It.** Illustrated by Mimi Orlando. Children's First Press, 1978.

The focus of this cookbook for use with children is on good-tasting, healthy foods. The over 100 recipes call for ingredients that are as natural as possible. The pages are color-coded to indicate level of difficulty. The appealing names of the recipes—dinosaur soup and bags of gold—should win over the most reluctant eaters.

Bernick, Deborah, and Carol Hershad. **Bodyworks: The Kid's Guide to Food and Physical Fitness.** Illustrated by Heidi Johanna Selig. Random House, 1979.

Originally written for an upper-elementary curriculum package, this health guide and nutrition resource is infused with fascinating facts and humor.

Berry, Erick. **Eating and Cooking Around the World.** John Day, 1963.

   Some unusual cooking and eating practices, from igloo kitchens to Jamaican oil can cooking, will introduce preschoolers to food from other lands.

Coody, Betty. **Using Literature with Young Children.** 2nd ed. Wm. C. Brown, 1979.

   Storytelling is explored through language arts, puppets, arts, and food experiences for young children. The chapter on food experiences is one of the only sources to combine food and literature for preschoolers.

Ellison, Virginia H. **The Pooh Cookbook.** Illustrated by Ernest H. Shepard. Dutton, 1969.

   Inspired by Milne's Pooh books, the author adds fitting quotations and comments to the appropriate recipes for "smackerels," "provisions for picnics and expotitions," parties, and specialties. You will finally discover what goes into a Cottleston pie!

Frank, Marjorie. **I Can Make a Rainbow.** Illustrated by Gayle Seaberg. Incentive, 1976.

   This craft book includes creative approaches to food with suggestions for the teacher to adapt activities for classroom use or relate the activity to a curriculum area.

Hayes, Phyllis. **Food Fun.** Illustrated by Irene Trivas. Watts, 1981.

   These simple recipes and craft projects using food are easy to use with young children. The step-by- step approach indicates when an adult will need to help the child.

Hill, Barbara. **Cooking the English Way.** Lerner, 1982.

   English recipes from tea treats to supper dishes are included along with basic facts about English eating. This book is part of Lerner's ethnic cooking series for older children, but will be a useful resource for preschool teachers and librarians.

Jenkins, Karen S. **Kinder-Krunchies: Health Snack Recipes for Children.** Distributed by Discovery Toys, c. 1982.

   Developed as a pilot project by the San Diego County Department of Education, this book includes discussion suggestions, skills development, and a complete step-by-step picture approach to each recipe.

Johnson, Barbara. **Cup Cooking: Individual Child-Portion Picture Recipes.** Early Educators Press, 1978.

   These individual-portion recipes were specially developed for use by young children in day-care centers, preschools, and elementary schools. Following the sequence of pictures, young children can work through the instructions with a minimum of adult supervision. Most of the recipes need only an electric fry pan or portable toaster oven so the cooking will be possible in nearly any setting.

Johnson, Hannah Lyons. **Let's Bake Bread.** Lothrop, Lee, and Shepard, 1973.

   Clear photographs and step-by-step instructions show how to bake bread. This book can be used by seven-year-olds on their own, or with younger children if an adult supervises.

Lansky, Vicki. **Feed Me I'm Yours.** Illustrated by Pat Seitz. Meadowbrook Press, 1974.

   Delicious, nutritious and fun things to cook up for infants and toddlers, including baby foods from scratch, finger foods, and unusual breakfast treats as well as seasonal food ideas and kitchen crafts. Parents and teachers have found this a valuable resource book.

Meyer, Carolyn. **Lots and Lots of Candy.** Illustrated by Laura Jean Allen. Harcourt Brace Jovanovich, 1976.

The history of candy is traced from the Egyptians to our own day of candy factories. Recipes for a variety of sweet treats include old favorites—fudge and peanut brittle—in addition to the more exotic marzipan and pralines.

Munsen, Sylvia. **Cooking the Norwegian Way.** Lerner, 1982.

Some Swedish and Finnish recipes are included, but most of the fare is Norwegian: open-faced sandwiches, flatbread and meatballs. Like the Lerner ethnic cookbooks, this book gives basic facts about the country and its eating habits.

Penner, Lucille Recht. **The Honey Book.** Hastings House, 1980.

Everything you wanted to know about the history and production of honey is told with recipes from around the world—all using this natural sweetener.

Perl, Lila. **Hunter's Stew and Hangtown Fry: What Pioneer America Ate and Why.** Illustrated by Richard Cuffari. Seabury, 1977.

Five chapters arranged by area of the country trace the eating habits of pioneer Americans from the southern mountains to the west to the eastern seaboard.

Perl, Lila. **Junk Food, Fast Food, Health Food: What America Eats and Why.** Houghton Mifflin, 1980.

This book continues the author's other books on American eating patterns by looking at twentieth-century trends in snacks, health foods, and fast foods. Natural-food recipes and a list of common food additives are included.

Perl, Lila. **Slumps, Grunts, and Snickerdoodles: What Colonial America Ate and Why.** Illustrated by Richard Cuffari. Seabury, 1975.

This history of early American eating introduces children to succotash, johnnycake, Indian pudding and other colorful dishes. Teachers will find this a fascinating resource book for teaching younger children.

Scheib, Ida. **The First Book of Food.** Rev. ed. by Carole E. Walker. Illustrated by Robert Byrd. Watts, 1974.

Food production and preservation are discussed, as well as basic nutrition facts.

Schroeder, Rosella J., and Marie C. Sanderson. **It's Not Really Magic: Microwave Cooking for Young People.** Dillon, 1981.

Basic microwave-cooking instructions and safety precautions, as well as clearly-written recipes, make this cookbook easy for the older child to use independently. The approaches can also be used with younger children under adult supervision.

Steinkoler, Ronnie. **A Jewish Cookbook for Children.** Illustrated by Sonja Glassman. Julian Messner, 1980.

Arranged by various Jewish holidays, this specialty cookbook gives step-by-step instructions for such succulent dishes as apple noodle pudding, potato pancakes, charoset, and pita bread. A brief explanation of each holiday is given.

Stubis, Patricia, and Talivadis Stubis. **Sandwichery.** Parents, 1975.

Recipes for common and uncommon sandwiches such as Beauty-and-Beast sandwiches are introduced through riddles and whimsical illustrations.

Tornborg, Pat. **The Sesame Street Cookbook.** Illustrated by Robert Dennis. Platt and Munk, 1979.

Sesame Street characters and scenes present easy and nutritious recipes young children will happily make with your help. Cookie Monster's Uncookies and Oscar's Junk-Food Pie need no baking. Other recipes require a hot plate or oven.

Travers, P. L., and Maurice Moore-Betty. **Mary Poppins in the Kitchen.** Illustrated by Mary Shepard. Harcourt Brace Jovanovich, 1975.

Selections from Mary Poppins stories about the Banks children helping in the kitchen are interspersed with daily menus and recipes. A few simple recipes to use with young children that are "very British" include Egg Flip and Welsh Rarebit.

Waldee, Lynne Marie. **Cooking the French Way.** Lerner, 1982.

French meals from *le petit dejeuner* (breakfast) to *le diner* (dinner) are described with delicious recipes for quiche and crepes.

Walker, Barbara. **The Little House Cookbook.** Illustrated by Garth Williams. Harper & Row, 1979.

Excerpts from the Little House books and illustrations by Garth Williams add to the appeal of the pioneer recipes and food lore. The chapter introductions provide lively background about the country store, the pioneer kitchen, fishing, and growing food in the nineteenth century. Because of the popularity of the television series, children enjoy these books at an early age.

Weston, Reiko. **Cooking the Japanese Way.** Lerner, 1983.

This Lerner ethnic cookbook, like the others in the series, provides recipes, eating methods, and a pronunciation guide to the names of Japanese foods.

What's to Eat? And Other Questions Kids Ask about Food. The U.S. Department of Agriculture Yearbook, 1979.

Eight topics span the history of food, nutrition, gardening, food production and food habits around the world with fun activities to do with children.

Yu, Ling. **Cooking the Chinese Way.** Lerner, 1982.

Another in the Lerner ethnic-cooking series, this cookbook simplifies Chinese recipes and notes optional ingredients while preserving authenticity.

Zubrowski, Bernie. **Messing Around with Baking Chemistry.** Illustrated by Signe Hanson. Little, Brown, 1981.

Experiments and recipes for the junior scientist who is curious about the fizzes and gases in baking powder, soda, and yeast will help answer young children's questions about how cakes and bread rise.

POETRY AND STORY COLLECTIONS ABOUT FOOD

Adoff, Arnold. **Eats.** Illustrated by Susan Russo. Lothrop, Lee, and Shepard, 1979.

Adoff's reflections on food are free-verse treasures about measuring, mixing, gardening, and eating. Some of the poems, such as the directions for making a sunnyside-up egg, read as concrete poems. Most of the selections will be appreciated more fully by school-aged children, but some are fun with preschoolers, too.

Bennett, Jill. **A Packet of Poems.** Oxford, 1982.

> Appealing graphics combine with tasty morsels of poems all about food. Sections include "Hot Pot," "Leftovers," and "A Matter of Taste." Even the cover will make kids want to gobble this up—it looks like a checkerboard box of cereal!

Cole, William. **Poem Stew.** Illustrated by Karen Ann Weihaus. Lippincott, 1981.

> In this feast of poems about food and manners, Cole has brought together funny verse about "Rhinoceros Stew" by Mildred Luton, "Vegetables" by Shel Silverstein, and many others.

Greene, Ellin. **Clever Cooks: A Concoction of Stories, Charms, Recipes, and Riddles.** Illustrated by Trina Schart Hyman. Lothrop, Lee, and Shepard, 1973.

> Favorite folktales about cooks and cooking will inspire the teacher/librarian to tell or adapt these yarns for young children. Several of the stories are available in picture-book form, e.g., "The Old Woman Who Lost Her Dumpling" as The Funny Little Woman.

Lobel, Arnold. **Gregory Griggs and Other Nursery Rhyme People.** Greenwillow, 1978.

> Thirty-four nursery rhymes include several characters obsessed with food: the gluttonous Hannah Bantry, the finicky Miss Tuckett, and the sweet-tooth, Jack-a-Dandy.

Prelutsky, Jack. **The New Kid on the Block.** Illustrated by James Stevenson. Greenwillow, 1984.

> Prelutsky attacks food with such broad humor that even young children will readily enjoy his unlikely concoctions.

SKILLS LIST

Self-Awareness Skills
Gross Motor Skills
Health and Safety Skills
Tasting and Smelling Skills
Color Recognition Skills
Size and Shape Recognition Skills
Rhythm and Rhyming Skills
Counting Skills
Following Directions Skills
Group Cooperation Skills
Musical Skills
Artistic Skills
Role and Dialogue Invention Skills
Sequencing Skills
Classification Skills
Word Recognition Skills

BREAKDOWN OF ACTIVITIES BY SKILLS AREA

Refer to Alphabetical Index of Activities for page numbers.

Self-Awareness Skills

Alphabet Soup Bowl Just for Fun
Apple Bob
Bigfoot Sandwich
Birthday Cakes in a Cup
Body Food
Breakfast Song
Child-Safe Candles for the Tree
Different and the Same
Doin' the Chocolate Shake
Fortunate Fortunes
Fussy Eaters' Song
Gingerbread Boy and Gingerbread Girl on a
      Tree
H Team vs. the Junk Food Junkies
Hello Jello
How to Dump What You Won't Eat
I Feel Good . . . I'm Growing Up
If You Want to Grow Up Healthy
I'm a Good Egg
Indigestion
It's a Piece of Cake
Jack-O'-Lantern Pie
Kid Soup
Kitchen Band Song
Kitchen Work Song
Lick 'Em Up
Magic Pots Cooking in Many Lands
My Birthday Action Rhyme
Nellie or Nathan Noodlehead
Nimble Noodleheads
Oh Where, Oh Where Is My Peanut Butter?

Peanut Butter Letters
Picky Paul
Picky Paul Pizza
Pluck the Turkey and Do a Trick
Popcorn Bowl-Frolic
Pot on the Stove
Teddy Bear Picnic Game
Wake Up the Yeast Giant!
We're Growing a Little Garden
Who Eats Worms?
You-Are-What-You-Eat Puppet

Gross Motor Skills

Ants Go Softly Round and Round
Apple Bob
Blueberry-Picking Song
Body Food
Breakfast Song
Bring It Right Here!
Bubble, Bubble Pot
Candy-Cane Capers Relay
Casserole Roll
Chicken Feed
Christmas Stocking Relay
Christmas Treats Good to Eat
County Fair
Crumb Catcher
Day Barnaby Bear Fell in the Batter Bowl
Deviled Eggs—Chicken Legs Game
Different and the Same
Disappearing D-O-N-U-T
Doin' the Chocolate Shake

Easy as Pie
Egg Frolic
Egg Roll
Eggs and More Eggs—Surprise!
First Thanksgiving
Food for Thought
Fortunate Fortunes
Frozen Thanksgiving Meal
Fruit Fun
Giant Musical Sandwich Game
Gingerbread Boy and Gingerbread Girl on a
    Tree
Glass of Sunshine Fingerplay
Going on a Picnic
Good Licken
Groaning-Board Groan
Gum Drop Sticky Teeth Rhyme
Hand-Me-Down Food
Hello Jello
Honey Bee Dance
Hot Dog Song
I Feel Good . . . I'm Growing Up
If You Want to Grow Up Healthy
It's a Piece of Cake
Kid Soup
Kitchen Band Song
Kitchen Work Song
Leftover Hopscotch
Let Us Make a Salad Bowl
Lick 'Em Up
Lunch Is Fun
Lunchtime Rhyme
Marshmallow Ghosts
Mexican Jumping Bean
Monster Messy Face
More-Than-Enough Sandwich
My Birthday Action Rhyme
Nimble Noodleheads
Ogre Roar
Oh Where, Oh Where Is My Peanut Butter?
Pachyderm Peanut Pitch
Pancakes, What a Treat!
Peas Porridge Hot
Piggy Piggy
Pizza Pie to Perform
Pluck the Turkey and Do a Trick
Pop Goes the Popcorn
Popcorn Bowl-Frolic
Popcorn-Cranberry Chain
Pot on the Stove
Queen Bee—A Honey of a Game!
Roll-the-Can Ice Cream
Snap, Crackle, Pop Around
Soggy Cornflake Song
Soup-Can Roll—Just for Fun
Spider and Fly

Teddy Bear Picnic Game
Toast Pop-up Game
Unhatched Egg
We're Growing a Little Garden
Where Does It Grow?
Who Eats Worms?
Who Put the Cookies in the Cookie Jar?

Health and Safety Skills
Any Food Kabob
Applecrafts through the Holidays
Apple Mac, the Puppet
Arthur's Christmas Cookie Ornaments
Basic Mix for Granola
Big Batch Pancake Mix
Big Sweet Tooth
Bigfoot Sandwich
Breadbasket Sampler
Bumps on a Log
Carrots for Every Bunny
Catch-the-Sun Salad
Cedric Celery, the Garden Snake
Chicken Soup with Rice
Child-Safe Candles for the Tree
Chinese Noodle Pick-Up
Chocolate Pancakes
Christmas Wreath Cookies
Dried Apple Rings
Easy Won Ton Soup
Eating of the Green
Food to Eat on the Run
Frances in a Frame
Freezer Fruits
Fruit Fun
Fussy Eaters' Song
Garden Salad Open-Faced Sandwich
Gardens You Can Grow Inside
Good Food Finger Puppet
Green Magic Dip
H Team vs. the Junk Food Junkies
Healthy-Four Game
Hello Jello Bars
Hobo Bags
Honey Bee Dance
How to Dump What You Won't Eat
I Feel Good . . . I'm Growing Up
I Like What's in My Lunch Box
Ice Cream Concoctions
If You Want to Grow Up Healthy
I'm Going to the Market, Super-Dooper-Doo
Indigestion
Ketchup, Ketchup, Everywhere . . . Only Six
    Jars to Spare
Leftover Stew
Let Us Make a Salad Bowl

Make Your Own Soup Mix
Mouse Bites
My Lunch Box
Pancakes that Might Run Away
Pasta Pig-Out
Peanut Butter Letters
Peanut Butter Porcupines
Peanut Butter Wallop
Picky Paul
Picky Paul Pizza
Pig Party
Pig Tails
Pleasing Pancakes
Pop Goes the Popcorn
Popcorn Bowl-Frolic
Porcupine Balls
Potato Pancakes
Quick Alphabet Soup
Really Easy Strawberry Jam
Right-Out-of-the-Garden Salad
Sam-I-Am Deviled Green Eggs
SandWitches You Can Make
Silly Jungle Dinner
Somewhat Inflated Tale of J. S. and His Wife
  Nan
Sponge Cake
Square Meal
Stone Soup
Taco Bar
Terrible Tale of Joshua Nickel
Trail Mix
Treat Bag Treasure Hunt
Well-Rounded Meal
Witch Brew
You-Are-What-You-Eat Puppet

Tasting and Smelling Skills

Any Food Kabob
Applecrafts through the Holidays
Basic Mix for Granola
Big Batch Pancake Mix
Bigfoot Sandwich
Birthday Cakes in a Cup
Blueberry-Picking Song
Body Food
Breadbasket Sampler
Bumps on a Log
Catch-the-Sun Salad
Cedric Celery, the Garden Snake
Cereal Surprises
Chicken Soup with Rice
Chinese Noodle Pick-Up
Chocolate Haystacks
Chocolate Pancakes
Christmas Wreath Cookies

Colorful Cake Walk
Cookie Muncher Game
Crunch! Squirt! Squish!
Dried Apple Rings
Easy Won Ton Soup
Eating of the Green
Flower Pot Cakes
Food Fair from Many Lands
Food to Eat on the Run
Frances in a Frame
Freezer Fruits
Funny Feeling Foods
Garden Salad Open-Faced Sandwich
Gingerbread Boy and Gingerbread Girl on a
  Tree
Gingerbread Boy Treasure Hunt
Gingerbread House on a Plate
Green Magic Dip
Hello Jello Bars
Hobo Bags
Ice Cream and Something to Go with It!
Ice Cream Concoctions
Jack-O'-Lantern Cake
Make Your Own Soup Mix
Monster Mickey Bread
Mouse Bites
Mudluscious!
Pancakes that Might Run Away
Pasta Pig-Out
Peanut Butter Letters
Peanut Butter Porcupines
Peanut Butter Wallop
Pickle Creature to Eat
Picky Paul
Picky Paul Pizza
Pig Party
Pig Tails
Pleasing Pancakes
Pooh's Hunny Jar and the Bees' Bee Hive
Popcorn Bowl-Frolic
Porcupine Balls
Potato Pancakes
Quick Alphabet Soup
Really Easy Strawberry Jam
Right-Out-of-the-Garden Salad
Roll-the-Can Ice Cream
Sam-I-Am Deviled Green Eggs
SandWitches You Can Make
Silly Jungle Dinner
Stone Soup
Taco Bar
Trail Mix
Tree for All Reasons and Seasons to Celebrate
Witch Brew
World of Good Food to Share

Color Recognition Skills

Alphabet Soup Bowl Just for Fun
Applecrafts through the Holidays
Apple Mac, the Puppet
Arthur's Christmas Cookie Ornaments
Aunt Annie, the Picnic Ant
Baker, Baker
Blueberry-Picking Song
Child-Safe Candles for the Tree
Christmas Wreath Cookies
Colorful Cake Walk
Country Market
Double Scooper Ice Cream Cone
Eating of the Green
Good Food Finger Puppet
Green Magic Dip
Groaning Board Mural
Halloween Treat Song
Humpty Dumpty Back Together Again
Ice Cream Super Scoopers
I'm a Good Egg
Incredible Everything-You-Want-in-One Pie
Ketchup, Ketchup, Everywhere . . . Only Six
    Jars to Spare
Let Us Make a Salad Bowl
Little Red Hen
Lolly Pop Puppet
Mexican Jumping Bean
Mudluscious
My Lunch Box
Natural Food Dye Decorating
Pancakes that Might Run Away
Paper Pickle Creature Puppet
Picky Paul
Pizza Pie to Perform
Placemats from India
Popcorn-Cranberry Chain
Pysanky Adapted: Daisy, Daisy, I Love You
Sam-I-Am Deviled Green Eggs
Sandwich Sign
SandWitches You Can Make
Shopping Lists All Around
Silly Jungle Dinner
Square Meal
Supermarket in the Library or Classroom
This Litter Piggy Went Home
Turkey Place Card for Thanksgiving
What Do You Like to Start the Day?
Why Pigs Are Pink

Size and Shape Recognition Skills

After the Shopping's Done
Arthur's Christmas Cookie Ornaments
Aunt Annie, the Picnic Ant
Best Part Is . . . What's Left
Big Sweet Tooth

Bigfoot Sandwich
Bread-and-Glue Dough
Breadbasket Sampler
Bubble, Bubble Pot
Carrots for Every Bunny
Cedric Celery, the Garden Snake
Colorful Cake Walk
Day Barnaby Bear Fell in the Batter Bowl
Disappearing D-O-N-U-T
Double Scooper Ice Cream Cone
Eggs and More Eggs—Surprise!
Funny Feeling Foods
Gingerbread Boy and Gingerbread Girl on a
    Tree
Gingerbread House on a Plate
Glass of Sunshine Fingerplay
Glutton Feast Song
Good Licken
Groaning-Board Groan
Hand-Me-Down Food
Happy Magic Pot
Hello Jello Bars
How Old Mother Hubbard's Dog Finally Got
    Dinner
How-to-Set-the-Table Placemat
Humpty Dumpty Together Again
Humpty Dumpty Triple Treat
Hungry-Mouth Cat
Ice Cream Super Scoopers
I'll-Eat-You-Up Chant
Incredible Everything-You-Want-in-One Pie
Jack-O'-Lantern Cake
Jack-O'-Lantern Pie
Leftover Hopscotch
Leftover Stew
Let Us Make a Salad Bowl
Lighter-than-Air Cake
Lost, Left, and All Gone
Lunchtime Surprise
Magic Microwave
Monster Mickey Bread
More-Than-Enough Sandwich
My Lunch Box
Nellie or Nathan Noodlehead
Old Lady and the Fly: A Jarring Experience
Old Lady from a Bag
Pancakes that Might Run Away
Paper-Plate Pig
Peanut Butter Porcupines
Picky Paul
Picky Paul Pizza
Pokey, Pokey, the Bread Song
Pooh's Hunny Jar and the Bees' Bee Hive
Popcorn-Cranberry Chain
Pysanky Adapted: Daisy, Daisy, I Love You

SandWitches You Can Make
Shopping Lists All Around
Silly Jungle Dinner
Somewhat Inflated Tale of J. S. and His
　　Wife Nan
Square Meal
Sugar Snowperson
Supermarket in the Library or Classroom
This Litter Piggy Went Home
Three Pigs on a Tube
Too Many Cooks
Turkey Place Card for Thanksgiving
Unhatched Egg
Utensil Art Prints
Very Hungry Bear
Wake Up the Yeast Giant!
Well-Rounded Meal
What's Inside Jack Horner's Pie?
Where Does It Grow?
Who Put the Cookies in the Cookie Jar?
Why Doesn't It Grow on Trees?
Why Pigs Are Pink
World's Great Bread Basket
You-Are-What-You-Eat Puppet

Rhythm and Rhyming Skills

All-Kinds-of-Soup Song
Alphabet Soup Song
Ants Go Softly Round and Round
Apple Bob
Baker, Baker
Banana Split
Best Part Is . . . What's Left
Big Sweet Tooth
Breakfast Song
Bring It Right Here!
Bubble, Bubble Pot
Casserole Roll
Chocolate Soup
Christmas Treats Good to Eat
Clean the Fridge
Come On and Do the Cake Walk
Cookie Muncher Game
Country Market
County Fair
Crumb Catcher
Different and the Same
Dippy Donut Song
Disappearing D-O-N-U-T
Doin' the Chocolate Shake
Easy as Pie
Eat, Eat, Eat Your Food
Eggs and More Eggs—Surprise!
Fantastic Food Dream
Fast-Food Quick Trip

First Thanksgiving
Food Fair from Many Lands
Food from the U.S.A.
Fruit Fun
Fudge Song
Fussy Eaters' Song
Gingerbread Boy and Gingerbread Girl on a
　　Tree
Gingerbread Boy in Verse
Gingerbread-Man Story with Masks
Glass of Sunshine Fingerplay
Glutton Feast Song
Good Licken
Groaning-Board Groan
Gum Drop Sticky Teeth Rhyme
H Team vs. the Junk Food Junkies
Halloween Treat Song
Hand-Me-Down Food
Happy, Happy Hanukkah
Hello Jello
Honey Bee Dance
Hot Dog Song
How Do You Eat an Ice Cream Cone?
How to Dump What You Won't Eat
Humpty Dumpty Triple Treat
Hungry-for-Pie Song
I Feel Good . . . I'm Growing Up
I Like What's in My Lunch Box
If You Want to Grow Up Healthy
I'll-Eat-You-Up Chant
I'm Going to the Market, Super-Dooper-Doo
Indigestion
Irish Potato Frolic
It's a Piece of Cake
Jack-O'-Lantern Pie
Just My Dish
Kid Soup
Kitchen Band Song
Kitchen Work Song
Leftover Food, It Ain't What It Used to Be
Let's Go and Pack a Picnic
Let's Make Christmas Pudding
Lunch Is Fun
Lunchtime Rhyme
Magic Microwave
Magic Pots Cooking in Many Lands
Marshmallow Ghosts
Mexican Fiesta
More-Than-Enough Sandwich
My Birthday Action Rhyme
Nimble Noodleheads
Ogre Roar
Oh Where, Oh Where Is My Peanut Butter?
Old Lady and the Fly: A Jarring Experience
Old Lady from a Bag

Old Mother Hubbard Retold
Pancakes, What a Treat!
Pasta Song
Peas Porridge Hot
Piggy Piggy
Pizza Pie to Perform
Pokey, Pokey, the Bread Song
Popcorn-Cranberry Chain
Pot on the Stove
Shopping List for Porcupines and Other
    Peculiar Animals
Silly, Silly Things to Eat
Soggy Cornflake Song
Something for Santa
Somewhat Inflated Tale of J. S. and His
    Wife Nan
Song for Making Mud Pie
Spider and Fly
Street Cries for Modern Children
Terrible Tale of Joshua Nickel
Three Pigs on a Tube
Toast Pop-up Game
Tree for All Reasons and Seasons to Celebrate
Wake Up the Yeast Giant!
We're Fixing a Thanksgiving Dinner Feast
What a Cake!
What Do You Like to Start the Day?
What's Inside Jack Horner's Pie?
Where Does It Grow?
Who Put the Cookies in the Cookie Jar?
World of Good Food to Share
World's Great Bread Basket

Counting Skills

Applecrafts through the Holidays
Baker, Baker
Banana Split
Carrots for Every Bunny
Come On and Do the Cake Walk
Country Market
County Fair
First Thanksgiving
Glass of Sunshine Fingerplay
Gum Drop Sticky Teeth Rhyme
H Team vs. the Junk Food Junkies
Hand-Me-Down Food
Happy, Happy Hanukkah
Healthy-Four Game
Hungry-Mouth Cat
Irish Potato Frolic
Jack-O'-Lantern Pie
Ker Choo Ee!
Ketchup, Ketchup, Everywhere . . . Only Six
    Jars to Spare
Kid Soup
Let Us Make a Salad Bowl

Marshmallow Ghosts
Mexican Jumping Bean
Ogre Roar
Pancake Stack
Paper-Plate Pig
Pasta Song
Peas Porridge Hot
Picky Paul
Piggy Pie
Pluck the Turkey and Do a Trick
Shopping List for Porcupines and Other
    Peculiar Animals
Shopping Lists All Around
Square Meal
Three Pigs on a Tube
Too Many Cooks
Very Hungry Bear
Well-Rounded Meal

Following Directions Skills

Alphabet Animal Soup
Alphabet Soup Bowl Just for Fun
Amazing Table
Ants Go Softly Round and Round
Apple Bob
Applecrafts through the Holidays
Apple Mac, the Puppet
Arthur's Christmas Cookie Ornaments
Baker, Baker Doll
Baker Hat for Children
Blueberry-Picking Song
Body Food
Bread-and-Glue Dough
Camel Chowder
Candy-Cane Capers Relay
Casserole Roll
Chicken Feed
Child-Safe Candles for the Tree
Christmas Stocking Relay
Christmas Treats Good to Eat
Clean the Fridge
Colorful Cake Walk
Cookie Muncher Game
Country Market
County Fair
Crumb Catcher
Crunch! Squirt! Squish!
Day Barnaby Bear Fell in the Batter Bowl
Deviled Eggs—Chicken Legs Game
Different and the Same
Disappearing D-O-N-U-T
Doin' the Chocolate Shake
Double Scooper Ice Cream Cone
Easy as Pie
Eat-Your-Words Game
Egg Carton Art

Egg Frolic
Egg Roll
Eggbert the Baker
Eggs and More Eggs—Surprise!
First Thanksgiving
Food for Thought
Fortunate Fortunes
Frozen Thanksgiving Meal
Fruit Fun
Garbage-Bag Bib
Gardens You Can Grow Inside
Giant Musical Sandwich Game
Gingerbread Boy and Gingerbread Girl on a
      Tree
Gingerbread-Boy Treasure Hunt
Gingerbread-Man Story with Masks
Glass of Sunshine Fingerplay
Gobble Up: Fast-Food Lunch Muncher
Going on a Picnic
Good Food Finger Puppet
Good Licken
Groaning-Board Groan
Groaning Board Mural
Gum Drop Sticky Teeth Rhyme
Hand-Me-Down Food
Haunted House Milk Carton
Healthy-Four Game
Hello Jello
Honey Bee Dance
Hot Dog Song
How-to-Set-the-Table Placemat
Humpty Dumpty Together Again
Hungry-Mouth Cat
I Feel Good . . . I'm Growing Up
Ice Cream Super Scoopers
If You Want to Grow Up Healthy
I'll-Eat-You-Up Chant
Incredible Everything-You-Want-in-One Pie
Irish Potato Frolic
It's a Piece of Cake
Junk Food Rubby in the Tummy
Ker Choo Ee!
Kid Soup
Kitchen Band Song
Leftover Hopscotch
Let Us Make a Salad Bowl
Let's Go and Pack a Picnic
Lick 'Em Up
Litter Eater
Little Red Hen
Lolly Pop Puppet
Lunch Is Fun
Magic Cooking Pot
Magic Pots Cooking in Many Lands
Make Your Own Soup Label
Marshmallow Ghosts
Mexican Jumping Bean

Monster Messy Face
More-Than-Enough Sandwich
Mud Pie
Mudluscious!
Muncher
My Birthday Action Rhyme
My Lunch Box
Natural Food Dye Decorating
Nellie or Nathan Noodlehead
Nimble Noodleheads
Ogre Roar
Pachyderm Peanut Pitch
Pancake Stack
Pancakes, What a Treat!
Paper Pickle Creature Puppet
Paper-Plate Pig
Parrot Piñata
Peas Porridge Hot
Piggy Piggy
Pizza Pie to Perform
Placemats from India
Pluck the Turkey and Do a Trick
Pooh's Hunny Jar and the Bees' Bee Hive
Pop Goes the Popcorn
Popcorn Bowl-Frolic
Popcorn-Cranberry Chain
Pot on the Stove
Pysanky Adapted: Daisy, Daisy, I Love You
Queen Bee—A Honey of a Game!
Roll-the-Can Ice Cream
Sand Cake
Sandwich Sign
Shopping Lists All Around
Snap, Crackle, Pop Around
Soggy Cornflake Song
Soup-Can Roll—Just for Fun
Spider and Fly
Sponge Cake
Sugar Snowperson
Super Spaghetti Cake
Supermarket in the Library or Classroom
Teddy Bear Picnic Game
This Bag Is for the Dogs
This Litter Piggy Went Home
Toast Pop-up Game
Too Many Cooks
Treat Bag Treasure Hunt
Turkey Place Card for Thanksgiving
Unhatched Egg
Utensil Art Prints
Very Hungry Bear
Well-Rounded Meal
We're Growing a Little Garden
What Do You Like to Start the Day?
What's Inside Jack Horner's Pie?

Where Does It Grow?
Who Eats Worms?
Who Put the Cookies in the Cookie Jar?
Why Pigs Are Pink
You-Are-What-You-Eat Puppet

Group Cooperation Skills
Alphabet Animal Soup
Ants Go Softly Round and Round
Candy-Cane Capers Relay
Christmas Stocking Relay
Clean the Fridge
Crumb Catcher
Crunch! Squirt! Squish!
Day Barnaby Bear Fell in the Batter Bowl
Deviled Eggs—Chicken Legs Game
Egg Roll
Giant Musical Sandwich Game
Gingerbread-Boy Treasure Hunt
Groaning Board Mural
Honey Bee Dance
I Feel Good . . . I'm Growing Up
Ker Choo Ee!
Kid Soup
Kitchen Band Song
Little Red Hen
Magic Microwave
Magic Pots Cooking in Many Lands
Pancake Stack
Piggy Piggy
Pizza Pie to Perform
Popcorn-Cranberry Chain
Queen Bee—A Honey of a Game!
Snap, Crackle, Pop Around
Soup-Can Roll—Just for Fun
Spider and Fly
Three Pigs on a Tube
Toast Pop-up Game
Treat Bag Treasure Hunt
Tree for All Reasons and Seasons to Celebrate
Very Hungry Bear

Musical Skills
All-Kinds-of-Soup Song
Alphabet Soup Song
Ants Go Softly Round and Round
Banana Split
Big Sweet Tooth
Blueberry-Picking Song
Breakfast Song
Bring It Right Here!
Bubble, Bubble Pot
Chocolate Soup
Clean the Fridge
Colorful Cake Walk
Come On and Do the Cake Walk

County Fair
Crumb Catcher
Did You Ever Eat . . .
Dippy Donut Song
Disappearing D-O-N-U-T
Doin' the Chocolate Shake
Eat, Eat, Eat Your Food
Fast-Food Quick Trip
Food from the U.S.A.
Fudge Song
Fussy Eaters' Song
Giant Musical Sandwich Game
Glutton Feast Song
H Team vs. the Junk Food Junkies
Halloween Treat Song
Honey Bee Dance
Hot Dog Song
How to Dump What You Won't Eat
Hungry-for-Pie Song
I Feel Good . . . I'm Growing Up
If You Want to Grow Up Healthy
Indigestion
Kitchen Band Song
Kitchen Work Song
Leftover Food, It Ain't What It Used to Be
Let's Go and Pack a Picnic
Let's Make Christmas Pudding
Nimble Noodleheads
Oh Where, Oh Where Is My Peanut Butter?
Old Lady and the Fly: A Jarring Experience
Old Lady from a Bag
Pancake Chase
Pasta Song
Pluck the Turkey and Do a Trick
Pokey, Pokey, the Bread Song
Pop Goes the Popcorn
Popcorn-Cranberry Chain
Silly, Silly Things to Eat
Soggy Cornflake Song
Song for Making Mud Pie
Spider and Fly
We're Fixing a Thanksgiving Dinner Feast
We're Growing a Little Garden

Artistic Skills
Alphabet Soup Bowl Just for Fun
Applecrafts through the Holidays
Apple Mac, the Puppet
Arthur's Christmas Cookie Ornaments
Aunt Annie, the Picnic Ant
Baker, Baker Doll
Baker Hat for Children
Bread-and-Glue Dough
Catch-the-Sun Salad
Child-Safe Candles for the tree
Chinese New Year Tree Centerpiece

Chocolate Pudding Just for Fun
Christmas Wreath Cookies
Double Scooper Ice Cream Cone
Egg Carton Art
Eggbert the Baker
Garbage-Bag Bib
Gingerbread House on a Plate
Gobble Up: Fast-Food Lunch Muncher
Good Food Finger Puppet
Groaning Board Mural
Haunted House Milk Carton
How-to-Set-the-Table Placemat
Humpty Dumpty Together Again
Hungry-Mouth Cat
Incredible Everything-You-Want-in-One Pie
Jack-O'-Lantern Cake
Junk Food Rubby in the Tummy
Litter Eater
Lolly Pop Puppet
Magic Cooking Pot
Make Your Own Soup Label
Mud Pie
Mudluscious!
Muncher
My Lunch Box
Natural Food Dye Decorating
Nellie or Nathan Noodlehead
Paper Pickle Creature Puppet
Paper-Plate Pig
Parrot Piñata
Pickle Creature to Eat
Placemats from India
Pooh's Hunny Jar and the Bees' Bee Hive
Popcorn-Cranberry Chain
Pysanky Adapted: Daisy, Daisy, I Love You
Sand Cake
Sandwich Sign
SandWitches You Can Make
Sponge Cake
Sugar Snowperson
Super Spaghetti Cake
This Bag Is for the Dogs
This Litter Piggy Went Home
Turkey Place Card for Thanksgiving
Utensil Art Prints
Well-Rounded Meal
Why Pigs Are Pink
You-Are-What-You-Eat Puppet

Role and Dialogue Invention Skills

Amazing Table
Ants Go Softly Round and Round
Apple Bob
Apple Mac, the Puppet
Baker, Baker
Blueberry-Picking Song

Bubble, Bubble Pot
Chicken Feed
Crunch! Squirt! Squish!
Day Barnaby Bear Fell in the Batter Bowl
Egg Frolic
First Thanksgiving
Food Fair from Many Lands
Fortunate Fortunes
Frozen Thanksgiving Meal
Fruit Fun
Gingerbread Boy and Gingerbread Girl on a
    Tree
Gingerbread Boy in Verse
Gingerbread-Man Story with Masks
Gobble Up: Fast-Food Lunch Muncher
Going on a Picnic
Good Licken
Groaning-Board Groan
Gum Drop Sticky Teeth Rhyme
H Team vs. the Junk Food Junkies
Honey Bee Dance
How Old Mother Hubbard's Dog Finally Got
    Dinner
Humpty Dumpty Triple Treat
I Feel Good . . . I'm Growing Up
Ice Cream and Something to Go with It!
Ice Cream Super Scoopers
If You Want to Grow Up Healthy
I'm Going to the Market, Super-Dooper-Doo
Ker Choo Ee!
Kitchen Band Song
Let Us Make a Salad Bowl
Lick 'Em Up
Little Red Hen
Lolly Pop Puppet
Lunchtime Surprise
Make Your Own Soup Label
Marshmallow Ghosts
Nimble Noodleheads
Ogre Roar
Old Lady and the Fly: A Jarring Experience
Old Lady from a Bag
Old Mother Hubbard Retold
Out-of-This-World Soup
Pancake Chase
Pancake Stack
Picky Paul
Piggy Piggy
Pizza Pie to Perform
Pluck the Turkey and Do a Trick
Popcorn Bowl-Frolic
Shopping List for Porcupines and Other
    Peculiar Animals
Somewhat Inflated Tale of J. S. and His
    Wife Nan
Spider and Fly
Super Spaghetti Cake

Supermarket in the Library or Classroom
Teddy Bear Picnic Game
Terrible Tale of Joshua Nickel
Three Pigs on a Tube
Too Many Cooks
Unhatched Egg
Very Hungry Bear
Wake Up the Yeast Giant!
We're Fixing a Thanksgiving Dinner Feast
We're Growing a Little Garden
What a Cake!
Who Eats Worms?
Why Doesn't It Grow on Trees?

Sequencing Skills

Amazing Table
Baker, Baker
Banana Split
Best Part Is . . . What's Left
Blueberry-Picking Song
Carrots for Every Bunny
Cereal Surprises
Chocolate Soup
Clean the Fridge
Day Barnaby Bear Fell in the Batter Bowl
Disappearing D-O-N-U-T
First Thanksgiving
Fudge Song
Gardens You Can Grow Inside
Gingerbread Boy in Verse
Gingerbread-Man Story with Masks
Glass of Sunshine Fingerplay
Going on a Picnic
Good Licken
H Team vs. the Junk Food Junkies
Hand-Me-Down Food
Happy Magic Pot
Honey Bee Dance
Hot Dog Song
How Old Mother Hubbard's Dog Finally Got
    Dinner
How-to-Set-the-Table Placemat
Humpty Dumpty Triple Treat
Ice Cream and Something to Go with It!
Ice Cream Super Scoopers
If You Want to Grow Up Healthy
I'll-Eat-You-Up Chant
I'm Going to the Market, Super-Dooper-Doo
Jack-O'-Lantern Pie
Ker Choo Ee!
Ketchup, Ketchup, Everywhere . . . Only Six
    Jars to Spare
Leftover Food, It Ain't What It Used to Be
Leftover Stew

Let's Go and Pack a Picnic
Let's Make Christmas Pudding
Lighter-than-Air Cake
Little Red Hen
Lost, Left, and All Gone
Lunchtime Rhyme
Lunchtime Surprise
Magic Cooking Pot
Magic Microwave
More-Than-Enough Sandwich
Old Lady and the Fly: A Jarring Experience
Old Lady from a Bag
Old Mother Hubbard Retold
Out-of-This-World Soup
Pancake Chase
Pancake Stack
Pasta Song
Picky Paul
Piggy Pie
Piggy Piggy
Pokey, Pokey, the Bread Song
Popcorn Bowl-Frolic
Pot on the Stove
Queen Bee—A Honey of a Game!
Soggy Cornflake Song
Somewhat Inflated Tale of J. S. and His
    Wife Nan
Song for Making Mud Pie
Square Meal
Teddy Bear Picnic Game
Terrible Tale of Joshua Nickel
Three Pigs on a Tube
Toast Pop-up Game
Too Many Cooks
Tree for All Reasons and Seasons to Celebrate
Very Hungry Bear
Wake Up the Yeast Giant!
We're Fixing a Thanksgiving Dinner Feast
We're Growing a Little Garden
What a Cake!
Why Doesn't It Grow on Trees?

Classification Skills

After the Shopping's Done
All-Kinds-of-Soup Song
Alphabet Animal Soup
Alphabet Soup Song
Breadbasket Sampler
Breakfast Song
Camel Chowder
Different and the Same
Dippy Donut Song
Easy as Pie
Eat-Your-Words Game
Egg Frolic

Food Fair from Many Lands
Food for Thought
Food from the U.S.A.
Fruit Fun
Garden Salad Open-Faced Sandwich
Giant Musical Sandwich Game
Going on a Picnic
H Team vs. the Junk Food Junkies
Healthy-Four Game
How Old Mother Hubbard's Dog Finally
 Got Dinner
Hungry-for-Pie Song
I Feel Good . . . I'm Growing Up
If You Want to Grow Up Healthy
I'm Going to the Market, Super-Dooper-Doo
Irish Potato Frolic
Leftover Hopscotch
Lunchtime Rhyme
More-Than-Enough Sandwich
Mouse Bites
Old Mother Hubbard Retold
Out-of-This-World Soup
Pasta Pig-Out
Pasta Song
Shopping List for Porcupines and Other
 Peculiar Animals
Shopping Lists All Around
Supermarket in the Library or Classroom
Well-Rounded Meal
We're Fixing a Thanksgiving Dinner Feast
What Do You Like to Start the Day?
Where Does It Grow?
Who Put the Cookies in the Cookie Jar?
World of Good Food to Share
World's Great Bread Basket

Word Recognition Skills

Alphabet Animal Soup
Alphabet Soup Bowl Just for Fun
Alphabet Soup Song
Breadbasket Sampler
Camel Chowder
Cereal Surprises
Disappearing D-O-N-U-T
Easy as Pie
Eat-Your-Words Game
Food Fair from Many Lands
H Team vs. the Junk Food Junkies
How to Say "Eat" in Different Languages
How-to-Set-the-Table Placemat
I'm a Good Egg
It's a Piece of Cake
Kid Soup
Let Us Make a Salad Bowl
Make Your Own Soup Label
Mexican Fiesta
Monster Mickey Bread
Muncher
Nimble Noodleheads
Out-of-This-World Soup
Pachyderm Peanut Pitch
Pancakes, What a Treat!
Pasta Pig-Out
Pasta Song
Peanut Butter Letters
Piggy Pie
Quick Alphabet Soup
Sandwich Sign
Shopping Lists All Around
Supermarket in the Library or Classroom
This Bag Is for the Dogs
This Litter Piggy Went Home
Turkey Place Card for Thanksgiving
World's Great Bread Basket

ALPHABETICAL INDEX OF ACTIVITIES SHOWING ASSOCIATED SKILLS

This index is designed so that it can be used in two ways: All the activities in the book—games, songs, crafts, projects, recipes, etc.—are listed alphabetically, each with its page number. Thus we have an activities index. In addition, the skills enriched by the activities in *Mudluscious* are listed across the top of each two-page column, and for each activity Xs mark the associated skills. Accordingly, we have a chart for immediate skill identification.

ACTIVITY	Health and Safety Skills	Self-Awareness Skills	Rhythm and Rhyming Skills	Tasting and Smelling Skills	Artistic Skills	Musical Skills	Color Recognition Skills	Classification Skills	Size and Shape Recognition Skills	Counting Skills	Gross Motor Skills	Group Cooperation Skills	Sequencing Skills	Following Directions Skills	Word Recognition Skills	Role and Dialogue Invention Skills
After the Shopping's Done (p. 220)								X	X							X
All-Kinds-of-Soup Song (p. 117)			X			X		X								
Alphabet Animal Soup (p. 128)								X				X		X	X	
Alphabet Soup Bowl Just for Fun (p. 129)		X			X		X								X	
Alphabet Soup Song (p. 114)														X	X	X
Amazing Table (p. 194)			X			X		X					X			
Any Food Kabob (p. 146)	X			X												X
Ants Go Softly Round and Round (p. 15)			X			X					X	X		X		X
Apple Bob (p. 169)			X								X			X		X
Apple Mac, the Puppet (p. 51)	X	X			X		X							X		X
Applecrafts through the Holidays (p. 178)	X			X	X		X			X				X		
Arthur's Christmas Cookie Ornaments (p. 183)	X				X		X		X					X		
Aunt Annie, the Picnic Ant (p. 28)					X		X		X							
Baker, Baker (p. 93)										X			X			X
Baker, Baker Doll (p. 107)			X		X									X		
Baker Hat for Children (p. 108)					X								X	X		
Banana Split (p. 57)			X	X		X				X						
Basic Mix for Granola (p. 13)	X															

Best Part Is . . . What's Left (p. 123)

Big Batch Pancake Mix (p. 12)

Big Sweet Tooth (p. 55)

Bigfoot Sandwich (p. 205)

Birthday Cakes in a Cup (p. 110)

Blueberry-Picking Song (p. 216)

Body Food (p. 87)

Bread-and-Glue Dough (p. 109)

Breadbasket Sampler (p. 109)

Breakfast Song (p. 1)

Bring It Right Here! (p. 173)

Bubble, Bubble Pot (p. 149)

Bumps on a Log (p. 145)

Camel Chowder (p. 128)

Candy-Cane Capers Relay (p. 177)

Carrots for Every Bunny (p. 37)

Casserole Roll (p. 124)

Catch-the-Sun Salad (p. 54)

Cedric Celery, the Garden Snake (p. 53)

Cereal Surprises (p. 9)

Chicken Feed (p. 200)

Chicken Soup with Rice (p. 131)

Child-Safe Candles for the Tree (p. 182)

Chinese New Year Tree Centerpiece (p. 163)

Chinese Noodle Pick-Up (p. 165)

Chocolate Haystacks (p. 69)

Chocolate Pancakes (p. 13)

Chocolate Pudding Just for Fun (p. 88)

ACTIVITY	Role and Dialogue Invention Skills	Word Recognition Skills	Following Directions Skills	Sequencing Skills	Group Cooperation Skills	Gross Motor Skills	Counting Skills	Size and Shape Recognition Skills	Classification Skills	Color Recognition Skills	Musical Skills	Artistic Skills	Tasting and Smelling Skills	Rhythm and Rhyming Skills	Self-Awareness Skills	Health and Safety Skills
Chocolate Soup (p. 122)			X	X							X			X		
Christmas Stocking Relay (p. 177)			X		X	X										
Christmas Treats Good to Eat (p. 175)			X			X								X		
Christmas Wreath Cookies (p. 185)			X							X		X	X			X
Clean the Fridge (p. 111)			X	X	X						X			X		
Colorful Cake Walk (p. 106)			X					X		X	X		X			
Come On and Do the Cake Walk (p. 105)							X				X			X		
Cookie Muncher Game (p. 66)			X										X	X		
Country Market (p. 214)			X	X	X	X	X			X				X		
County Fair (p. 159)			X	X	X	X	X				X			X		
Crumb Catcher (p. 200)			X		X						X			X		
Crunch! Squish! Squish! (p. 86)	X				X											
Day Barnaby Bear Fell in the Batter Bowl (p. 99)	X		X	X	X	X		X								
Deviled Eggs—Chicken Legs Game (p. 25)			X		X	X							X			
Did You Ever Eat . . . (p. 142)											X					
Different and the Same (p. 158)			X			X			X					X	X	
Dippy Donut Song (p. 63)									X		X			X		

Disappearing D-O-N-U-T (p. 62)

Doin' the Chocolate Shake (p. 65)

Double Scooper Ice Cream Cone (p. 67)

Dried Apple Rings (p. 222)

Easy as Pie (p. 61)

Easy Won Ton Soup (p. 131)

Eat, Eat, Eat Your Food (p. 133)

Eat-Your-Words Game (p. 87)

Eating of the Green (p. 52)

Egg Carton Art (p. 10)

Egg Frolic (p. 5)

Egg Roll (p. 161)

Eggbert the Baker (p. 108)

Eggs and More Eggs—Surprise! (p. 4)

Fantastic Food Dream (p. 83)

Fast-Food Quick Trip (p. 22)

First Thanksgiving (p. 171)

Flower Pot Cakes (p. 110)

Food Fair from Many Lands (p. 159)

Food for Thought (p. 187)

Food from the U.S.A. (p. 158)

Food to Eat on the Run (p. 145)

Fortunate Fortunes (p. 161)

Frances in a Frame (p. 12)

Freezer Fruits (p. 222)

Frozen Thanksgiving Meal (p. 172)

Fruit Fun (p. 39)

Fudge Song (p. 63)

Funny Feeling Foods (p. 88)

Fussy Eaters' Song (p. 191)

ACTIVITY	Health and Safety Skills	Self-Awareness Skills	Rhythm and Rhyming Skills	Tasting and Smelling Skills	Artistic Skills	Musical Skills	Color Recognition Skills	Classification Skills	Size and Shape Recognition Skills	Counting Skills	Gross Motor Skills	Group Cooperation Skills	Sequencing Skills	Following Directions Skills	Word Recognition Skills	Role and Dialogue Invention Skills
Garbage-Bag Bib (p. 130)					X									X		
Garden Salad Open-Faced Sandwich (p. 53)	X			X				X								
Gardens You Can Grow Inside (p. 221)	X												X	X		
Giant Musical Sandwich Game (p. 25)						X		X			X	X		X		
Gingerbread Boy and Gingerbread Girl on a Tree (p. 174)		X	X	X					X		X			X		X
Gingerbread Boy in Verse (p. 137)			X										X			X
Gingerbread-Boy Treasure Hunt (p. 143)				X								X		X		
Gingerbread House on a Plate (p. 184)				X	X				X							
Gingerbread-Man Story with Masks (p. 134)			X		X								X	X		X
Glass of Sunshine Fingerplay (p. 3)			X						X	X	X		X	X		
Glutton Feast Song (p. 198)			X			X			X	X						
Gobble Up: Fast-Food Lunch Muncher (p. 29)					X									X		X
Going on a Picnic (p. 20)								X			X		X	X		X
Good Food Finger Puppet (p. 50)	X				X		X				X		X	X		
Good Licken (p. 103)			X						X					X		X

Green Magic Dip (p. 53)

Groaning-Board Groan (p. 200)

Groaning Board Mural (p. 202)

Gum Drop Sticky Teeth Rhyme (p. 64)

H Team vs. the Junk Food Junkies (p. 40)

Halloween Treat Song (p. 169)

Hand-Me-Down Food (p. 126)

Happy, Happy Hanukkah (p. 176)

Happy Magic Pot (p. 149)

Haunted House Milk Carton (p. 180)

Healthy-Four Game (p. 49)

Hello Jello (p. 75)

Hello Jello Bars (p. 91)

Hobo Bags (p. 146)

Honey Bee Dance (p. 65)

Hot Dog Song (p. 18)

How Do You Eat an Ice Cream Cone? (p. 59)

How Old Mother Hubbard's Dog Finally Got Dinner (p. 208)

How to Dump What You Won't Eat (p. 192)

How to Say "Eat" in Different Languages (p. 160)

How-to-Set-the-Table Placemat (p. 220)

Humpty Dumpty Together Again (p. 10)

Humpty Dumpty Triple Treat (p. 4)

Hungry-for-Pie Song (p. 61)

Hungry-Mouth Cat (p. 144)

ACTIVITY	Role and Dialogue Invention Skills	Word Recognition Skills	Following Directions Skills	Sequencing Skills	Group Cooperation Skills	Gross Motor Skills	Counting Skills	Size and Shape Recognition Skills	Classification Skills	Color Recognition Skills	Musical Skills	Artistic Skills	Tasting and Smelling Skills	Rhythm and Rhyming Skills	Self-Awareness Skills	Health and Safety Skills
I Feel Good . . . I'm Growing Up (p. 48)	X		X		X	X			X		X			X	X	X
I Like What's in My Lunch Box (p. 22)														X		X
Ice Cream and Something to Go with It! (p. 58)	X			X									X			
Ice Cream Concoctions (p. 70)			X	X									X			
Ice Cream Super Scoopers (p. 56)	X		X	X				X		X						X
If You Want to Grow Up Healthy (p. 35)	X		X			X			X		X			X	X	X
I'll-Eat-You-Up Chant (p. 133)			X	X				X						X		
I'm a Good Egg (p. 11)		X								X					X	
I'm Going to the Market, Super-Dooper-Doo (p. 213)	X		X	X					X					X		X
Incredible-Everything-You-Want-in-One Pie (p. 66)			X					X		X		X				
Indigestion (p. 199)											X			X	X	X
Irish Potato Frolic (p. 161)			X						X					X	X	
It's a Piece of Cake (p. 107)		X	X				X							X	X	
Jack-O'-Lantern Cake (p. 183)								X				X	X			
Jack-O'-Lantern Pie (p. 168)			X	X			X	X						X	X	
Junk Food Rubby in the Tummy (p. 202)												X				
Just My Dish (p. 127)														X		

- Ker Choo Ee! (p. 76)
- Ketchup, Ketchup, Everywhere . . . : Only Six Jars to Spare (p. 191)
- Kid Soup (p. 113)
- Kitchen Band Song (p. 218)
- Kitchen Work Song (p. 218)
- Leftover Food, It Ain't What It Used to Be (p. 124)
- Leftover Hopscotch (p. 128)
- Leftover Stew (p. 123)
- Let Us Make a Salad Bowl (p. 36)
- Let's Go and Pack a Picnic (p. 19)
- Let's Make Christmas Pudding (p. 174)
- Lick 'Em Up (p. 71)
- Lighter-than-Air Cake (p. 103)
- Litter Eater (p. 144)
- Little Red Hen (p. 94)
- Lolly Pop Puppet (p. 68)
- Lost, Left, and All Gone (p. 126)
- Lunch Is Fun (p. 15)
- Lunchtime Rhyme (p. 16)
- Lunchtime Surprise (p. 22)
- Magic Cooking Pot (p. 162)
- Magic Microwave (p. 150)
- Magic Pots Cooking in Many Lands (p. 148)
- Make Your Own Soup Label (p. 129)
- Make Your Own Soup Mix (p. 131)
- Marshmallow Ghosts (p. 169)
- Mexican Fiesta (p. 158)
- Mexican Jumping Bean (p. 161)

ACTIVITY	Role and Dialogue Invention Skills	Word Recognition Skills	Following Directions Skills	Sequencing Skills	Group Cooperation Skills	Gross Motor Skills	Counting Skills	Size and Shape Recognition Skills	Classification Skills	Color Recognition Skills	Musical Skills	Artistic Skills	Tasting and Smelling Skills	Rhythm and Rhyming Skills	Self-Awareness Skills	Health and Safety Skills
Monster Messy Face (p. 201)			X			X										
Monster Mickey Bread (p. 109)		X											X	X		
More-Than-Enough Sandwich (p. 17)			X	X		X		X	X							
Mouse Bites (p. 206)									X				X			X
Mud Pie (p. 69)			X									X				
Mudluscious! (p. 88)			X							X		X	X			
Muncher (p. 26)		X	X									X				
My Birthday Action Rhyme (p. 102)			X			X								X		
My Lunch Box (p. 27)			X					X		X		X				X
Natural Food Dye Decorating (p. 10)			X							X		X				
Nellie or Nathan Noodlehead (p. 88)			X					X				X			X	
Nimble Noodleheads (p. 85)	X	X	X			X					X			X	X	
Ogre Roar (p. 201)	X		X			X	X							X		
Oh Where, Oh Where Is My Peanut Butter? (p. 77)						X					X			X	X	
Old Lady and the Fly: A Jarring Experience (p. 196)	X			X				X			X			X		
Old Lady from a Bag (p. 195)	X			X				X			X			X		
Old Mother Hubbard Retold (p. 210)	X			X					X					X		

Activity	1	2	3	4	5	6	7	8	9	10	11	12	13	14	15
Out-of-This-World Soup (p. 117)								X					X	X	
Pachyderm Peanut Pitch (p. 202)														X	X
Pancake Chase (p. 137)						X					X		X	X	X
Pancake Stack (p. 6)										X			X	X	X
Pancakes that Might Run Away (p. 145)	X			X			X		X			X			
Pancakes, What a Treat! (p. 6)			X			X					X	X	X	X	X
Paper Pickle Creature Puppet (p. 90)									X					X	
Paper-Plate Pig (p. 144)					X			X						X	
Parrot Piñata (p. 164)					X									X	
Pasta Pig-Out (p. 164)								X							X
Pasta Song (p. 157)	X		X	X		X		X			X	X		X	X
Peanut Butter Letters (p. 205)	X	X													X
Peanut Butter Porcupines (p. 91)	X			X				X						X	
Peanut Butter Wallop (p. 30)	X														
Peas Porridge Hot (p. 8)			X							X	X				
Pickle Creature to Eat (p. 91)					X									X	
Picky Paul (p. 189)	X	X		X	X		X	X	X	X		X			X
Picky Paul Pizza (p. 206)	X	X		X				X							
Pig Party (p. 205)	X					X					X		X	X	
Pig Tails (p. 206)	X			X				X		X	X		X	X	
Piggy Pie (p. 170)			X									X			X
Piggy Piggy (p. 8)			X									X			
Pizza Pie to Perform (p. 156)		X					X			X	X	X	X	X	X
Placemats from India (p. 163)					X								X	X	
Pleasing Pancakes (p. 12)	X			X										X	
Pluck the Turkey and Do a Trick (p. 177)		X				X	X	X			X	X		X	X
Pokey, Pokey, the Bread Song (p. 97)						X									
Pooh's Hunny Jar and the Bees' Bee Hive (p. 68)					X		X	X						X	
Pop Goes the Popcorn (p. 39)	X					X					X			X	X

ACTIVITY	Role and Dialogue Invention Skills	Word Recognition Skills	Following Directions Skills	Sequencing Skills	Group Cooperation Skills	Gross Motor Skills	Counting Skills	Size and Shape Recognition Skills	Classification Skills	Color Recognition Skills	Musical Skills	Artistic Skills	Tasting and Smelling Skills	Rhythm and Rhyming Skills	Self-Awareness Skills	Health and Safety Skills
Popcorn Bowl-Frolic (p. 50)	X		X	X		X					X		X		X	X
Popcorn-Cranberry Chain (p. 177)			X		X	X		X		X	X	X		X		
Porcupine Balls (p. 145)						X							X			X
Pot on the Stove (p. 154)			X	X		X								X	X	
Potato Pancakes (p. 186)													X			X
Psyanky Adapted: Daisy, Daisy, I Love You (p. 9)			X					X		X		X				
Queen Bee—A Honey of a Game! (p. 65)			X	X	X	X										
Quick Alpabet Soup (p. 131)		X											X			X
Really Easy Strawberry Jam (p. 222)													X			X
Right-Out-of-the-Garden Salad (p. 53)													X			X
Roll-the-Can Ice Cream (p. 70)			X			X				X		X	X			
Sam-I-Am Deviled Green Eggs (p. 11)										X		X	X			X
Sand Cake (p. 90)			X					X				X				
Sandwich Sign (p. 27)		X	X							X						
SandWitches You Can Make (p. 30)							X		X	X		X	X			X
Shopping List for Porcupines and Other Peculiar Animals (p. 213)	X						X	X	X					X		
Shopping Lists All Around (p. 219)		X	X				X	X	X	X						

Activity	1	2	3	4	5	6	7	8	9	10	11	12	13	14	15
Silly Jungle Dinner (p. 90)	X			X			X		X						
Silly, Silly Things to Eat (p. 74)			X			X									
Snap, Crackle, Pop Around (p. 7)											X	X		X	
Soggy Cornflake Song (p. 7)			X			X					X	X	X	X	
Something for Santa (p. 175)					X										
Somewhat Inflated Tale of J. S. and His Wife Nan (p. 187)	X		X						X			X	X		X
Song for Making Mud Pie (p. 61)			X	X											
Soup-Can-Roll—Just for Fun (p. 128)						X					X	X	X		
Spider and Fly (p. 143)			X			X					X	X			X
Sponge Cake (p. 90)	X								X						
Square Meal (p. 74)	X				X		X								
Stone Soup (p. 131)	X			X						X		X	X		
Street Cries for Modern Children (p. 215)			X												
Sugar Snowperson (p. 182)					X				X					X	
Super Spaghetti Cake (p. 89)					X									X	X
Supermarket in the Library or Classroom (p. 219)							X	X	X						X
Taco Bar (p. 165)	X			X											
Teddy Bear Picnic Game (p. 25)		X									X				X
Terrible Tale of Joshua Nickel (p. 81)	X		X										X		X
This Bag Is for the Dogs (p. 130)					X									X	
This Litter Piggy Went Home (p. 204)					X		X		X					X	
Three Pigs on a Tube (p. 139)			X						X	X		X	X	X	X
Toast Pop-up Game (p. 106)			X									X	X	X	X
Too Many Cooks (p. 115)				X					X	X			X	X	X
Trail Mix (p. 29)	X											X			
Treat Bag Treasure Hunt (p. 176)	X														X

ACTIVITY	Role and Dialogue Invention Skills	Word Recognition Skills	Following Directions Skills	Sequencing Skills	Group Cooperation Skills	Gross Motor Skills	Counting Skills	Size and Shape Recognition Skills	Classification Skills	Color Recognition Skills	Musical Skills	Artistic Skills	Tasting and Smelling Skills	Rhythm and Rhyming Skills	Self-Awareness Skills	Health and Safety Skills
Tree for All Reasons and Seasons to Celebrate (p. 167)				X	X								X	X		
Turkey Place Card for Thanksgiving (p. 181)		X	X							X		X				
Unhatched Egg (p. 5)	X		X			X										
Utensil Art Prints (p. 220)			X					X				X				
Very Hungry Bear (p. 140)	X		X	X	X			X								
Wake Up the Yeast Giant! (p. 94)	X			X				X						X		
Well-Rounded Meal (p. 52)			X				X	X	X			X				X
We're Fixing a Thanksgiving Dinner Feast (p. 171)	X			X					X		X			X		
We're Growing a Little Garden (p. 217)	X		X	X		X					X				X	
What a Cake! (p. 83)	X			X										X		
What Do You Like to Start the Day? (p. 2)			X						X	X				X		
What's Inside Jack Horner's Pie? (p. 178)			X					X						X		
Where Does It Grow? (p. 217)			X			X		X	X					X		
Who Eats Worms? (p. 86)	X		X			X									X	
Who Put the Cookies in the Cookie Jar? (p. 60)			X			X		X	X					X		

Why Doesn't It Grow On Trees? (p. 79)

Why Pigs Are Pink (p. 203)

Witch Brew (p. 183)

World of Good Food to Share (p. 155)

World's Great Bread Basket (p. 98)

You-Are-What-You-Eat Puppet (p. 50)

LITERATURE INDEX

Agnew, Seth M., 16
Ahlberg, Allan, 72
Ahlberg, Janet, 72
Aldridge, Josephine, 72
Aldridge, Richard, 72
Allard, Harry, 212
Ambrus, Victor, 138
An Apple a Day, 39
Apple Pigs, 35
Apples, 123
Armitage, David, 56
Armitage, Ronda, 56
Arthur's Christmas Cookies, 173, 183
Asbjornsen, P. C., 133
Asch, Frank, 73, 90, 167, 212
Avocado Baby, 40

Babar Learns to Cook, 154
Bake Off, 40
Balian, Lorna, 62, 170
Bang, Betsy, 154
Barrett, Judi, 39, 78, 122, 215
Bembelman's Bakery, 92, 93, 94
Benedictus, Roger, 73
Benjamin, Alan, 78
Benny Bakes a Cake, 99
Berger, Terry, 18
Big Pig, 193
Biggest Sandwich Ever, 16
Bileck, Marvin, 78
Black, Irma Simonton, 212
Blue Bug's Vegetable Garden, 216
Blueberries for Sal, 216
Blueberry Bears, 215
Blueberry Cake That Little Fox Baked, 98

Brandenburg, Franz, 18, 138
Bread and Jam for Frances, 187, 188
Breakfast for Sammy, 8
Brierley, Louise, 122
Brown, Marc, 73, 173
Brown, Marcia, 112, 133
Bun, 132, 133
Burgess, Anthony, 56
Burningham, John, 40, 212, 218

Calhoun, Mary, 154
Carle, Eric, 5, 21, 192
Carlson, Nancy, 167
Carrot Seed, 35
Cauley, Lorinda Bryan, 40
Cereal Box, 7
Charlip, Remy, 193
"Cheese, Peas, and Chocolate Pudding,"
        Humpty Dumpty's Storybook, 189, 206
Chicken Soup with Rice, 113, 131
Chocolate Chip Cookie Contest, 59
Christmas Cookie Sprinkle Snitcher, 173
Cloudy with a Chance of Meatballs, 78
Cole, Joanna, 193
*Comic Adventures of Old Mother Hubbard
        and Her Dog,* 208
Cranberry Thanksgiving, 170
Cupboard, 218

Da Rif, Andrea, 98
Daly, Kathleen, 21
Day Jimmy's Boa Ate the Wash, 73
Dauer, Rosamond, 193
De Brunhoff, Laurent, 154

De Paola, Tomie, xviii, 5, 35, 92, 93, 112, 148, 154, 207, 208
De Regniers, Beatrice, 138
Degen, Bruce, 73
Devlin, Harry, 170
Devlin, Wende, 170
Domanska, Janina, 154
Dorros, Arthur, 73
Douglass, Barbara, 59
Dragon Stew, 78, 83

Each Peach Pear Plum, 72
Eat!, 188
Eating Out, 73
Eberts, Marjorie, 73
Egg Thoughts and Other Frances Songs, 3, 12
Ernest and Celestine's Picnic, 19

Farmer Goff and His Turkey Sam, 60
Fat Cat, 193
Fat Magic, 78
Fifty Million Sausages, 73
Fin Mc Coul, 154
Flory, Jane, 138
Friedman, Ina R., 155
Frog and Toad Together, 60
Fudge Dream Supreme, 56
Funny Little Woman, 147, 155

Gackenbush, Dick, 188
Galdone, Paul, xvii, 7, 93, 133, 138, 148, 155
Garth Pig and the Ice Cream Lady, 138
Gelman, Rita Golden, 16
George and Martha, 113
Giant Jam Sandwich, 16
Giant Sandwich, 16
Giant Vegetable Garden, 36
Gibbons, Gail, 93
Gingerbread Boy, 132, 133
Ginsburg, Mirra, 148
Gisler, Margaret, 73
Glorious Christmas Soup Party, 112
Goffstein, M. B., 176
Golly Gump Swallowed a Fly, 193
Good Lemonade, 212
Gordon, Margaret, 18
Grandma, Felix, and Mustapha Biscuit, 138
Great Giant Watermelon Birthday, 74
Green, Melinda, 93
Green Eggs and Ham, 3, 11

Gregory the Terrible Eater, xviii, 187, 189
Gretz, Susanna, 213
Grey, Judith, 59, 98

Hale, Linda, 112
Happy Baker, 92, 93
Harriet's Halloween Candy, 167, 183
Hirsch, Marilyn, 176
Hoban, Lillian, 173
Hoban, Russell, 3, 188
Hogrogian, Nonny, 123
Homer Price, 147
How My Garden Grew, 216
How My Parents Learned to Eat, 155
How the Grinch Stole Christmas, 173
How to Make Elephant Bread, 71, 73
How to Make Possum's Honey Bread, 94
Hums of Pooh, 62
Hungry Leprechaun, 154

I Know an Old Lady Who Swallowed a Fly, 193
I Will Not Go to Market Today, 212
Ice Creams for Rosie, 56
In the Night Kitchen, 99, 109
In the Witch's Kitchen: Poems for Halloween, 167

Jamberry, 73
Janice, 170
Jeremy Isn't Hungry, 189
Johnson, Tony, 167
Journey Cake, Ho!, 132, 134, 146

Kahl, Virginia, 173
Kennedy, Jimmy, 18
Kent, Jack, 73, 193
King Lion and His Cooks, 122
Koshland, Ellen, 78
Krasilovsky, Phyllis, 98, 215
Kraus, Robert, 173
Krauss, Ruth, 35
Kroll, Stephen, 78
Kwitz, Mary De Ball, 8

Lambs for Dinner, 138
Land Where the Ice Cream Grows, 56
Lapp, Eleanor, 215
Lasker, Joe, 112

Laughing Latkes, 176
Lemerise, Bruce, 22
Lentil Soup, 112
Lindgren, Barbro, 59
Little Bear's Thanksgiving, 170
Little Chick's Breakfast, 8
Little Old Man Who Couldn't Read, 212
Little Red Hen, 93
Little Red Riding Hood, 138
Lobel, Anita, 134
Lobel, Arnold, 60, 213
Lord, John Vernon, 16
Love from Aunt Betty, 98

Maestro, Betty, 138
Maestro, Julio, 138
Magic Cooking Pot, 148
Magic Lollipop, 78
Magic Meatballs, 78
Magic Porridge Pot, 148
Magic Stove, 148, 150
Man Who Cooked for Himself, 215
Man Who Entered a Contest, 98, 110
Mandry, Kathy, 73
Marshall, James, 113, 193
McCloskey, Robert, 147, 216
McCully, Emily Arnold, 19
McGowen, Tom, 78
McPhail, David, 7
Meg and Mog, 168
Miller, Alice P., 60
Milne, A. A., 62
Mitchell, Barbara, 155
Moe, Jorgen, 133
Mooncake, 73
Moore, Inga, 216
Mosel, Arlene, 155
Moskowitz, Stewart, 62
Mother Mother I Feel Sick Send for the Doctor Quick Quick Quick, 193
Mother Rabbit's Son Tom, 188
Mouse Family's Blueberry Pie, 60
Mrs. Pig's Bulk Buy, xviii, 189, 191, 203
Mud Pies, 59
Munchety Munch, 74
My Kitchen, 218
My Lunch Box, 21, 27

Nail Soup, 113
Nicoll, Helen, 168
Nobens, C. A., 93
Noble, Trinka Hakes, 73
Nolan, Dennis, 193

Oatmeal Is Not for Mustaches, 74
Old Fasnacht, 155
Old MacDonald Had an Apartment House, 215
Old Woman and the Red Pumpkin, 147, 154
Old Woman and the Rice Thief, 154
On Market Street, 213
Orbach, Ruth, 35
Oxenbury, Helen, 73

Painter's Trick, 113
Pancake, 132, 134
Pancakes, Crackers, and Pizza: A Book about Shapes, 73
Pancakes for Breakfast, xviii, 5
Pancakes, Pancakes, 5
Parker, Nancy Winslow, 98
Paterson, Diane, 188
Patz, Nancy, 74
Pickle Creature, 78, 90
Pickle Things, 73
Picnic, 19
Picnic, Hurrah, 18
Pienkowski, Jan, 168
Pinkwater, Daniel, 78
Plum Pudding for Christmas, 173
Pomerantz, Charlotte, 134
Pop Corn and Ma Goodness, 36
Popcorn, 167
Popcorn Book, 35
Potato Pancakes All Around, 176
Potato Talk, 78
Poulet, Virginia, 216
Preston, Edna Mitchell, 36
Pretzels, 73
Pumpernickel Tickle and Mean Green Cheese, 71, 74

Rain Makes Applesauce, 78
Rayner, Mary, xviii, 138, 189
Reasons and Raisins, 72
Rees, Ennis, 78
Ribtickle Town, 78, 89
Rice, Eve, 99
Rockwell, Anne, 216
Rockwell, Harlow, 216, 218
Rockwell, Thomas, 74
Runaway Pancake, 132, 133

Sam's Cookie, 59
Sand Cake, 73, 90
Sandwich, 16

Sawyer, Ruth, 132, 134
Schatell, Brian, 60
Scheer, Julian, 78
Scrambled Eggs Super!, 3, 11
Sendak, Maurice, 99, 113
Seuss, Dr., 3, 10, 173
Seymour, Dorothy, 16
Sharmat, Mitchell, xviii, 189
Sheldon's Lunch, 22
Shopping Basket, 212
Socks for Supper, 73
Sometimes It's Turkey, Sometimes It's Feathers, 170
Spinelli, Eileen, 170
Stamaty, Mark, 62
Stevens, Carla, 94
Stevenson, James, 113
Stone Soup, 112, 131
Strega Nona, 148, 157
Sugar Mouse Cake, 99
Supree, Burton, 193
Sweet Touch, 62

Teddy Bear Baker, 99
Teddy Bears Go Shopping, 213
Teddy Bears' Picnic, 18
Tether, Graham, 56
Thanksgiving at the Tappletons, 170
Three Bears, xvii, 7
300 Pound Cat, 193
Three Little Pigs, 138
Three Wishes, 155
Too-Great Bread Book, 92, 93, 94
Too-Loose the Chocolate Moose, 62
Toto, Joe, 73
Towle, Faith M., 148
Tuna Fish Sandwiches, 16
Turnip, 154
Turtles' Picnic and Other Nonsense Stories, 18

Van Witsen, 189
Vanishing Pumpkin, 167
Vegetable Thieves, 216
Ventura, Marisa, 113
Ventura, Piero, 113
Very Hungry Caterpillar, 192
Vincent, Gabrielle, 19

Watanabe, Shiego, 22
Watch Out for the Chicken Feet in Your Soup, 92, 93, 112
Weissman, Cynthia, 8
We'll Have a Friend for Lunch, 138
Welber, Robert, 19
Westcott, Nadine, 36, 193
What a Good Lunch!, 22
What Shall We Have for Breakfast?, xvii, 3
What's for Lunch, 21
What's Left, 122
Whiff, Sniff, Nibble and Chew: The Gingerbread Boy Retold, 134
Who Needs Donuts?, 62
Wilberforce Goes on a Picnic, 18
Williams, Barbara, 189
Williams, Vera B., 74
Winter Picnic, 19
Wolcott, Patty, 16
Worthington, Phoebe, 99
Worthington, Selby, 99

Yaffe, Alan, 78
Yuck!, 113
Yum Yum, 72
Yummers, 193
Yummy Yummy, 98

Zemach, Harve, 113
Ziefert, Harriet, 74
Zimelman, Nathan, xvii, 3
Zion, Gene, 99